The Who's Who of the Anglo-Zulu War

The Who's Who of the Anglo-Zulu War

Part II

Colonials and Zulus

by

Ian Knight and Adrian Greaves

Pen & Sword
MILITARY

First published in Great Britain in 2007 by
Pen & Sword Military
an imprint of
Pen & Sword Books Ltd
47 Church Street
Barnsley
South Yorkshire
S70 2AS

Typeset in 11/13 Sabon by
Lamorna Publishing Services

Printed and bound in England by
CPI UK

For a complete list of Pen & Sword titles please contact
PEN & SWORD BOOKS LIMITED
47 Church Street, Barnsley, South Yorkshire, S70 2AS, England
E-mail: enquiries@pen-and-sword.co.uk
Website: www.pen-and-sword.co.uk

Contents

The Colonials

The Zulus

Glossary

Afrikaans

Afrikaans – language spoken by the descendants of the original European settlers at the Cape; predominantly Dutch with the addition of some French, German, Indonesian and local African words and constructions.

Afrikaner – descendant of the first predominantly Dutch-speaking white settlers at the Cape. Often known as 'Boers'.

Boer – literally a country person or farmer, the common name applied to the descendants of the first white Dutch-speaking settlers at the Cape.

Drift – a ford or crossing place.

Laager – a defensive formation improvised by drawing wagons into a circle. Also used during the Anglo-Zulu War to refer to an entrenched or fortified position generally.

isiZulu

ibutho (pl. amabutho) – Zulu guild, grouped together according to the common-age of its members, providing part time national service to the Zulu kings or to other important amakhosi. Often translated in a military context as 'regiment'.

ikhanda (pl. amakhanda) – Zulu royal homestead (literal 'head', meaning of state authority) serving as an administrative centre and often as a barracks for amabutho.

impi – matters pertaining to war, or a group of men gathered together as an armed force.

induna (pl. izinduna) – a state functionary or official appointed to a position of authority by the Zulu king or other amakhosi.

inkosi (pl. amakhosi) – hereditary chief or ruler.

oNdini/Ulundi – alternative versions of the name of King Cetshwayo's principle royal homestead, from the common root *undi*, meaning 'a high place'. The residence was commonly known as oNdini by the Zulus; Lord Chelmsford initially used this version in correspondence but once the campaign was underway took to calling it Ulundi. The battle which took place there on 4 July is generally referred to by this name.

umuzi (pl. imizi) – ordinary Zulu family homestead.

Foreword

On 1 September 1873 Cetshwayo kaMpande was installed as king of the Zulu nation. At the end of several days of traditional ceremonies – which confirmed his authority in the eyes of his people – he went through a rather farcical 'coronation' supervised by Theophilus Shepstone, a representative of the neighbouring British colony, Natal. That Cetshwayo himself had felt the need to submit, as an independent monarch, to such a validation by an outside power was indicative of the changing status of the Zulu kingdom in southern Africa.

In the 1820s it had been the dominant power on the eastern seaboard, between the Kahlamba mountains and the sea; by the 1870s, it was surrounded on two sides by European colonies. The steady encroachment of white settler societies on the Zulu borders had impacted heavily upon the Zulu kingdom, altering the complex relationship between the Zulu kings and the African societies subsumed into the colonies, providing a haven for political refugees from Zululand and, through their aggressive trading economies, undermining the economic basis of royal power within Zululand itself. Cetshwayo had thought it wise to secure the blessing of his British neighbours to consolidate his position against internal rivals; it was a grave political error for it gave the British an opportunity to interfere in the internal affairs of Zululand.

In 1879 the process reached its logical conclusion. The British, expanding their hold across southern Africa, had come to see the Zulu kingdom as a threat to their objectives; while King Cetshwayo struggled to maintain with them a good relationship,

Imperial strategists plotted his downfall. On 11 December 1878 he was presented with an ultimatum, which required him either to disband the structures upon which royal authority was based, or to fight to defend them. As the British had anticipated, he chose to fight. On 11 January 1879 the British Empire invaded Zululand.

The Anglo-Zulu War saw a total of over 12,000 British and Colonial troops participate in this hard-fought campaign and casualties were high on both sides, with many incapacitated by disease rather than conflict on the British side. Statistics reflecting the Zulu participation in the war are, of course, impossible to assess, but it is estimated that over 40,000 Zulu men, in total, took part in the defence of their country. Zulu losses throughout the war are estimated to have been as high as 10,000. On one day alone – 22 January, the day of Nyezane, Isandlwana, Rorke's Drift and Zunguin mountain – the toll from the fighting on all three fronts amounted to perhaps 3,500 dead and many hundreds more wounded. In addition, by the end of the war most of the great *amakhanda* – the royal homesteads which served as a centre for state administration – were destroyed, together with hundreds of ordinary Zulu homesteads. Tens of thousands of Zulu cattle, which constituted the wealth of the Zulu nation, were carried away by the invaders. And, while for the British the war was merely one element in their struggle to maintain a global Empire – the professional soldiers themselves moved on to other wars, the politicians to other crises – the impact on the Zulu kingdom was permanent and devastating. The British invasion of 1879 was the most destructive single act in a process of European penetration and conquest which began in the 1820s and lasted into the twentieth century, and which in the end saw the Zulu people dispossessed, their political institutions destroyed, and their economy subverted to the needs of the invaders.

The lives of the Zulus who fought in the war were scarcely recognized beyond the confines of their immediate families. Yet the impact of all wars is, above all, a human one, and the purpose of this book is to assess something of that impact upon the lives of a small number of those individuals who took part – and, indeed, to assess their impact upon it. It is primarily intended as a companion piece for students and readers of the conflict, and it makes no claims to comprehensiveness. And because Zulu tradition was, until recently, an oral one it is often impossible to provide even the most basic outline of the lives of Zulu participants. Instead, we offer a selection of experiences which we hope is, in some way, representative, and our criteria for inclusion has, on occasion, been arbitrary. While we have tried to include all of the major figures, the movers and shakers who shaped the conflict, we have also included many individuals whose lives appeared to us particularly interesting or, in the case of the Zulus, could be adequately documented.

The repercussions of the British invasion were not limited to 1879, and indeed many of those Zulus who distinguished themselves fighting for their country in 1879 were to fall victim to the violence unleashed by the post-war settlement. Ironically, they were slaughtered not by foreign invaders, but by their own countrymen. Many of the *amakhosi, izikhulu* and *izinduna* of the old kingdom were killed during the sacking of oNdini in the civil war of 1883. Others, like Sitshitshili kaMnqandi – a hero of the Battle of Hlobane in 1879, but later murdered as a government collaborator by Zulu rebels in 1906 – were forced by the reality of defeat into difficult choices. Those choices have continued to affect the lives of their descendents to this day.

In the case of the Colonial participants, their activities are rather better recorded, especially local newspaper accounts and diaries. Some, like George Mossop – who served as a young trooper in an irregular unit in 1879 – offer stories of little strategic or political consequence, but undeniable human interest. It is hard to read his account of the Battle of Hlobane, *Running the Gauntlet*, without wondering what became of him in later life. Indeed, the lives of many Colonials reflect, no less than the Zulus, the changing balance of power in southern Africa in that crucial last quarter of the nineteenth century.

We are grateful for the help we have received in researching this work, both from students of the war, and from the descendants of those involved. Lee Stevenson has most generously made available his own meticulous research into the lives of veterans of the Battle of Rorke's Drift, while Ian Woodason – who runs a website dedicated to the graves and memorials of those who fought in the war – also made free with his own inspiring archives. So, too, did Ian Castle, particularly with regard to Natal's Volunteer forces. George Button provided information on his forebear, George Mossop, and Vernon Wilson allowed us access to family research into the colourful career of George Hamilton Browne. The late Prince Gilenja Biyela passed on family traditions regarding his grandfather *inkosi* Mkhosana kaMvundlana, Paul Cebekhulu information on his grandfather, *inkosi* Zibhebhu kaMaphitha, and Mnandi Ngobese provided perspectives on his father, *inkosi* Mehlokazulu kaSihayo. Ian Knight would like to acknowledge his particular debt to his old friend and mentor, the late 'SB' Bourquin, who first opened a road for him into the green hills of Zululand, and to Professor John Laband, the doyen of Zulu historical studies, for his help and encouragement.

This work is dedicated to all who participated in this campaign, be they British, Colonial or Zulu, great men or small, brave or not so brave; all fought in the honest belief that what they were doing was right.

Ian Knight and Adrian Greaves.
Chichester and Tenterden, 2006

The Colonials

Adendorff, Gert Wilhelm

Adendorff was born at Graaf Reinett, in the Eastern Cape, on 10 July 1848. His grandfather, Michiel Joseph Adendorff, was a German surgeon who had set sail from Europe for the Far East but, on arriving at the Cape, had disembarked to assist with an outbreak of fever, and had remained there. He had settled at Graaff Reinet where his son, also Michiel, was born in 1799. Michiel Jnr. married a woman of French descent, Charlotte Rouverie, in 1829 and together they had thirteen children, of whom Gert Wilhelm was the tenth.

During the 9th Frontier War (1877-78), an irregular unit, the Kaffrarian Rifles, was recruited among the German community on the Eastern Cape, and Gert Adendorff volunteered; he may also have served in the Diamond Fields Horse. In 1878, with hostilities imminent against the Zulus, Rupert Lonsdale was sent to the Cape to recruit whites from the recently disbanded local irregular units to serve as officers and NCOs in a new auxiliary force. Adendorff's name appears on a list of men recruited for the Royal Swazi Levy – under the impression they were destined for Swaziland – who arrived in Natal on the steamer *Nubian* at the end of November 1878. In fact, they were needed for the recently authorized Natal Native Contingent, and Adendorff was given the rank of lieutenant in the 3rd Regiment, attached to the Centre Column.

Adendorff's role in the subsequent fighting has been the subject of particularly intense mythologizing, but in fact there is no reason to doubt a considerable body of evidence which suggests

1

he was present at the Battles of both Isandlwana and Rorke's Drift. He was certainly present in camp at Isandlwana on the morning of the 22nd, and is mentioned by name as having brought a report from the piquet on the iNyoni escarpment regarding Zulu movements on the heights. It is possible that, as a German speaker, his command of English was not good, and this may have been the first of many elements that has led to confusion regarding his role. His own account of the day – in a letter published anonymously – is entirely consistent with other sources, and indeed brutally honest. Adendorff says that he stayed in the camp until the British line collapsed, then tried to make his escape. His horse was killed as he rode down into the Manzimnyama valley, but he commandeered another at gunpoint from a mounted auxiliary. He then attached himself to Hlubi's Tlokoa, one of the few mounted groups who escaped the battle-field in any order. Hlubi's men forced a way through the Zulu right 'horn' and rode across country to Rorke's Drift. When they approached the river, Adendorff and another survivor rode ahead to warn Lieutenant Chard's party at the ponts; Hlubi's men crossed by the Drift downstream, then dismounted to rest.

The doubts about Adendorff's presence at Rorke's Drift seem to have started early enough, as whispers among officers of his own regiment, and have been enshrined in Donald Morris' classic account of the war, *The Washing of the Spears*. Morris claimed to have evidence to this effect, but never published it. Chard himself, however, went out of his way to single out Adendorff as the only man among the Isandlwana survivors who stayed to assist in the defence; the fact that he was a complete stranger to the rest of the garrison, and occupied a post inside the storehouse during the battle, accounts for his apparent invisibility otherwise. Trooper Fred Symons of the Natal Carbineers – part of Lord Chelmsford's command – confirms Adendorff's presence at the mission on the morning of the 23rd, while Walter Stafford – himself an Isandlwana survivor, who served with Adendorff's brother in August in 1880 and knew Adendorff himself in later life – had no doubts about his story. It is also significant that Lieutenant Henry Harford, acting as adjutant of the 3rd NNC, noted in his almanac that Adendorff was present at Rorke's Drift. Nor is there any evidence to suggest that he was ever considered for official censure regarding his conduct on 22-23 January.

The fact that Adendorff's account, when published, was greeted with contempt by the settler community in Natal probably accounts for his later reticence on the subject. He took little part in the rest of the war, giving up military service when the 3rd NNC was disbanded for poor performance in the aftermath of Isandlwana.

In 1882, he surfaced as a clerk working for the Gold Commission, and apparently living with other members of the Adendorff family who had settled the Newcastle region of northern Natal. He later moved to the Transvaal and married a widow, Hester Grobler, and was living in Pretoria, working as a government clerk, when the Anglo-Boer War broke out. The war split the Adendorff family, some fighting for the British and others for the Boers, although Gert Wilhelm seems to have remained in his civilian post and surrendered it when the British advanced to Pretoria. The war caused him financial loss, however, for after hostilities ended he appealed to the British authorities for compensation for a cart requisitioned by the Boers and two horses taken by British troops.

Adendorff died about 1914. It is not unusual for the lives of individual colonial troops to remain obscure to history but Adendorff's reputation has suffered unduly; he was in fact the only man on the British side to have fought at both Isandlwana and Rorke's Drift.

Brickhill, James Alexander

Brickhill was born in Port Elizabeth, Eastern Cape, on 17 October 1836. As an adult he worked as a government interpreter in Natal. On 3 July 1861 he married Jane Anne Buchanan in Pietermaritzburg. On the outbreak of the Zulu war he volunteered his services and was attached as interpreter to the No. 3 (Centre Column). He was present in the camp at Isandlwana when it was attacked on 22 January 1879 and left a graphic account of his harrowing escape. After the war he served as an interpreter to a commission which delineated the Transvaal/Swazi border. He died in Durban on 27 November 1892.

Bulwer, Sir Henry Ernest Gascoyne

Henry Bulwer was born in 1836, the younger son of W. E. Lytton Bulwer of Heydon, Norwich. He was educated at Charterhouse public school and Trinity College before embarking upon a career in the colonial civil service. In 1860 he became official British resident in the Ionian Islands, and in 1865 private secretary to his uncle, Lord Dalling Bulwer, who was ambassador to Constantinople. He then served as Receiver-General in Trinidad, Administrator of the Government of Dominica, Governor of Labuan and Consul-General in Borneo.

In 1875 he took up the post of Lieutenant Governor of Natal, then the senior administrative post in the Colony. He arrived at a time when the Confederation scheme was already in the wind but would prove a determined opponent of British intervention in Zululand. Although an Imperialist by training, Bulwer did not accept that the long-term interests of Natal's population, both black and white, lay in vigorous military expansion. In particular, he was dismissive of the rhetoric of Sir Bartle Frere – who from 1877 was his immediate superior as High Commissioner to Southern Africa – and saw little to merit Frere's claims that the Zulu kingdom presented a menace to Natal's security. Bulwer recognized Frere's aggressive intentions towards the Zulus but did not consider his policy justified; moreover, he was worried about the vulnerability of Natal's settler society should war break out, and of the long-term consequences to the relationship between Natal's African population and the Zulu, with whom their history was inextricably entwined. Following the annexation of the Transvaal in April 1877, it was Bulwer who offered to mediate between the Transvaal and the Zulu kingdom in an attempt to diffuse tension over the 'disputed territory'. The result was the Boundary Commission which subsequently met at Rorke's Drift, and after sifting the evidence found largely in favour of the Zulu position. Nevertheless, the announcement of these findings was delayed by Frere until he felt able to qualify them with a series of demands which were finally presented to Zulu representatives as the ultimatum of December 1878.

Once Frere had decided openly to embark on a course of confrontation, his senior military officer Lord Chelmsford began planning for the invasion of Zululand and the defence of Natal. Although both men of impeccable manners, Chelmsford found Bulwer a stubborn opponent who demanded strict adherence to protocol and refused to allow Chelmsford free reign in Natal. Bulwer obstructed Chelmsford's attempts to mobilize Natal's African population as an auxiliary force, or to allow Natal's white volunteer troops – whose terms of service limited their deployment to the defence of Natal – to join the invasion. In both cases Frere and Chelmsford combined to outmanoeuvre Bulwer in the Natal Legislative Assembly, although the auxiliary units – the NNC – were only authorized in November 1878, and had scarcely assembled when the war began. Bulwer insisted that the white volunteer troops be balloted on their willingness to serve across the border in Zululand and that those who refused should not be compelled to do so; in the event most agreed. Later, when Lord Chelmsford began to reassert himself following the low-point in British fortunes after Isandlwana, Bulwer refused to allow auxiliary troops serving as Border Guards to make raids into Zululand. Small wonder that Chelmsford complained that 'Sir H. Bulwer, from my first arrival in Natal has thrown every obstacle in my way'. In the event, to Bulwer's irritation, Chelmsford authorized raids in April and May without first securing Bulwer's consent. When the Zulu later made a counter-raid across the border at Middle Drift in June, Bulwer's reservations were vindicated.

In the event, Chelmsford's increasingly strained relationship with Bulwer, and the difficult working relationship between the military and colonial authorities, was one factor which influenced the decision to replace Lord Chelmsford as commander-in-chief in southern Africa. However, Chelmsford won his victory at Ulundi on 4 July before he could be superseded; his successor, Wolseley, privately confided to his journal that Bulwer had probably been right in his opposition to raiding. Bulwer's advice on the post-war settlement was influential in Wolseley's decision to partition Zululand.

Bulwer's period as Lieutenant Governor of Natal ended in 1880, but in 1882 he was given a post with even greater responsibilities, that of Governor of Natal and Special Commissioner for

Zululand. Although he had not been in favour of the invasion of Zululand, he now regarded any reversal of policy as a mistake and set himself firmly against the resurgence of the Zulu Royal House. In this he was influenced by Theophilus Shepstone. When the Colonial office in London decided in 1882 to restore King Cetshwayo to part of his former territories, Bulwer was charged with the responsibility of deciding the boundaries. As Professor Jeff Guy has pointed out, 'he acted reluctantly, dragging his feet at every step, determined to obstruct restoration if possible'. The restoration went ahead anyway, but Bulwer continued to support his officials in Zululand, most of whom were openly partisan against the king's party. Civil war broke out almost immediately, and Cetshwayo was defeated, fleeing to the protection of the British Resident in Eshowe where he died in February 1884.

Cetshwayo's successor, King Dinuzulu, appealed to republican Boers from the Transvaal to intervene in the civil war on his behalf, promising land as a reward; they did so, defeating Dinuzulu's enemy Zibhebhu at the Battle of Tshaneni in June 1884. The price to be paid was high, however, and the Boers demanded a vast tract of Zulu territory in payment. Bulwer openly expressed the opinion that the loss served the Royal House right, but nonetheless argued that the British government intervene. In 1887 Boer claims were limited and the rest of Zululand passed under British control.

Bulwer had already left Africa by then. His term as Governor of Natal had come to an end in 1885, and he took up a post as High Commissioner of Cyprus. He retired in 1892 and returned to Norfolk, where he died on 30 September 1914.

Browne, George Hamilton

George Hamilton Browne (the name was not hyphenated in early official documents, though it has often been written as such) remains one of the most intriguing and controversial characters to emerge from the Anglo-Zulu War. He was by nature an adventurer, and a garrulous one at that, whose own stories are the principle cause of the confusion that still surrounds his life and career.

George Hamilton Browne was born on 22 December 1844 in

Cheltenham, the son of Major George Browne of the 35th Regiment, and his wife Susannah. The Browne family seat was Comber House, in County Londonderry, Ireland, and George was one of nine children. He was given a public school education, but by his own account he gained 'far more laurels in the playing fields than in the lecture-rooms, for although I worked hard in a desultory way, still my best efforts were given to the play-ground and gymnasium'. He remained athletic in later life and took a keen interest in boxing.

From an early age, Browne had enjoyed the sights and sounds of military life at the barracks where his father was based, and when he left school he was sent to an academy in Lausanne with the intention of eventually joining the Army. If he can be believed, Hamilton Browne's youth was characterized by a romantic penchant for duelling and for dramatic entanglements with women that, between them, prevented him gaining entry into the Royal Military Academy at Woolwich. Instead, he ran away to join the Royal Horse Artillery as a driver, but was discovered by a relative and was discharged as under-aged. There followed, he said, a duel over a lady, and a rapid flight across the Channel, which resulted in enlistment in the Papal Zouaves – the first taste of an essentially mercenary lifestyle – and some action in the Italian War of Unification.

In January 1866 Browne arrived in New Zealand, and entered the most controversial period of his extraordinary career. New Zealand was, at that time, drawing towards the end of several decades of bitter warfare between European settlers and the indigenous Maori over the question of land ownership. Browne later wrote a book about that period – *With the Lost Legion in New Zealand* (c. 1911) – in which, curiously, he refers to himself throughout by a pseudonym. The reason for this has since become apparent, in that the adventures he ascribes to his alter ego were by no means all his own. He claimed to have served with the famous Forest Rangers, but no official record of service in his own name exists prior to 1872, by which time the fighting was over. If Browne saw service in the active phase of the wars between 1866 and 1872, as he claimed, it was not under his own name; it is, however, entirely possible that he enlisted under a false one. Whether he had witnessed them himself, or heard them from participants later, many of the incidents described in the book did not in any case occur to George Hamilton Browne, and the use of a pseudonym appears to have been a rather transparent attempt to deflect criticism that he was claiming other men's glory.

Whatever the truth of his adventures, the implication that he had considerably embellished them caused considerable offence in New Zealand when the book was published. What seems to have irritated Browne's former comrades as much as anything, was the fact that, at a time when white New Zealand society was striving to achieve a sense of common identity and respectability, Browne had portrayed the men of the old volunteer units as piratical rogues and vagabonds. One officer went so far as to claim, in response, that Browne was not entitled to the New Zealand campaign medal he habitually wore, but had misappropriated it by falsifying the records of a man with a similar surname who had died in service. Certainly, there can be no doubt that the love of a good yarn was often foremost in Browne's reminiscences, and that he had few qualms about bending the facts to suit.

Browne seems to have left New Zealand about 1870. He probably did then fight bushrangers for a spell in Australia – where he was wounded – and might perhaps have served on the American frontier in the wars against the indigenous Americans. A year or two later he was back in New Zealand, serving in the Armed Constabulary until discharged at his own request in 1875. He then tried his hand at running a pub, but the venture failed and he left New Zealand under something of a financial cloud. He was troubled throughout his life by money worries, and admitted that he was often 'reckless'. Nevertheless, he continued to refer to himself by the nickname 'Maori' Browne throughout the rest of his life.

At the beginning of 1878 he arrived in southern Africa. Here he met a number of former acquaintances among the 1/24th Regiment, then serving on the Cape Frontier, and volunteered as an officer in Pulleine's Rangers, an irregular unit formed by Colonel Henry Pulleine, 1/24th. At the end of 1878, with the 24th joining the troops assembling on the Zulu border, Browne again volunteered, this time securing the rank of major in the 1st Battalion, 3rd Regiment, Natal Native Contingent.

When Browne wrote a second book about his experiences – *A Lost Legionary in South Africa* (c. 1913) – he wisely decided to do so under his own name, aware, no doubt, of the controversy his earlier book had caused in New Zealand. Fortunately, his part in the Zulu campaign is well documented and supported by a wide variety of official reports, private diaries and correspondence. It is interesting to note, however, that where two accounts of the same incident exist written by Browne – an official one and a later one in his reminiscences – the one in the book is invariably prone to greater exaggeration.

Browne was present at the crossing of the Centre Column into Zululand at Rorke's Drift on 11 January 1879 (there is, incidentally, no independent evidence to support his comment that several of his men drowned in the crossing), and he was in the thick of the action at Sihayo's homestead on the 12th. Here he led several companies from his battalion into the centre of the Zulu position among the rocks at the foot of the Ngedla cliffs, only to find that most of his men fled before they reached the Zulus. On 21 January his battalion was appointed to sweep through the Malakatha and Hlazakazi range. His men were engaged in clearing Zulus from the Magogo and Silutshana hills on the 22nd when they were ordered to return to the camp at Isandlwana to assist in packing up for a general column advance.

Browne's men approached to within two or three miles of the camp before realizing that it was under attack. They then took up a position on a commanding ridge on the left of the road, and Browne's description – from his memoirs – of what he saw there remains one of the most chilling accounts to emerge from the war:

> Good God! What a sight it was. By the road that runs between the hill and the kopje, came a huge mob of maddened cattle, followed by a dense swarm of Zulus. These poured into the undefended right and rear of the camp and at the same time the left horn of the enemy and the chest of the army rushed in. Nothing could stand against this combined attack. All formation was broken in a minute, and the camp became a seething pandemonium of men and cattle struggling in dense

clouds of dust and smoke ...

That night, on the Nek below Isandlwana, Browne claimed to recognize the body of his old friend, Henry Pulleine.

The following morning the remnants of Lord Chelmsford's column returned to Rorke's Drift. They arrived to find the garrison had made a stout defence during the night – and that a large number of wounded Zulus lay out in the surrounding bush. Hamilton Browne's men, assisted by numbers of regular infantry, swept the bush and killed them all. Browne's comment that 'it was beastly but there was nothing else to do' reflects a ruthlessness which may have been learned in the tough fighting in New Zealand – whatever he saw of it – and which characterized his career.

In the aftermath of Isandlwana, Browne remained at Rorke's Drift, making occasional forays across the border to skirmish there ('on turning the body over we found it was a woman', he remarked after he and a companion shot two Zulus making ritual preparations; 'we neither of us expressed any regret ...') until ordered to the Cape to recruit men for a newly-raised unit, Lonsdale's Horse. He returned to the border in time to serve with Lord Chelmsford's expedition to relieve the besieged garrison at Eshowe, and was present at the Battle of kwaGingindlovu on 2 April. Sent back to the Cape, with a party of irregulars due to be discharged, Browne was badly injured when he was crushed between a mule and its shipboard stall.

Browne spent several months convalescing at the Cape, during which time he met Dolphina Spolander, whom he married on 25 June 1879. The couple later had six children, although Browne spent much of his time away from the marriage, adventuring in southern Africa. He served in the BaSotho 'Gun War' of 1880, and in Sir Charles Warren's Bechuanaland expedition of 1884. In 1885 he was appointed adjutant of the Diamond Fields Horse. In 1888 he served briefly in Zululand again, during the Dinuzulu rebellion, where he met Robert Baden-Powell.

In 1890, he joined the British South Africa Company's Pioneer expedition to occupy Mashonaland (Zimbabwe, formerly Rhodesia), the beginning of several years' involvement in Rhodesian affairs. He served under Major Forbes in the war against the amaNdebele ('Matabele') in 1893 and in 1896 commanded volunteers under Baden-Powell during the Rebellion. Baden-Powell remembered him with obvious affection from the 1888 expedition, and photographed Browne 'as he liked to be photographed', pointing a gun at a cowering African. While Baden-Powell clearly regarded him as a colourful and rather extreme character, whose views were not necessarily typical of the regular soldiery, his attitude reflects a darker understanding that it was by men such as Browne that empires are won and held.

Browne seems to have remained in Rhodesia throughout the Anglo-Boer War, before returning to the Cape. He had, apparently, lost much of his investment in the cattle diseases that swept through southern Africa at the end of the nineteenth century. At the Cape, there was worse to come; his wife Dolphina died in May 1904. This ushered in a new period of hardship for Browne, who appealed to the British Government for a pension, but was refused. About this time he seems to have sold his campaign medals, which perhaps explains why of those he wore in later life – now in a private collection – only his BSA Co. was as officially issued; indeed, the official status of his medals remains something of a mystery. He was so reduced in circumstances at one point as to seek help from the Salvation Army.

In 1909 his luck turned, and he married Sarah Wilkerson, a lady of independent means, and they returned to England. The meeting was apparently a romantic one; Sarah Wilkerson is said to have corresponded with Browne after the Zulu campaign, for she had been engaged to a man whose life Browne had 'saved'. Her fiancée had later been killed in the Sudan, and Sarah had never married; seeing the news of Browne's misfortunes she had contacted him again.

Browne was by now in retirement, his health impaired by the hardships of the life he had endured, and he embarked upon writing up 'his' experiences, although his tone suggests a certain disillusion with the practical rewards of a lifetime spent servicing Imperial adventures:

I had made the Crown and flag my fetish from early childhood, and in my own stupid and conceited mind reckoned it to be my bounded duty to fight for them, and that

11

so long as the war continued I must continue to serve, no matter what it cost me in pecuniary and personal losses. This infatuation has stuck to me all my life, and is as quick now as it was then, my life in consequence, so far as gaining the good things of this world goes being a wretched failure ... as for your country, represented as it is by a gang of greedy, self-seeking politicians, you may starve in the gutter or rot in the workhouse. Therefore, my romantic new chum, when you see the chance to make money on the one hand, and fighting for your country on the other, you go for the money. There are plenty of bally fools such as I have been to do the fighting. Your paltry services won't be missed...

George Hamilton Browne's last years were spent with his wife in Jamaica, where he died in a nursing home in February 1916. His recklessness with money must have continued to the very end, if the story that his wife had been a wealthy woman is to be believed, for a few years after his death Sarah, back in England, was reduced to repairing soldiers' worn clothing in a munitions depot. A friend appealed on her behalf to the New Zealand government for support in recognition of George's role in the old Maori Wars. In view of the controversy surrounding his time there, the Government declined.

Colenso, Agnes Mary

Agnes Colenso was the youngest of Bishop John William Colenso's daughters, and was born in September 1855 in Pietermaritzburg, shortly after the family arrived in Natal. She shared a common upbringing with her siblings in an environment dominated by Christian faith and intellectual debate. She was a fluent Zulu linguist, and although by nature shy, she followed the family tradition, established by her father and inherited by her eldest sister Harriette, of campaigning for just dealings with the Zulu Royal House. None of the Colenso daughters married, and Agnes lived much of her life with Harriette, with whom she formed a formidable partnership championing, in particular, the cause of King Cetshwayo's successor, King Dinuzulu. In 1884 the Colenso residence at Bishopstowe burned down, but Harriette and Agnes continued to live on the property until evicted under the Church Properties Act in 1910. They moved to Sweetwaters, Pietermaritzburg, and pursued mission work until their deaths within a few weeks of each other in 1932; Harriette died on 2 June and Agnes on 26 July.

Colenso, Frances Ellen

Frances Colenso was the second daughter of Bishop John William Colenso and his wife Sarah. She was born in Norfolk in 1849, when her father was a country parson, and emigrated to Natal with the family in 1855. Frances grew up against the background of life at Colenso's Ekukhanyeni mission, outside Pietermaritzburg. Apart from a brief spell in school in England (1862-1865, when her father was defending himself against the charge of heresy) she was educated at home in an atmosphere characterized by a greater degree of intellectual stimulation than was common for female children of the age. The Colenso children absorbed both the religious faith and commitment to social justice which framed their parents' beliefs, and from an early age Frances and her sisters assisted with the mission work. In 1873 the family befriended Major Anthony Durnford RE, who had recently arrived in the colony as Natal's Chief Engineer. Durnford was soon at the centre of events which propelled Bishop Colenso – and his family – to the forefront of controversial colonial politics. During the 'rebellion' of *inkosi* Langalibalele kaMthimkhulu of the amaHlubi, Durnford was sent in command of a detachment of colonial troops to prevent the amaHlubi fleeing across the Kahlamba Mountains, and away from Natal's jurisdiction. In a skirmish on the Bushman's Pass on 4 November 1873 several of Durnford's troops were killed and Durnford was himself wounded. Settler society was alarmed by the incident and blamed Durnford; the intensity of the punishment inflicted upon the amaHlubi prompted Colenso to publicly question the justice of colonial policy.

The Langalibalele affair marked the politicization of Colenso's daughters, and their increasing involvement in their father's affairs. It was about this time that Frances – who preferred to be called Nell – formed a deep attachment to Durnford. Although popular mythology has elevated this relationship to the great love affair of the Anglo-Zulu War, it is unlikely that it ever developed beyond an intense friendship constrained by mutual circumstance. Durnford was older than Nell and married to an estranged wife whom he could not divorce, and both parties were bound by propriety and honour; indeed, in the aftermath of the Bushman's Pass affair, honour was all that Durnford had left.

Nevertheless, Frances Colenso was moved by the apparent injustice of Durnford's predicament to write a fictionalized defence of his actions; Durnford asked that it should not be published in his lifetime, and it emerged only in 1880 as *My Chief and I*, written under the pseudonym Atherton Wylde. *My Chief and I* is today regarded as a prototype of southern African feminist writing and political polemic. Durnford's death at Isandlwana, the attempts by Lord Chelmsford's staff to blame him for the disaster, and the injustice of the British invasion of Zululand in general, prompted Frances to adopt an increasingly outspoken stance. On hearing that items had been moved from Durnford's body, discovered on the field on 21 May 1879, she became convinced that these included papers damaging to Lord Chelmsford's reputation, and campaigned for the contents to be made public; the existence of such documents was vigorously denied by the men who had found Durnford's body.

Frances left Natal in October 1879, apparently in part to escape her grief, but during her time in England she allied herself to Durnford's brother, Edward, who was also seeking to clear his name. Together they produced *A History of the Zulu War and its Origins*, which was a critique of British policy and vindication of Anthony Durnford. As Zululand collapsed into civil war as a result of the post-war settlement, Frances returned to Natal and, encouraged by her father, began work on another book, *The Ruin of Zululand*, which was not published until after the Bishop's death. She was by this stage already suffering from tuberculosis, which she had contracted while nursing a sick soldier in 1878, and while she continued with her sisters to campaign on behalf of the Zulu people, her health steadily declined. She died in 1887.

Colenso, Harriette Emily
Harriette was the eldest child of Bishop John Colenso and his wife

Sarah. She was born in Norfolk, England, in June 1847 and emigrated to Natal with her family in 1855. She grew up at Bishopstowe, outside Pietermaritzburg, and while interested in music, dancing and art – all conventional feminine pursuits of the age – she developed a strong character and was greatly influenced by her parents' religious and humanitarian beliefs. From the mid-1860s she acted as her father's secretary, sharing his growing commitment to African affairs following the Langalibalele 'rebellion' of 1873. A fluent Zulu linguist, she was known to the Africans as Dlwedlwe, 'her father's walking stick', reflecting both her supportive role and strength of personal character. When Colenso defended Langalibalele's actions, it was Harriette who cared for the *inkosi*'s children following his banishment to Robben Island. Together with her sisters, she supported her father's campaign against British intervention in Zululand in 1879, and in November 1880 she accompanied her father on a visit to the exiled monarch in Cape Town. Harriette then supervised the publication of a *Digest of Zulu Affairs* which was strongly critical of British policy. With Bishop Colenso's death in June 1883 his work passed to his children, and particularly his daughters Harriette, Frances and Agnes. After the death of King Cetshwayo in 1884, Harriette campaigned on behalf of his son, Dinuzulu. The Colensos were increasingly isolated within colonial society – an isolation which intensified with the death of Frances in 1887. When, in 1888, King Dinuzulu's Royalist revolt in Zululand collapsed, it was to Harriette Colenso that he chose to surrender, slipping through cordons of British troops and catching the train to Pietermaritzburg. Harriette played a prominent part in orchestrating his defence against charges of treason, but Dinuzulu was found guilty and exiled to St Helena. With Agnes' support, Harriette continued to agitate for his defence, campaigning in Natal and England for his release. Between 1890 and 1913 she produced fourteen pamphlets criticizing British conduct in Zululand, and she was regarded with irritation by the colonial officials whose failings she mercilessly exposed. In 1898, King Dinuzulu returned to Natal but was arrested again in 1907 and was charged with having incited the poll tax disturbances of the previous year. Once again Harriette

was at the forefront of his defence, organizing his legal represen-
tation and arguing his case in the press. Largely as a result of her
efforts King Dinuzulu was found guilty on only five out of
twenty-three charges against him, and sentenced to internal exile.

Colenso's house at Bishopstowe was burnt down in 1884.
Harriette and Agnes continued to live on the property until
evicted in 1910 under the Church Properties Act. They continued
their mission work at Sweetwaters, Pietermaritzburg, until
Harriette's death in June 1932. Agnes died a few weeks later.

Colenso, Bishop John William

John William Colenso's career was characterized throughout his
life by intense and often bitter controversy, both religious and
political. He was born on 24 January 1814 in St Austell,
Cornwall, the eldest of four children. His father was a mining
agent who lost the family savings when a tin mine he had invested
in was flooded; his mother died when he was a teenager. From an
early age Colenso displayed both a remarkable strength of
character and a strong interest in religion. Impelled by the
family's straightened circumstances, he took work as a teacher at
the age of seventeen, but he was determined to attend the
University of Cambridge, an ambition he achieved only after his
extended family pooled their meagre resources. At Cambridge he
proved a prize-winning scholar with a flair for mathematics but
his early career remained marred by financial struggle. In 1839 he
was admitted as a Deacon in the Church of England, and took up
a post as a tutor of mathematics at Harrow school. This proved
a financial disaster as he over-extended himself in buying a house
which promptly burned down; three years' later he was back at
Cambridge, in debt, and scraping a living as a maths teacher.
During this time, however, he met Sarah Frances Bunyon who
shared Colenso's passion for learning and theology, and whom he
married in 1846, when his financial position at last stabilized.
The couple had five children – two boys and three girls – and
Colenso's daughters played a significant part in the history of the
Zulu Royal House.

Over several years Colenso enjoyed the parish living at Forncett
St Mary in Norfolk, where in 1852 he was visited by Robert

Grey, first Anglican Bishop of Cape Town. Grey was impressed by Colenso's energy and determination, and asked him to accept the newly created bishopric of the colony of Natal. Excited by the prospect of mission work among the Zulus, Colenso accepted. On 13 November 1853 he was consecrated at Lambeth by the Archbishop of Canterbury in a ceremony in which the Bishops of Cape Town, Oxford, London, Lincoln, Adelaide and Guiana participated. Within months he was in Natal on a rapid reconnaissance, riding about the country, meeting local clerics, colonial officials and *amakhosi* alike. He returned to England to raise funds, and in March 1855 set sail with his wife and growing family. He built a mission at Bishopstowe, outside Pietermaritzburg, which he called Ekukanyeni, 'the home of light'.

Colenso threw himself into his new responsibilities with typical energy. Recognizing the practical difficulties of preaching the gospel to isiZulu speakers, he first produced a book of Zulu grammar, then began to translate the Gospels. As well as planning a chain of mission stations across Natal, he began a school at Bishopstowe to teach the sons of influential *amakhosi*. Under his tutelage for a while was Prince Mthonga kaMpande, one of Prince Cetshwayo's rivals to the succession of the Zulu throne, who had fled Zululand following the 'war of the princes' in 1856. At this point Colenso enjoyed a firm friendship with Theophilus Shepstone, who supported Colenso's attempts to spread Christianity – and with it British political influence – through education.

Colenso had arrived in Natal at a time of deep theological divisions within the Anglican Church, and from the outset this created an uneasy relationship with his settler congregation. This was intensified by Colenso's own refusal to shirk from the contentious consequences of his own rigorously logical approach to Christian theology. He was assisted in his attempts to translate the gospel by one of his congregation, William Ngidi, whose questions during the process caused Colenso to doubt the literal truth of some aspects of the Old Testament. In 1861, as a result of his own soul-searching, he published a critique of St Paul's Epistle to the Romans, followed between 1862 and 1879 by seven

17

volumes examining the Pentateuch and the Book of Joshua. His views provoked a violent reaction among High Church supporters within the Anglican Church and alienated his immediate superior, the Bishop of Cape Town. In 1863 he was charged with heresy and travelled to England to defend himself. Although found guilty and sentenced to excommunication, this verdict was later found to be legally unsound, and he was reinstated in 1869. Nevertheless, a considerable faction remained opposed to his return to Natal, where rival clergy formed a separate group, the Church of the Province of South Africa, and consecrated a rival Bishop, William Macrorie, who took the title Bishop of Maritzburg. Colenso continued to preach at St Peter's Cathedral in Pietermaritzburg but at the height of the schism his sermons were often accomplished in the face of determined opposition from his rivals.

Colenso's approach to missionary theology remained pragmatic, which further isolated him from his colleagues. Most missionaries, for example, were adamant that converts should abandon polygamy and set aside all but their first wife; Colenso recognized the injustice of this and merely required that a convert took no more wives after becoming a Christian.

Colenso became actively involved in the politics of Natal following the 'rebellion' of the amaHlubi *inkosi* Langalibalele kaMthimkhulu in 1873. Colenso felt that Langalibalele had been driven into a corner by colonial policies, and that his act of rebellion – seeking to place himself outside the authority of the Natal administration by crossing the Kahlamba Mountains into BaSotholand – had been punished by disproportionate severity. His decision to publicly defend Langalibalele led to a rift with Theophilus Shepstone, whose policies provided the context for the rebellion. From 1873 Colenso became increasingly outspoken as a champion of African rights. Although, as Professor Jeff Guy has pointed out, his liberalism was limited by his faith in the righteousness of the British Empire – he saw injustice as an aberration of British principles, rather than as an inevitable consequence of colonialism – he would remain a remarkably courageous champion of liberty who deservedly received the African name Sobantu, 'father of the people'.

From 1877 – when Britain annexed the Transvaal Republic – Colenso became an increasingly forthright critic of the Confederation policy, discerning in it a ploy to destroy the Zulu kingdom which he attempted to expose by constantly questioning the motives of Imperial officials. He became a trusted correspondent of King Cetshwayo, who sought his advice during the accelerating crisis. Colenso was unable to prevent the outbreak of hostilities in January 1879. In the aftermath of Isandlwana, on 12 March 1879 – a day appointed by Natal's Lieutenant Governor as one of humiliation and prayer – Colenso delivered a powerful sermon which laid bare the hypocrisy of British policy in Zululand, and found common ground in the suffering of bereaved Natal families with those of the fallen Zulus. At the end of hostilities, in October 1879, Colenso and his family organized for the body of their friend, Colonel Anthony Durnford, to be exhumed from the battlefield at Isandlwana and re-interred in Pietermaritzburg.

The defeat of the Zulus only intensified Colenso's campaigning on their behalf. He remained one of the few supporters of the Zulu Royal House during King Cetshwayo's exile, encouraging both the king in his captivity and his supporters in Zululand. In November 1880 he and his daughter Harriette personally visited the king in captivity in Cape Town. Over the next two years, several deputations of Royalist supporters walked from Zululand to Bishopstowe, hoping to find sympathy for their predicament which was denied to them by colonial officials. In fact, however, although Colenso remained outspoken, his influence in official circles – dominated in Natal by Theophilus Shepstone's family and by the disinterest of the Gladstone administration in London – was negligible. Refusing to give way to frustration he became increasingly preoccupied with Zulu affairs, to the detriment of his health. He welcomed Cetshwayo's partial restoration in February 1883, but recognized that the constraints placed upon the king would prevent him addressing the deep divisions which had prevailed within the country since 1879. In June 1883 Colenso became ill, and on the 20th he died. He was buried in front of the altar of St Peter's Church. King Cetshwayo expressed his sorrow at his passing; within weeks, however, King Cetshwayo was defeated at the rebuilt oNdini homestead by his rival, *inkosi* Zibhebhu kaMaphitha.

Colenso's legacy was one of moral courage and intellectual strength in the cause of social justice; it was taken up in his lifetime by his children, and – perhaps more significantly – laid the foundation for a tradition of outspoken Christian liberalism that has remained a theme in modern South African history.

D'Arcy, Henry Cecil, VC

Henry Cecil Dudgeon D'Arcy was born at Wanganui, New Zealand, on 11 August 1850, into a family with an established military tradition. His grandfather, Captain Edward D'Arcy, served with the 43rd Regiment under Wellington in the Peninsula, and fought at New Orleans in the War of 1812 where he was severely wounded, losing both his legs. Cecil's father, Major Oliver Barker D'Arcy, was born in Ireland in 1811 and was a career soldier, serving at various times with the 18th, 65th, 73rd, Regiments and the Cape Mounted Rifles (then an imperial, rather than colonial, regiment). Major Barker and his wife had no less than nine children, born at various points around the Empire in accordance with his service; Cecil was born in New Zealand at the time of the 65th Regiment's participation in the Maori Wars. From 1859 they moved to South Africa and the Cape Frontier, where Major D'Arcy retired and settled. Cecil D'Arcy and his brothers grew up in King William's Town and its surroundings against a background of frontier life. Cecil and his elder brother Robert both grew up strong and adventurous and enjoyed the outdoor life, and were renowned for their disregard of danger. One revealing anecdote from their childhood recalls how they decided, as teenagers, to swim the flooded Qora River with knapsacks on their backs; they were promptly swept away and would have drowned had not a boat's crew spotted them struggling in the waters at the river mouth and rescued them. Most of Major D'Arcy's sons entered either the Cape military or civil service, and Cecil was working as a clerk in Grahamstown when the 9th Frontier War broke out in 1877. He promptly resigned his job and volunteered to join a local irregular unit, the Albany Mounted Volunteers, as a trooper. He soon rose to the rank of sergeant major, and in December of that year transferred to another irregular unit, the Frontier Light Horse, which had recently been raised by Major Fred Carrington of the 24th Regiment. D'Arcy was offered a commission, and served with the Frontier Light Horse throughout the closing stages of the war, which consisted mainly of extended sweeps through the bush in search of Xhosa guerrilla bands. On one occasion the Frontier Light Horse was camping in the bush and was troubled by the attentions of a sniper. The story has it that the senior officer asked for three men to step forward – the bravest man in the corps, the best shot, and the man with the best eyesight. The man with the best eyesight happened to be a padre, and Cecil volunteered as the 'brave man'. He was promptly directed to stand on a barrel, in plain view of the sniper, tempting him to make a shot; when he did, the padre spotted the source of the gun smoke, and the marksman promptly shot the sniper dead. When the Xhosa chief Sandile was killed in June 1878 – his death deprived the Xhosa of their last focus of resistance – Cecil D'Arcy commanded a troop of the Frontier Light Horse which paraded at his funeral.

In July 1878 the Frontier Light Horse was ordered to Natal and thence to the Transvaal to join the column assembling under Colonel Hugh Rowlands VC for the attack on the Pedi king Sekhukhune. In the event Rowlands' campaign was unsuccessful – he had too few troops for the job and his advance was hampered by lack of water and by horse-sickness – and in November the Frontier Light Horse was re-allocated to Colonel Wood's column on the Zulu border. Wood's column crossed the Ncome River into Zululand on 6 January – five days before Bartle Frere's ultimatum to King Cetshwayo officially expired – and he began a programme of aggressive patrolling, harassing local Zulu groups towards the Hlobane Mountain, and dispersing the Zulu raiders who assembled in the Ntombe valley. The Frontier Light Horse was extensively employed in this work; Cecil kept a souvenir upon which he carved his battle honours, and which testifies to his personal involvement in these actions. He was present at the entry into Zululand on 6 January, the patrols to Domba's Kop (possibly Dumbe mountain, north of Hlobane) and Makatees' Kop (a distinctive peak between Khambula and

Lüneburg), and the retaliatory raid against Prince Mbilini's followers in the Ntombe valley on 15 February. He also commanded part of the force that escorted Prince Hamu kaNzibe into Khambula on 10 March, following his surrender.

On 28 March the Frontier Light Horse took part in the attack on Hlobane Mountain under Buller, ascending a steep pass at the eastern flank at first light and in a thunderstorm. Buller secured the summit of the mountain in the face of resistance from the local abaQulusi Zulus, but the unexpected arrival of the main Zulu army, en route from oNdini to attack Khambula, forced him to abandon it. Among those who spotted the approaching army in the valley below was Cecil D'Arcy, who drew Buller's attention to it with the comment 'It's all up with us this time, Colonel'. Buller's men were forced to retire down a steep staircase of rock at the western tip of the mountain, later dubbed 'the Devil's Pass'. D'Arcy himself only just managed to escape:

> I saw, I thought, all our men down, and then considered I had to think of myself, and got half-way down when a stone about the size of a small piano came bounding down; I heard a shout from above, 'Look out below', and down the beastly thing came right on my horse's leg, cutting it right off. I at that same time got knocked down the hill by another horse, and was nearly squeezed to death. I had taken the bridle off, and was about to take the saddle, when I heard a scream; I looked up and saw the Zulus right in among the white men, stabbing horses and men. I made a jump and got down somehow or other, and ran as hard as I could with seventy rounds of ball cartridge, a carbine, revolver, field-glasses, and heavy boots.

At the bottom of the hill one of his men caught D'Arcy a horse, but he was no sooner mounted than he was obliged to dismount again and give it up to a man wounded in the leg. Buller himself then took D'Arcy up behind his saddle and carried him clear before returning to try to stem the rout; D'Arcy was then carried away in turns by Lieutenant Blaine of the Frontier Light Horse and Major Tremlett RA. For his part in D'Arcy's rescue, Buller himself was awarded the Victoria Cross.

Exhausted and traumatized by their experience, the survivors of the Frontier Light Horse were in vengeful mood the following day when the Zulu army attacked Khambula. During the pursuit in the closing stages of the battle, D'Arcy set the tone with a ruthlessness which, for all its brutality, seriously damaged the future capacity of the Zulu army to resist:

> ...once they retired all the horsemen in the camp followed them for eight miles, butchering the brutes all over the place. I told the men, 'No quarter boys, and remember yesterday', and we did knock them about, killing them all over the place. In the line where I followed them there were 157 dead bodies counted next day.

The defeat at Khambula exhausted the Zulu army, allowing Lord Chelmsford to complete his plans for a renewed offensive. The British columns were reorganized and Wood's column re-designated the Flying Column. The Frontier Light Horse, including D'Arcy, took part in extensive patrolling to clear the country of Zulu scouts prior to the new British advance across the Ncome on 1 June. In a change to his previous policy, Lord Chelmsford authorized the large-scale destruction of Zulu homesteads in an attempt to undermine civilian support for the war. Like most of the irregulars, Cecil D'Arcy burned a great many Zulu huts, and the story is told of one occasion when he entered a homestead alone, calmly smoking his pipe as he went from one hut to another, setting each alight, despite sniping from the outraged inhabitants in the hills nearby. Seeing him there, a fellow officer ran up to him and called out 'For Heaven's sake, D'Arcy, give me a light and let me die smoking too!' On 5 June the Frontier Light Horse took part in a protracted skirmish along the valley of the uPoko stream, below eZungeni hill, during which Lieutenant Frith of the 17th Lancers was killed. On 27 June it was part of a force which destroyed the concentration of Zulu royal homesteads in the emaKhosini valley.

By the end of June the British advance had reached the White Mfolozi River, beyond which lay oNdini, where the Zulu army was again assembling to resist them. On 3 July Buller led a large force of irregulars across the river to scout out the terrain and to determine the Zulu intentions; the Frontier Light Horse and Cecil

D'Arcy went with him. The mounted men scattered Zulu marksmen defending bluffs above the river, and pursued a number of herdsmen and scouts across the undulating grassland beyond. The scouts retired towards the homestead of kwaNodwengu, and Buller became suspicious that the British were being led into a trap. He ordered the mounted men to halt, and as he did so the Zulu uMxapho regiment rose from the grass ahead of them, where they had been lying in ambush. The Zulus fired a ragged volley that startled the horses, and several men were thrown. D'Arcy saw Trooper Raubenheim fall to the ground and lay stunned; he dismounted and tried to heave Raubenheim's inert weight onto his saddle. He succeeded, but as he tried to mount himself, the horse, unaccustomed to the weight and startled by the approaching warriors, bucked and both men fell. D'Arcy fell on his holstered revolver, injuring his side. Nonetheless, he tried once more to lift Raubenheim, further injuring his back in the process. By this time the Zulus were only yards away, and D'Arcy reluctantly gave up the struggle, letting Raubenheim fall to the ground, and riding away in the nick of time. As the Zulus rushed past, Raubenheim was killed; his body was discovered the following morning having been mutilated to provide potent medicine for the pre-battle ritual preparation of the Zulu army.

D'Arcy's injuries were severe enough to keep him in camp the following day when Lord Chelmsford crossed the White Mfolozi with the bulk of his forces and decisively defeated the Zulus at the Battle of Ulundi.

The action on 3 July produced a crop of VC recommendations, Lord Beresford, D'Arcy and Sergeant Edmund O'Toole of the Frontier Light Horse all being recommended for their attempts to save the lives of unhorsed men during the retreat. All three were confirmed, and the awards to D'Arcy and O'Toole were particularly welcomed in the colonial press, which felt that the heroism of the colonial forces had not been fully recognized throughout the war. D'Arcy was presented with his award by General Sir Garnet Wolseley in Pretoria on 11 December 1879. In a fulsome speech, Wolseley commented that:

I am sure, Mr D'Arcy, that not only South Africa, but in every other colony of the British Empire, it will now be understood, from the gift of this decoration by Her Majesty, that Her Majesty does not reserve this honour for Imperial Troops alone, but is anxious to distinguish the courage and devotion of the soldiers of Her Colonial Empire.

Privately, however, Wolseley confided to his journal, rather sourly, that 'I don't think his was a good case for this distinction as he did not succeed in saving the life of the man he dismounted to assist'.

The Zulu campaign had seriously affected Cecil D'Arcy's health. He remained troubled by his back injury, and he was apparently suffering from the effects of bilharzia – probably contracted in childhood – and malaria. He also suffered from asthma. The controversy surrounding his award seems to have left him disillusioned with his experiences in Zululand, and he may well have been suffering from periodic bouts of depression. Nevertheless, in May 1880 he accepted a commission as captain in the Cape Mounted Rifles. In July, a detachment from the regiment was dispatched to BaSotholand, where a number of Sotho chiefs had recently risen in rebellion rather than be disarmed at the dictates of the Cape Colony. Cecil D'Arcy fought with his regiment throughout the 'Gun War', and on one occasion, during the attack on Chief Lerothodi on 31 October 1880, D'Arcy found himself among a party cut off by the precipitate retreat of a body of volunteer troops. D'Arcy and another officer ordered their men to dismount and form a square, and they were able to hold off repeated attacks by a much larger number of Sotho warriors.

The 'Gun War' ended in controversy for the Cape Mounted Rifles, with wrangling and recriminations among the officers. Although he never commented upon it, this may have influenced D'Arcy's decision to resign his commission on 15 April 1881. He bought a small farm near Stutterheim and lived a solitary life, still plagued by ill health. He began to drink heavily. At the beginning of August he went to stay with the Revd. Mr Taberer at the St Matthew's Mission outside Keiskamma Hoek. It was the depths of the Cape winter, and the Taberers thought the bracing hill-country air might be good for D'Arcy.

25

On the evening of Saturday 6 August D'Arcy retired for the night, complaining of feeling tired. The following morning, Mr Taberer took a coffee to D'Arcy's room but found it empty and the bed not slept in. Taberer was not unduly worried until D'Arcy failed to return that day and in the afternoon he alerted the police. An extensive search followed, but despite reports of a lone white man seen wandering in the hills, D'Arcy was not found. Then, on 28 December 1881 an African, searching for honey, found the remains of a man in a narrow cleft in a cliff-face about six miles from Mr Taberer's mission. A gold watch and signet ring found on the body identified the remains as those of Cecil D'Arcy. What had led him into the hills that night remains a mystery, but it had been a bitterly cold one with a light fall of snow, and he had probably died of exposure.

Curiously, in 1925 a Mr V. G. Sparks was playing cricket at Newcastle, in northern Natal, when he spotted an elderly man, apparently down on his luck, who looked familiar. To his surprise, when he went to speak to the man Sparks claimed to recognize him as Cecil D'Arcy. Confronted, the man admitted his identity, and claimed that he had faked his death more than forty years before. He had, he said, stumbled across a corpse at the foot of the cliffs and on the spur of the moment decided to escape his worries and place his watch and ring upon the dead man. D'Arcy then begged Sparks to keep his identity secret, as he wished to remain 'dead to the world', before he shuffled off again into obscurity.

The Sparks story is perhaps best judged in the tradition of other reported sightings of famous men long after their supposed deaths, from Butch Cassidy to Lord Lucan. D'Arcy's death was, by 1925, an established mystery, and whatever personal acquaintance Sparks had shared with him had been decades before – the identity of the mysterious stranger of 1925 is unlikely ever to be known. It does, however, at least add a bizarre postscript not altogether out of keeping with Cecil D'Arcy's curious and tragic end.

Dartnell, John George

Dartnell was born in 1837 in Ontario, Canada, his father, George Russell Dartnell, being an Inspector General of Military

Hospitals. In 1855, Dartnell purchased a commission as an ensign in the 86th Regiment, and was serving with them in 1857 when the Indian Mutiny broke out. The Regiment was heavily involved in operations in central India under Sir Hugh Rose, and Dartnell himself was badly wounded in the storming of the rebel stronghold at Jhansi. Dartnell had been assigned to one of a number of storming parties which were attempting to climb the city walls with scaling ladders; although the storming parties reached the walls successfully, the rebels repeatedly pushed their ladders away. At last, one ladder was secured, and Dartnell clambered quickly up, throwing himself into a group of rebels at the top. He was immediately attacked and suffered no less than four sword cuts, including a bad wound to his left hand, and was hit in the chest by a matchlock bullet, which was fortunately deflected by the plate on his sword belt. By this time, however, others had climbed up the ladder and joined the mêlée, driving the rebels off and saving Dartnell's life. He was recommended for the Victoria Cross, but not awarded it, although he was personally commended by Sir Hugh Rose.

At the close of the Mutiny, Dartnell remained in India, transferring first to the 16th Regiment, and later to the 27th. He also took part in the Bhutan expedition of 1865 as an ADC to the commanding officer. In 1865, he married Clara Steer, daughter of the Judge of the Supreme Court of Calcutta.

In 1869 Dartnell sold his commission and retired from the Army with the rank of brevet major. He decided to try his hand at farming in the colonies, and he and Clara set sail for Natal, where Dartnell bought a farm. Although not unsuccessful, it was a lonely life, and Clara Dartnell complained of the isolation. When, following the rebellion of *inkosi* Langalibalele kaMthimkhulu in 1873, the Natal authorities decided to establish a regular force to police the colony, Dartnell applied for the job. He was appointed largely on the strength of his extensive military experience, and the result was the Natal Mounted Police, which, although not strictly a military body, was then the only full-time professional armed unit maintained by the Natal administration. Dartnell recruited most of the men in England, since service did not seem attractive to those already in the colony, and through hard work Dartnell turned them into an efficient force which eventually commanded respect throughout the colony. Dartnell himself emerged as a popular leader among his men, and soon established himself as a prominent voice on military matters within colonial society.

With the invasion of Zululand imminent, the Natal government made hurried preparations for the defence of the colony. The various administrative counties were divided up into defensive districts, and Dartnell was given command of Defensive District No. 1 in the Klip River County. This was a huge swathe of country which stretched from Ladysmith in the west along the north bank of the Thukela as far as the Mzinyathi and the border with Zululand. At the same time, however, the government recognized that Dartnell might be called upon to pass over this duty to a deputy if he was needed to serve in the field. And indeed he was; it soon became clear to Lord Chelmsford that he was dangerously short of mounted troops, and that the locally-raised mounted units – the Police and Volunteers – would be an invaluable addition to his forces. The conditions of service for both the Volunteer units and Police dictated that they could not be forced to serve outside the colony's borders, and even though Chelmsford persuaded the Natal administration to sanction the move, the men had to be balloted to see if they were prepared to fight in Zululand. Most agreed, stipulating that they would only do so under Dartnell's command.

In November 1878 both the Police and various Volunteer corps were mobilized, and Dartnell with them. The Police were attached to the No. 3 Column assembling at Helpmekaar, together with a number of Volunteer units. Lord Chelmsford placed all the mounted men under the command of a 'special service' officer, Lieutenant Colonel J. C. Russell of the 12th Lancers, who had been sent out from the UK for extra staff duties – and in doing so promptly offended the Colonial troops, who had only agreed to join the invasion on condition they were led by Dartnell. Russell himself was more accustomed to the habits and style of command of a fashionable cavalry unit, and the Volunteers and Police had not taken to his manner; but the incident had as much to do with the need among the colonial troops for their unique status to be recognized. Their responsibility was to colonial authority, not the regular military. Chelmsford smoothed over the row by appointing Dartnell to his staff, while leaving Russell in charge in the field.

On 21 January Dartnell was given command of the extended foray through the Malakatha and Hlazakazi hills that heralded Chelmsford's intended forward move from Isandlwana. Since their sweep was to cover a large tract of rugged country, the most mobile elements in the column were chosen – the Police, Volunteers and NNC – and as the senior and most experienced colonial officer present, Dartnell was a logical choice for command. Dartnell set out at dawn on the 21st, with orders to return to Isandlwana that evening and report on any Zulu movements.

Once they reached the hills, Dartnell's command divided, the NNC sweeping round the high bastion of Malakatha hill, and working up the hot thorn-valleys beyond, towards the Mangeni gorge at the far end of the range. The mounted men swept across the undulating summit of Hlazakazi hill. All parties were ordered to rendezvous at the head of the Mangeni gorge. The sweep encountered no hostile Zulus, but by the time the NNC arrived at the rendezvous, late in the day, Police scouts had pushed into the hills above Mangeni. Here they saw the first signs of a Zulu presence. Dartnell placed the NNC on the eastern edge of the Hlazakazi range, and took the mounted men forward to probe the Magogo and Silutshana hills. They had not gone far when a line of warriors appeared on a crest above them. Dartnell at once withdrew, and so did the Zulus.

It was now late evening, and Dartnell was faced with a very real dilemma. Lord Chelmsford expected him to return to Isandlwana, but the reconnaissance had so far learned tantalizingly little of the Zulu movements, beyond their presence. If Dartnell then withdrew, he would negate the intelligence value of the expedition, since it was unlikely that the Zulus would remain in position overnight. He also risked the prospect of an attack in the rear, on the road back to camp, by an unknown number of the enemy.

Instead, he decided to join the NNC on the edge of Hlazakazi, to bivouac for the night and to send word of his discovery to Lord

Chelmsford, asking for assistance.

This was a reasonable decision under the circumstances, but it was to have serious repercussions on the conduct of the Isandlwana campaign. Chelmsford received the report in the small hours of the morning of the 22nd, and decided to split his force, hurrying out with a light column to reinforce Dartnell in the hope of catching the main Zulu army by surprise. In the event, by the time Chelmsford arrived at Mangeni, the Zulus of the night before had indeed melted away, and Chelmsford spent a frustrating morning – in which Dartnell and the Police were fully employed – chasing them through the hills. And while he did so, the main Zulu army fell upon and destroyed the camp at Isandlwana.

Chelmsford had little choice but to evacuate his command – including Dartnell's men – to Natal as quickly as possible. In the immediate aftermath of the disaster, the remnants of the Centre Column were left at Rorke's Drift. Dartnell himself remained there until early February when he returned to Ladysmith to supervise preparations for its defence in the event of an expected Zulu counter-attack. No such attack was forthcoming, and once the panic in settler society began to subside, Dartnell returned to Helpmekaar to take part with the Colonial troops in a series of probes across the Mzinyathi River which heralded the British recovery. On 14 March Major Black of the 24th crossed the border with a small patrol that included Dartnell and ten men of the Police. Black's intention was to investigate the state of the Isandlwana battlefield. As they passed through the Batshe valley they exchanged shots with Zulu scouts, who promptly ran onto high ground and lit signal fires. The old battlefield proved a disturbing sight, the dead not yet fully decomposed; on their way back the patrol came under fire from Zulus summoned by the signal fires. Black advised Lord Chelmsford that a further delay in attempting a burial of the dead was desirable. Ten days later, however, with Chelmsford poised to advance to the relief of Eshowe and keen to mount diversions along the border, another foray was mounted to Isandlwana. This was a much larger expedition – 2,000 men – and was commanded by Dartnell. The column swept through the countryside around Isandlwana, burning homesteads along the way, and returned across the Mzinyathi at Sothondose's ('Fugitives') Drift.

Although a hasty expedition to recover serviceable wagons and bury some of the dead took place in May, it was not until June that a serious attempt was made to bury the bodies at Isandlwana. By that stage the tide of war was swinging inexorably against the Zulus, and it was considered safe enough to try. Major Black made a series of expeditions from Rorke's Drift, and on the first day he was accompanied by Dartnell and representatives from the Police and Volunteers who sought out and buried a number of Colonial dead.

With the end of the Anglo-Zulu War, Dartnell returned to his role as Natal's senior military officer. With the outbreak of the BaSotho 'Gun War' in 1880, Dartnell led detachments of Police into the Drakensberg foothills, patrolling the passes – sometimes in atrocious weather – to ensure that the Sotho made no raids into Natal. At the end of the year, with the outbreak of the Boer rebellion in the Transvaal, Dartnell and the Police were attached to the troops assembled by General Sir George Colley in Natal. On 24 January 1881 the Police scouted the pass at Laing's Nek, Colley's intended route through the Drakensberg and into the Transvaal. In the event the Boers occupied the pass and blocked Colley's advance; when he unsuccessfully attacked it on the 28th, the Police were held in reserve. However, Colley was reluctant to employ local troops in the campaign for fear of poisoning long-term relations between the British settlers and Boers after the war. Throughout the rest of the campaign Dartnell and the Police were employed on scouting duties.

In May 1881 Dartnell was appointed a Companion of the Most Distinguished Order of St Michael and St George by Queen Victoria.

In 1891 Dartnell and a small escort were stationed on Natal's southern border to prevent violent disturbances in neighbouring Pondoland from spilling across the border. The Police presence was sufficient to prevent Pondo raids into Natal. In 1894 Natal's police forces were reorganized, and the old NMP officially replaced by the newly designated Natal Police. Dartnell himself was given the rank of chief commissioner.

With the outbreak of the Anglo-Boer War in 1899, Dartnell's local knowledge was greatly in demand, and he was appointed to the staff of the GOC Natal. He was close to General Sir William Penn Symons when Symons was shot and mortally wounded at Talana Hill, the first battle of the war, on 20 October 1899.

When the British troops withdrew from northern Natal towards Ladysmith, Dartnell was attached to the staff of General Sir George White. He was present throughout the subsequent siege, and after the relief served with the columns which drove the Boers back across the Biggarsberg and into the Transvaal.

In 1901 Dartnell was given command of a column which swept the eastern Transvaal along the Delagoa Bay railway line, and down towards the Zululand border. In August 1901 he took command of the Imperial Light Horse. Escorting provisions to Harrismith in the Free State, he clashed with a Boer commando at Elands' River. When Louis Botha made a strike into Zululand in September 1901, Dartnell and the Imperial Light Horse were sent from Harrismith to Eshowe, but Botha's advance had already been halted by the time it arrived. Sent back to Harrismith, Dartnell was engaged in further skirmishing along the Elands' River.

In 1903 Dartnell finally retired from Natal service with the rank of major general. He returned to England with the intention of enjoying his pension. When, however, the Poll Tax disturbances threatened to break into open violence in early 1906, Dartnell again offered his services. Sponsored by a Natal newspaper, he returned to Africa bringing with him a consignment of newly invented Rexer light machine guns. While this was a propaganda coup for white Natal, made deeply nervous at the prospect of an uprising and overreacting fiercely, Dartnell played little part in the subsequent field operations beyond advising the commanders at a senior level. The rebellion, such as it was, was ruthlessly suppressed, the final act in the long process of the conquest of the African peoples of Natal and Zululand in which Dartnell had more than once played his part.

Dartnell retired to England and settled in Folkestone, Kent, where he died on 7 August 1913 at the age of seventy-five.

Dunn, John Robert

John Dunn, the famous 'White Chief of the Zulus' came to the Zulu kingdom as an outsider, an *umlungu* – a European – with no previous history, power, wealth or influence, yet he rose to such a position of prominence that he came to rule hundreds of square miles in King Cetshwayo's name. His origins were humble enough. His father, Robert Newton Dunn, was born in Inverness, Scotland, in 1795. In 1820 he left home – and perhaps a broken marriage – and joined nearly 4,000 other immigrants in a government-sponsored scheme to settle the Eastern Cape of South Africa. The '1820 settlers' were established as a buffer between the existing colony and the independent chiefdoms of the amaXhosa. Many settlers found that the land allocated to them was insufficient to sustain them, but Robert Dunn seems to have prospered, and in 1824 he married Anne Biggar, the daughter of a prominent settler, Alexander Biggar. Biggar himself was a colourful character, destined to leave his mark, too, on the early white settlement of Natal; a one-time paymaster of the 85th Regiment, he had fought in the Napoleonic Wars and War of 1812 but had been cashiered following a row over missing regimental funds. A restless, charismatic character with little respect for authority, Biggar had railed against the British administration on the Cape Frontier, particularly in the aftermath of the 6th Frontier War (1834-35). Many settlers, both English-speaking and Afrikaners, lost property in the Xhosa attacks, and blamed the British for failing to protect them, and this conflict was important in shaping the attitudes which led to the Great Trek. Biggar, too, decided to leave the Cape, but not with one of the Boer trek groups; in 1834, together with a small group of family and associates, including Robert and Anne Dunn, Alexander Biggar sailed to Port Natal.

Port Natal at that time was an adventurous spot. It supported a small group of white hunters and traders, who had landed there a decade before, and who lived by the sufferance of the Zulu kings. Their lifestyle reflected their circumstances; most of them lived in wattle and daub huts, had married African wives, and, after the Zulu manner, reckoned their wealth and status in cattle and adherents. Their principal economic activity was trading with the Zulu king, augmented by hunting for ivory and hides. Tough, individualistic and self-reliant, they acknowledged little authority beyond that of the Zulu kings – and that reluctantly – and the atmosphere at the settlement was relaxed to the point of anarchy.

The Dunns established themselves on the Berea ridge, overlooking the bay of Port Natal, and in 1834 Anne Dunn gave birth to a son, John; whether he was born before they left the Cape or after the couple arrived in Natal has never been satisfactorily determined. In 1838, disaster struck the Port Natal settlement. The recent arrival of the Voortrekkers from the Cape led to conflict with the Zulu kingdom and the Port Natal settlers made the mistake of siding with their fellow whites. The ensuing conflict saw a ramshackle settler army scattered by the Zulus, a Zulu attack on the settlement itself, and later the death of Alexander Biggar. After it was over, the Dunns returned to Port Natal, rebuilt their home, and prospered by selling imported ammunition to the Boers. In 1843 Natal was annexed as a British colony.

Young John Dunn had spent his formative years in the old settlement, and grew up assuming many of its multicultural characteristics. He had learned naturally to ride, shoot and fend for himself; he spoke Zulu as well as English, mixed with Africans as an equal, and accepted marriage between white men and African women as commonplace. In 1847 Robert Dunn died – trampled to death by an elephant – and after a while Anne Dunn returned to the Cape. John Dunn, who was fourteen when his father died, decided to remain in Natal. For a while he attempted to make a living as a hunter, hiring himself out as a guide to officers of the garrison at Port Natal, but this was too insecure an income, and in 1853 he took a position as a transport rider, taking goods to and from the Transvaal. The experience was to prove both disillusioning and decisive:

> On our return, when the time for my honorarium came, I was told I was not of age, and that by Roman-Dutch Law I could not claim the money. This so disgusted me that I determined to desert the haunts of civilization for the haunts of large game in Zululand...

When John Dunn left Natal, he took with him Catherine Pierce, the daughter of his father's business associate, Frank Pierce, by a Cape Malay woman. Dunn entered Zululand at the Lower Drift on the Thukela, and for nearly two years lived a semi-nomadic life, subsisting by his hunting. Like some of the early adventurers in the Port Natal community, he abandoned European clothes and spoke only the language of the people among whom he lived. This might have been his lot for the rest of his life, but for a bizarre quirk of fate. In 1854, Joshua Walmsley, a retired army officer recently appointed Border Agent at the Lower Drift by the Natal government, was hunting in Zululand with some friends. While they were camped at the AmaTigulu River, Walmsley apparently spotted a white Zulu, and one of his companions recognized him as John Dunn. Walmsley decided to detain him, and despite Dunn's protests, offered him the alternative of returning with him to live at his border post, or of being sent back to Durban, as Port Natal had now been renamed. Dunn chose the latter.

His relationship with Walmsley was to prove a pivotal one for Dunn. Walmsley, an eccentric himself, assumed the role of a father figure to his protégé, and took it upon himself to improve Dunn's education. Dunn worked as Walmsley's assistant, and again augmented his income by guiding hunting parties into Zululand. He was by now utterly familiar, not only with the language and customs of the Zulus, but with much of the country lying north of the lower reaches of the Thukela. His knowledge of the people and country, and his confidence in his own skill at arms, were to shape Dunn's crucial response to events that occurred, suddenly and dramatically, on his doorstep in 1856.

In 1856 the succession dispute among King Mpande's sons came to a head. Prince Mbuyazi, recognizing that he had secured insufficient support within the kingdom, attempted to flee to Natal with his supporters, and with his rival Prince Cetshwayo in hot pursuit. Mbuyazi reached the Thukela in late November but was prevented by the rains from crossing. He attempted to secure the support of the Natal authorities, but they refused to intervene.

As Border Agent, Walmsley suddenly found himself in the front line. He was aware of the government's official position, but he realized, too, that a human catastrophe was imminent; with Cetshwayo's uSuthu closing in, the iziGqoza were likely to be trapped on the river. The situation was complicated, too, by the presence on the Zulu bank of a group of white traders, who had been desperate to escape Zululand before the conflict, but were also trapped, along with their cattle and wagons, on the Zulu bank. When Dunn offered to intervene, Walmsley accepted his offer. Officially, Dunn was authorized only to try to mediate the quarrel between the two parties, but as Dunn himself recalled, Walmsley's private instructions were explicit – 'Make peace if you can, Dunn, but if you cannot succeed, fight like the devils, and give a good account of yourselves'. Since Dunn took with him thirty-five of Walmsley's African border policemen and 100 trained black hunters, it is clear he had very little hope of a peaceful outcome. He was not the only European to offer his services; several Boers had offered to fight for Mbuyazi, while a number of the traders stranded at the river were also prepared to fight. While their motives no doubt varied, all hoped to profit should Mbuyazi be victorious.

Mediation was, in fact, impossible and Cetshwayo's army arrived on 2 December. In the battle that followed, Dunn acquitted himself creditably, but barely escaped with his life. His armed retainers held Cetshwayo's men in check for a while, but the majority of Mbuyazi's warriors abandoned their position, retiring in confusion through their non-combatants, and sheltered in folds in the ground behind them. By the time they reached the river, all semblance of order had collapsed. Dunn's own account captures the horror of the final stage of the battle:

As soon as I got to the river I was at once rushed at by men, women, and children begging me to save them. Several poor mothers held out their babies to me offering them to me as my property if I would only save them. And now the uSuthu were fairly amongst us, stabbing right and left without mercy, and regardless of sex, and as I saw that my only chance was to try and swim for it, I urged my horse into the water, but no sooner in than I was besieged from all sides by men clinging to me, so that my horse was, to say the least, completely rooted to the spot. I now jumped off, stripped myself, all but hat and shirt, and taking nothing but my gun which I held aloft, and swam with one hand ...

Mbuyazi and thousands of his followers perished; the river carried their bodies away and out to sea, many were washed up on beaches for miles along the coast for days later. In one blow, Prince Cetshwayo had effectively destroyed the main opposition to his succession. In the aftermath of the battle, Dunn made a characteristically bold decision. Once they had recovered from their shocking experiences, the white traders realized that in the confusion the uSuthu had carried off the herds they had gathered at the river. As these amounted to several thousand head, they represented a considerable financial investment and the traders offered a reward of £250 to anyone who could recover them. John Dunn accepted. He crossed back into Zululand, and sought an audience with King Mpande. The old king was deeply moved to hear a first-hand account of the battle which had killed so many of his sons, but he explained that the cattle had been kept among Cetshwayo's supporters, near the coast.

Dunn had little option but to confront Cetshwayo himself. Given that he had only recently – and very effectively – fought against him, this required a certain amount of nerve, but in fact Prince Cetshwayo received him at the emaNgweni homestead politely enough. The heir apparent was reluctant to risk offending the Natal authorities, and could afford to be magnanimous. Dunn eventually emerged with 1,000 head of cattle, and finally claimed his reward.

It was probably Dunn's courage at this time that prompted Cetshwayo's next move. Dunn had not long been back in Natal when a royal messenger arrived from the king, bringing him an offer to move into Zululand, and act as his adviser on white affairs. At first glance, this seems a curious development, but in fact the succession crisis had brought home to Cetshwayo the extent to which European interests had penetrated all aspects of Zulu life. White hunters and traders operated widely in Zululand, and had become an important factor in the nation's economy, while mission societies constantly lobbied to be allowed to establish stations in the country. Cetshwayo felt the need for a white man upon whom he could rely to serve as an intermediary with the Europeans. Dunn's familiarity with the Zulu lifestyle, and his undoubted courage, made him ideal for the role. After giving the matter some thought, Dunn agreed, despite Walmsley's reservations. Dunn parted from his patron with regret; 'notwithstanding all his eccentricities', he recalled fondly, 'he was one of the most generous-hearted men I ever had anything to do with'.

Dunn established himself in the Ngoye hills, in the south-east of the country. This was an area that had suffered a population exodus as a result of the recent civil war, and it gave him the opportunity to build up support in something of a power vacuum. The area was rich in game, which enabled him to develop his hunting concerns, while at the same time it lay across the main road from the Lower Thukela drift to the Mahlabatini plain, where both Mpande and Cetshwayo established their capitals. Dunn was therefore ideally placed to monitor all European movements, and trade, into the country.

John Dunn had married Catherine Pierce in 1853, and soon after he moved to Zululand, he took his first Zulu wife, much to Catherine's outrage. In fact, the marriage merely confirmed the extent to which Dunn had adopted a cross-cultural lifestyle. Like the early settlers at Port Natal, among whom he grew up, he had assumed the role of a Zulu chief, and he accumulated power, prestige and adherents in the Zulu manner. In all, he would marry forty-nine Zulu wives, and by doing so carefully allied himself to important Zulu families along the coastal strip. As his influence grew, he established two homesteads – at Moyeni and Mangethe – and befriended important figures in the Zulu establishment who lived nearby, such as Prince Dabulamanzi kaMpande, who lived near Eshowe. From the late 1860s, he began to import firearms into the Zulu kingdom, on behalf of his patron, Prince Cetshwayo, a factor that materially strengthened Cetshwayo's position within the country, and later improved the firepower of the national army on the eve of war with the British.

Dunn's lifestyle reflected his increased affluence. He dressed in the fashion of an English country squire, buying clothes, guns and books on trading trips across the border, and at each of his homes he maintained a European house for his own living area. His Zulu wives were established in traditional settlements nearby. His legendary skill as a hunter attracted all manner of visiting European sportsmen, and he regularly entertained officers from the British garrison in Natal. As the traveller Bertram Mitford observed, there was nothing flamboyant about his manner:

> John Dunn is a handsome, well-built man, about five feet eight in height, with good forehead, regular features, and keen grey eyes; a closely cut iron-grey beard hides the lower half of his bronzed weather-tanned countenance, and a look of determination and shrewdness is discernible in every lineament. So far from affecting native costume, the chief was, if anything, more neatly dressed than the average colonist, in plain tweed suit and wide-awake hat. In manner he is quiet and unassuming, and no trace of self-glorification or 'bounce' is there about him.

The extent to which Dunn had integrated himself into the political hierarchy within Zululand became apparent in 1872, when King Mpande died. All of Cetshwayo's insecurities about his succession re-emerged as he feared new challenges might emerge at the last minute to prevent him becoming king. To bolster his position within the country, Cetshwayo invited colonial Natal to send representatives to attend the coronation ceremonies, as a tacit sign of support, and it was Dunn who mediated between the Natal representatives and the king. He also acted as a stabilizing factor within the country, reassuring Cetshwayo during the tensions that surrounded the ceremonies, and ensuring that meetings with powerful groups from the outlying regions passed off peacefully. He provided a carriage for Cetshwayo's use on the long march to the valley of the ancestors, and he arranged for a photographer to record the extraordinary events.

Although Dunn's position was now more influential than ever, he was unable to fend off the growing crisis with British Natal. As tension mounted throughout 1877 and 1878, Dunn urged King Cetshwayo to meet British demands wherever possible. Feeling within Zululand ran high against the aggressive stance adopted by the British, to the extent that by the end of 1878 many important councillors regarded Dunn with open suspicion and hostility. Despite the fact that Zulu society had proved quite capable of absorbing a white *inkosi* – it was more open in that respect than colonial society in Natal, which remained unwilling to treat Africans on equal terms – the threat of a direct confrontation between the different aspects of Dunn's lifestyle inevitably left him isolated. In the run up to war, Dunn continued to provide guns for the Zulu army, and it was to his Mangethe residence that the king's representatives first reported on their return from the ultimatum meeting of 11 December. The ultimatum, however, made Dunn's position impossible; if he stayed in Zululand, he risked being a scapegoat for Zulu anger against the whites, and if he chose to fight for Cetshwayo, the British would regard him as a traitor. Cetshwayo recognized this, and advised him that 'if it came to fighting I was to stand on one side'.

At the very end of December 1878, Dunn crossed into Natal with his dependants. He had entered Zululand twenty years before, accompanied by a young wife and a handful of African retainers; his following now numbered 2,000 people, and 3,000 cattle. The Natal authorities made land available to him south of the Thukela as a temporary settlement, but cattle promised by Lord Chelmsford to feed them failed to materialize – an omission that did little to restore Dunn's faith in colonial morality.

Dunn managed to stay aloof during the first phase of the war, preoccupied instead with the care of his followers. Following the disaster at Isandlwana, he came under increasing pressure from Lord Chelmsford to take an active part in the war. In particular, Dunn's knowledge of the coastal sector – his old fiefdom – became increasingly useful once it became clear that Chelmsford would have to mount an expedition to relieve Colonel Pearson's beleaguered garrison at Eshowe. Chelmsford would have to advance through country that Dunn knew intimately, while many of the local Zulu commanders were former friends of Dunn. Towards the end of March, therefore, Chelmsford formally requested Dunn to join his staff as an adviser on the Eshowe relief expedition. Dunn's reaction reflected the pragmatism that had characterized his entire career:

I began to think earnestly of the situation. I could see that I could be of service in pointing out the means of averting another disaster, and besides, I knew that in the fighting between the Boers and the English at the Bay (D'Urban) my father had suffered by remaining neutral, so I made up my mind to go with Lord Chelmsford to the relief of the Eshowe garrison.

This was, of course, a decision that the Zulus would regard as a betrayal, yet it is hard not to have some sympathy for Dunn's predicament. He knew that the odds of the Zulus ultimately winning the war were negligible; his only hope of regaining any of his former authority was to join the winning side. The alternative was to abandon everything he had built up. When Lord Chelmsford crossed the Lower Drift at the end of March, Dunn was with him. He took with him 200 of his trained hunters, who, as Dunn's Scouts, were to prove among the most useful African auxiliaries attached to the force. Having made his decision, Dunn played an active part in the expedition. The night before the Battle of kwaGingindlovu (1/2 April) he personally scouted out the Zulu dispositions, accompanied by one of Chelmsford's ADCs, Captain Molyneux. The following day, during the Zulu attack, Dunn stood on top of a wagon, picking off warriors at a range of 300 yards; 'I know I fired over thirty shots', he recalled, 'and missed very few'.

From kwaGingindlovu, Chelmsford advanced and relieved Eshowe. He had already decided not to hold the post, which was too advanced, and he ordered the garrison to retire. As a last gesture of defiance, Chelmsford himself personally commanded a sortie to attack eZulwini, the homestead of Prince Dabulamanzi, which was situated nearby. Dunn was persuaded to accompany the expedition. The troops found the homestead deserted and set it on fire, but as they did so shots struck among them from a group of Zulus watching from a nearby hill. Dunn recognized his old friend Prince Dabulamanzi among the marksmen, and the pair traded shots at long range. Neither man was struck, but Chelmsford's staff noted that the Zulus ducked several times during the exchange.

Yet Dunn was not able to escape entirely the consequences of his participation in the war. On the way back from Eshowe,

Chelmsford's force halted for the night by the deserted German mission station at eMvutsheni. The British troops bivouacked in a protective laager, with European piquet's thrown out, and a screen of Dunn's scouts beyond. During the night, a shot fired by a nervous piquet caused a mad scramble for the safety of the laager, and some of the troops mistook Dunn's scouts for the enemy. The result was an appalling tragedy:

> I was roused from a sound sleep by hearing firing and shouts. I seized my rifle and jumped up, but what was then my horror when I recognized the voices of some of my unfortunate native scouts calling out 'Friend! Friend!' which they had been taught to respond to the challenge of the sentries. I called out 'Good God! They are shooting my men down!' and ran out, calling out to the soldiers to stop firing. On passing the line of fire I came upon one of my men lying dead in the trench with a bayonet wound in his chest. On examining the lot, I found ten more wounded, two of whom died the next day ...

There was more to come. Passing his deserted homesteads on the way back to the border, Dunn found that the incensed Zulus had ransacked them and put them to the torch.

With British successes in the north of the country too – at Khambula on 29 March – the tide of war was swinging against the Zulus. Chelmsford had the time now to patiently prepare a new invasion, and Dunn was attached to the 1st Division, Chelmsford's new column that operated in the coastal sector. Although this column was not involved in any further fighting, Dunn was fully involved in the negotiations to persuade the chiefs of the coastal sector to surrender.

At the end of the war, Dunn not unnaturally hoped for his reward. Lord Chelmsford resigned his command soon after his victory at Ulundi (oNdini) on 4 July, and it was left to his successor, Sir Garnet Wolseley, to impose a peace settlement. Wolseley was constrained by a political brief that required him to reduce the threat posed by an independent Zululand, while at the same time avoiding the expense of outright annexation. At the end of August, his patrols captured King Cetshwayo, and the defeated monarch was sent to exile in Cape Town. Advised by colonial administrators in Natal, Wolseley had decided to divide Zululand out among thirteen client rulers, who were not only loyal to the British, but whose personal circumstances had made them opponents of the Royal House. Dunn fitted both categories. Wolseley who, on the whole, had a snobbish aversion to settler society, shared the admiration with which many officers had come to regard Dunn;

> I have never met a man who was more of a puzzle to me than Dunn. He has never been in England and most of his life he has passed in Zululand without any English or civilized society, and yet in his manner he is in every way the Gentleman. He is quiet, self-possessed and respectful without any servility whatever, and his voice is soft and pleasant. He is much more of the Gentlemen than any of the self-opinionated and stuck-up people who profess to be 'our leading citizens' in Natal ... He leads a curiously solitary life, but says he enjoys it thoroughly, being in every way his own king, without any policemen in his dominions to serve him with a writ or lay rough hands upon him for taking the law into his own hands ... He has as many wives and concubines as he wishes to keep and he has a clan about him who are all ready to obey his slightest nod. He pays periodical visits to Natal and has his books and letters and newspapers sent to him regularly. I wish I dared make [him] King of Zululand, for he [would] make an admirable ruler.

Yet Wolseley shied away from replacing King Cetshwayo entirely with Dunn. Much as a 'white Zulu' might have been a solution to his political problems, Dunn's unconventional lifestyle made such extensive support impossible. In particular, the Church community in Natal despised Dunn, not only for the way in which he had abandoned Christian morality in favour of traditional Zulu beliefs, but also for the autocratic way he ruled his territory. Dunn had little sympathy for missionaries, whose work, he believed, degraded the Zulu people, and whose part-time economic activities competed with his own. Moreover, many officials in the Natal government regarded Dunn with suspicion because of his former association with the king. In the event, the best that Wolseley could do was make Dunn one of the thirteen 'kinglets', whom he set up to rule in Zululand. Dunn was confirmed in possession of his old lands, and his authority was extended further westwards, along the banks of the Thukela. In the west, his property bordered that awarded to the Sotho chief, Hlubi, another outsider who was rewarded with territory by the British. In effect, Wolseley had created a buffer zone along the entire Natal/Zululand boundary, which he had given to the two men who could most be relied upon to support British policy.

Dunn accepted the award 'on condition that Cetywayo [sic] should never hold any position in the country again'. He returned with his followers and set about rebuilding his ruined home-steads, and in many ways those first post-war years were his most prosperous. His territory was the largest it had ever been, and there were now no checks to his hunting and trading activities. Typically, he was astute enough to realize that his elevation was likely to make him a lasting enemy of Zulu loyalists, and he ruled his chiefdom with the firmness of a Zulu autocrat. He formed an alliance with the powerful anti-royalist groups who now ruled the northern districts – Prince Hamu and Chief Zibhebhu – and between them they continually harassed ardent royalists in their districts. In particular, this earned Dunn the hatred of his former friend, Prince Dabulamanzi, who was steadfastly loyal to Cetshwayo, and who was now placed under Dunn's authority. Dunn's position, however, was a powerful one; when, in July 1881, a man named Sitimela claimed to be a descendant of the famous Mthethwa chief Dingiswayo, and threatened the stability of the entire coastal sector, Dunn simply attacked him and dispersed his followers.

Yet Wolseley's settlement, if it succeeded in one regard – dividing the Zulus against themselves – it failed in another, that of securing the broader stability of the region. The tensions it unleashed threatened to spill over into colonial Natal. In northern Zululand, in particular, the activities of the British appointees resulted in a stream of protests from royalist supporters, claiming they were oppressed. As early as 1882, the British government began to consider the possibility of restoring King Cetshwayo to Zululand to re-establish order. Dunn was bitter at the prospect:

Let self-considered wiser heads than mine say what they like, I am confident that if my services had been more utilized, even after the restoration of Cetywayo, [sic] I could greatly have assisted in bringing about a more peaceful settlement of affairs in Zululand, from my actual knowledge and feelings of the people. But no; I was set up by a certain faction, to suit their end, as a rival to Cetywayo, hence the consequences.

The restoration of King Cetshwayo in 1883 meant the end of Dunn's tenure as an independent *inkosi*, and his status was reduced to that of a regional chief under British authority. In the event, however, the king's restoration proved a disaster. Soon after he returned to Zululand, a civil war broke out between his supporters and those of Chief Zibhebhu. Cetshwayo was utterly defeated in a surprise attack on his reconstituted oNdini homestead in July 1883; he fled to the protection of the Reserve Territory, where he died a broken man.

Dunn continued to rule his following from Mangethe and Moyeni. He dabbled occasionally – and unsuccessfully – in the troubled politics of the following decade, but his personal lifestyle was undiminished. He died on 5 August 1895 from the effects of dropsy and heart failure at his Moyeni homestead. He was sixty-five; he was survived by twenty-three of his wives and seventy-nine children. By Zulu standards he was a rich man, and his legacy included a fortune in cattle and personal effects.

Yet he left another bequest, too, which was more problematic. Today his descendants number over 3,000 and their mixed blood has ensured them a difficult history, despised and denied during the apartheid years, and more recently resented by Zulu nationalists. In many ways, the full implications of John Dunn's extraordinary life have yet to be resolved.

Filter, Reverend Johann Heinrich

The Reverend Johann Heinrich Filter was the leader of the German Lutheran community at the Lüneburg settlement throughout the war.

Lüneburg was one of the most remote and vulnerable settlements along the north-western Zulu frontier, in the heart of the so-called 'disputed territory'. It was located on the fringes of

45

Transvaal, Zulu and Swazi authority, and had been established in an area with a history of disrupted settlement. Zulu, Swazi and Sotho speakers had originally overlapped along the Phongolo river, but in the 1820s the Zulu king Shaka had made a determined effort to bring the area under his control (his decisive battle against the Ndwandwe people in 1828 had taken place close to the site of modern Lüneburg). It was Shaka who had established the ebaQulusini royal homestead further south, and within a generation its adherents had taken on a distinct local identity and the name abaQulusi. This strong Zulu presence led to the effective withdrawal of Swazi settlements north across the Phongolo. In the 1840s, however, a new wave of settlements had seen the establishment of the Boer town of Utrecht to the south-west; by 1879 Utrecht was part of the Transvaal republic. King Mpande had originally allowed Utrecht Boers seasonal grazing rights extending towards the Phongolo, but by the 1870s their gradual encroachment deeper into Zulu territory was widely resented. Mpande's successor, King Cetshwayo, was determined to halt this creeping invasion, and the increasingly belligerent attitude of the British from 1877 only hardened his resolve.

Lüneburg itself, built at the foot of the Ncaka Mountain and close to the Ntombe River, was at the hub of this vortex. It had been established by Germans of the Hermannsburg Mission in 1869 – German settlement in Natal has a surprisingly established history, going back to the 1840s – and the Hermannsbergers had acknowledged the unsettled political landscape by seeking permission to settle from both King Mpande and the Transvaal Republic. The Hermannsburg ethos stressed the value of hard work, and by 1879 the Lüneburg community, although small, had prospered, the members augmenting their efficient farming methods with transport riding into the nearby Transvaal. Pastor Filter arrived to take spiritual charge of the community in 1870, and by 1879 the settlement boasted a fine German-style church.

In the tense months leading up to the outbreak of war in 1879 it was clear to both the Lüneburg community and the military that their position was extremely vulnerable. The main Zulu group, the abaQulusi further south, were ardent Zulu royalists, while the settlement was surrounded by smaller chiefdoms which seemed equally likely to support the Zulu cause. These included the adherents of Manyanyoba Khubeka in the Ntombe valley, and Prince Mbilini waMswati, who maintained homesteads close to the Ntombe and on Hlobane Mountain, among the abaQulusi. Throughout 1878 parties of abaQulusi, acting under King Cetshwayo's orders, built homesteads close to Lüneburg, seeking to emphasize the king's claim to the region.

The settlement's vulnerability undoubtedly framed Lord Chelmsford's invasion plans, and the presence of two British columns, operating on either side of it, was intended to offer it protection. Colonel H. E. Wood's Left Flank Column was assembled at Utrecht, to the south-west, while Colonel H. Rowlands' column moved to the hamlet of Derby, on the Transvaal/Swazi border, to the north-east of Lüneburg. In October 1878, before even the British ultimatum had been presented, Wood established a garrison at Lüneburg itself, and an earthwork, Fort Clery, was built close to the settlement. A further stone laager was built beside the church to serve as a refuge for the civilian population.

The weeks leading up to the expiry of the British ultimatum were particularly tense at Lüneburg, and with the British declaration of war on 11 January most of the outlying farmers abandoned their property and took refuge in the civilian laager. Skirmishes between British troops and Mbilini's followers and the abaQulusi began almost immediately; on 22 January Colonel Wood dispersed a Zulu force on the slopes of the Zungwini and Hlobane mountains. On the night of 10-11 February, however, Mbilini struck back, leading a raid against the abandoned white farms surrounding Lüneburg. His target was not the absent settlers themselves, but their African workers – most of them Christians – who had stayed on the farms, and who were both an easier target, and were particularly despised by Zulu traditionalists. Nearly seventy men, women and children were killed, despite a foray by the Lüneburg garrison. A counter-attack a few days later by Colonel Buller only succeeded in driving the Zulus into the security of the rugged hills along the Ntombe valley. Scarcely a month later, Mbilini regrouped and attacked a stranded convoy of the 80th Regiment on the banks of the Ntombe, just three miles from Lüneburg.

In March 1879 the northern front was the scene of renewed military activity which involved not only the abaQulusi, but the main Zulu army. After the Battles of Hlobane (28 March) and Khambula (29 March) Zulu morale in the area declined, but sporadic skirmishes continued around Lüneburg. On 4 April a combined force of abaQulusi and Mbilini's followers raided the outskirts of the settlement again. On the following day, however, a party from Lüneburg, including Pastor Filter's son Johann Heinrich August, intercepted a party of retreating raiders, and in the ensuing skirmish Prince Mbilini was mortally wounded and Tshekwane, a son of Sihayo, killed. Nevertheless, minor raids continued throughout the war, and indeed young Johann Filter was killed in an incident on 7 June. Manyanyoba's followers were among the last Zulus to formally surrender, and skirmishing continued in the Ntombe valley into September.

Pastor Filter's role in reinforcing the resolve of the German community in Lüneburg was undoubtedly crucial to the settlement's survival. Frederick Schermbrucker, who commanded the garrison at Fort Clery in January 1879, described Filter as 'a severe specimen of the Lutheran Pastor of the 16th Century type [who] was equally prepared to lead his flock spiritually to heaven and bodily against the Zulu'. Despite his resolve, however, Filter was greatly affected by the death of his son during the war, and died on 23 December 1879.

Filter, Johann Heinrich August

Filter (born 16 March 1862) was the son of Pastor Heinrich Filter of Lüneburg. During the hostilities of 1879, Johann Heinrich volunteered to serve as interpreter to the British forces stationed in the settlement. As such, he enthusiastically accompanied a number of patrols and forays directed against Zulu raiding parties operating in the district. He was present in the skirmish on 5 April when Tshekwane kaSihayo was killed and Prince Mbilini mortally wounded. On 7 June a large Zulu force raided the farm of a Mr Niebuhr, close to the outskirts of Lüneburg and within sight of the military camp. Johann Heinrich Filter set out with a number of African border policemen and intercepted the raiders as they tried to retire across the Ntombe. The Zulus turned to fight, and Filter and six African policemen were surrounded and killed. According to one story, Filter was recognized as the Pastor's son by some of his attackers, who were inclined to spare him; others recalled his role in the death of Prince Mbilini, and he was killed.

A monument to Filter was erected in the 1930s on the road between Lüneburg and the Ntombe. Also commemorated on the same monument is Trooper Larsen, a nineteen year old Dane serving in Schermbrucker's Horse. On 18 May Schermbrucker himself was patrolling from Lüneburg towards the Ntombe, accompanied by Captain Moore of the 4th Regiment and Larsen, who was acting as Schermbrucker's orderly. The party was ambushed in long grass close to the river and Schermbrucker's horse killed. With the Zulus scarcely 150 yards off, Schermbrucker ordered Larsen to dismount, mounted his horse, and ordered Larsen up behind. Larsen, who was apparently a good runner, was reluctant to risk the safety of the horse with a double-load, and offered instead to set off on foot towards Lüneburg. Schermbrucker and Moore had not gone far when Moore's horse was also killed, and Moore was forced in any case to mount behind Schermbrucker. Both men reached Lüneburg safely, but Larsen failed to arrive. That night Schermbrucker organized a search party but it was called off in the face of a severe rainstorm. Larsen's body was only recovered from the banks of the Ntombe some months later.

Fynn, Henry Francis Jnr.

Henry Fynn Jnr. was born at Colesburg, Cape Colony, on 14 November 1846. He was the son of one of the most prominent of the early British adventurers who had settled in Natal, Henry Francis Fynn Snr. Fynn Snr. had arrived in Natal in 1824 and had been instrumental in establishing the European settlement of Port Natal; his famous diary records his contact with the Zulu king Shaka kaSenzangakhona. Like many of the early white settlers, Fynn had originally adopted a polygamous lifestyle and married a number of Zulu girls; his descendants and followers formed a large community and many still live in modern Natal. In 1837, however, Fynn had married an English girl, Ann Brown, in Grahamstown on the Eastern Cape; she died just two years later, and Fynn then married her sister, Christiana, in 1841. Christiana was the mother of Henry Fynn Jnr.

Fynn Jnr. spent much of his early life in Natal, and he spoke both Zulu and Afrikaans fluently, while his background had given him a unique insight into the history and traditions of the African peoples. He entered the Natal Civil Service in 1854 as a clerk and interpreter and was posted first to the Umkomanzi division and then to Newcastle. In 1873 he had accompanied Theophilus Shepstone's expedition to 'crown' Cetshwayo, and had met the Zulu king for the first time. 1874 the Msinga district (officially 'Umsinga' in colonial literature) was made a magisterial division and Fynn was transferred there; in 1876 he was promoted its resident magistrate.

At that time Msinga was one of the most remote magistracies in Natal, and Fynn's judicial authority extended over the scattered settler community of the Biggarsberg ridge and abutted the Zulu border, along the banks of the Mzinyathi, and the African locations further south. Fynn had married Hannah Payne in June 1870, and their lives at Msinga were spartan; in the 1870s the post consisted of just a courthouse with two cells and four living rooms, their immediate white neighbour being a solitary policeman. Nevertheless, Henry and Hannah raised a large family between them and continued to live at Msinga into the 1890s. Fynn proved to be a perceptive magistrate with some insight and sympathy for the African people under his control. He was known by the Zulu name of 'Gwalagwala' from the crimson lourie feather he habitually wore in his hat – itself an emblem of royalty and courage.

In December 1878 Fynn was appointed interpreter at the meeting with King Cetshwayo's representatives at the Lower Thukela Drift at which the British ultimatum was presented. Fynn returned to Msinga, which had already become central to the British invasion plans. The hamlet of Helpmekaar on the Biggarsberg heights was designated as the assembly point for the No. 3 Column – which was to be accompanied by Lord Chelmsford himself – while the 3rd Regiment, NNC, mustered at

Sandspruit, within sight of Fynn's courthouse. Fynn himself received approval to fortify his court buildings with shutters in the event of a Zulu counter-attack. As the troops gathered, however, Fynn found himself increasingly in demand among the military, called upon to advise on local defence, on Zulu affairs, and to act as a liaison officer between the regulars and their colonial counterparts. When the column descended from Helpmekaar to Rorke's Drift in the first week of January, Chelmsford asked the Natal authorities to release Fynn temporarily from his post at Msinga to move there; within a few days, however, he changed his request to ask that Fynn accompany the advance into Zululand as a member of the general staff, 'seeing how essential it was in the public interest that he should be with me'. Fynn joined Chelmsford on the 19th, and interpreted at a meeting between Chelmsford and Gamdana kaXongo (brother of *inkosi* Sihayo kaXongo) which resulted in Gamdana's submission. On the morning of the 22nd, Fynn accompanied Chelmsford's advance to Mangeni. When he returned with Chelmsford to the camp at Isandlwana that night, they found it devastated by the unexpected Zulu attack.

Fynn hurried back to Msinga, arriving there on the 24th to find that troops under Colonel Bray of the 4th Regiment, who had been on the road on the 22nd, had taken refuge there and barricaded it against a possible Zulu attack. Fynn's wife had already learned of the disaster from a survivor, James Brickhill. Bray was not impressed by the post's defensive potential and on the 25th abandoned it in favour of a steep knoll on the far side of the Helpmekaar road (later the site of Fort Bengough). Fynn had little choice but to join him. Someone at this time described Fynn as 'unnerved' by his night spent among the fresh dead on the Isandlwana battlefield, and in an excited state from lack of sleep and food – as well he might have been. He soon recovered, however, and as no Zulu attack developed, Fynn threw himself into reorganizing the black Border Guards who patrolled the Mzinyathi drifts and who had been thrown into chaos by the British collapse. Towards the end of February he personally visited all their outposts to check on their dispositions and boost their morale. Despite their vulnerable position, the Border Guards made a valuable contribution to the British war effort at this time, resisting as they did incursions by small groups of Zulus from the opposite bank of the Mzinyathi who could not resist crossing the border in the hope of looting undefended African homesteads and European farms abandoned after Isandlwana.

With the British recovery of March and April, the focus of the war shifted away from the Mzinyathi border. Fynn remained at Msinga, and in May joined the first major burial expedition to the battlefields, where he was able to help identify some of the colonial dead. Once Chelmsford began his fresh invasion of Zululand in June, Fynn began to attempt to persuade the *amakhosi* living across the river to surrender. Most prevaricated and did not do so until long after news of the British victory at Ulundi became common knowledge. Nevertheless, at Rorke's Drift on 20 August, Fynn received the formal submission of a number of important *amakhosi*, including Matshana kaMondise and Matshana kaSitshakuza, both of whom lived near Isandlwana.

The end of the war bought a new order to the Mzinyathi frontier, and in October it was Fynn and his Border Levies who officially escorted Hlubi Molife to the Batshe valley, to take up the chieftainship awarded him by the British.

Fynn settled into life at Msinga once more, and his family continued to expand. Then, in early 1883, King Cetshwayo was restored to Zululand. His authority was severely limited, and large swathes of the northern and southern districts were placed outside his control. He was, moreover, required to accept a British resident – and Henry Fynn was given the job. As King Cetshwayo struggled to rebuild his oNdini homestead, Fynn set up camp a few miles away across the Mahlabatini plain. Fynn's standing clearly worked in his favour and he and Cetshwayo got on well, but in fact Fynn's position was to prove an impossible one, and he was at last out of his depth. The king's return accelerated the festering dispute between royalist supporters and anti-royalists who had waxed fat in his absence, and Fynn found himself powerless to intervene and unable to influence events. He sought doggedly to persuade King Cetshwayo not to arm in contravention of the conditions of his restoration, but in the end events overtook them both. On 21 July 1883 *inkosi* Zibhebhu attacked oNdini and scattered the royalists mustering there. King Cetshwayo himself was wounded and fled; Fynn was left to search among the bodies of the dead for important men he recognized.

The destruction of oNdini and the flight and subsequent death of King Cetshwayo brought to an end Fynn's time as resident. He returned to his old post at Msinga. His youngest child was born there in 1890; he died on 28 April 1915 in Pietermaritzburg.

Henderson, Alfred Fairlie

Alfred Henderson was born in Pietermaritzburg in December 1854, part of a prominent Natal settler family. He was educated in Pietermaritzburg, England and Germany, and worked the family farm until, in 1873, he was tempted to try his luck in the goldfields at Pilgrim's Rest in the eastern Transvaal, and later in the diamond diggings in Kimberley.

In 1879 Henderson commanded the Tlokoa troop of mounted auxiliaries under *inkosi* Hlubi Molife which was attached to Colonel A.W. Durnford's No. 2 Column. Durnford's command was initially based on the Middle Drift escarpment, above the Thukela border, but was moved to support the Centre Column, the mounted elements reaching Isandlwana on the morning of 22 January. Henderson's troop was under Durnford's personal command when the latter rode out to investigate reports of Zulu movements on the iNyoni range; when Durnford encountered the Zulu left, he retreated to make a stand in the Nyogane donga. Once his men's ammunition began to fail, however, and his position was in danger of being outflanked on both sides, he ordered his men to retreat. Hlubi's troop, accompanied by Henderson, forced its way through the Zulu right 'horn', and crossed the river at Rorke's Drift. Henderson was the officer who reported to Lieutenant John Chard, in command of the garrison at Rorke's Drift. When Hlubi's troop moved off to harass the Zulu advance, Henderson, together with Robert Hall, a meat contractor from Pietermaritzburg, helped direct other auxiliaries at the post to build the barricades. Henderson and Hall then rode out to see how Hlubi's troop was faring, but at that moment the

Zulu vanguard arrived and Hlubi's men fled for Helpmekaar. Hall and Henderson rode back to the mission to shout out a warning and stayed to fire off the last of their ammunition before also riding away. Henderson apparently fell in with a convoy taking ammunition and supplies to Rorke's Drift during the night – where this occurred is not entirely clear – and reached Helpmekaar on the 23rd.

Henderson developed typhoid shortly after Isandlwana and did not rejoin his troop until May. He took part in a number of patrols which heralded the renewed British invasion, and was present at the Battle of Ulundi on 4 July.

After the war Henderson opened a butchery business in Pietermaritzburg but was again tempted by the prospect of an easier fortune. In 1884 he left for Barberton, on the Transvaal/Swazi border, and in 1886 he joined the rush of Europeans seeking mineral concessions from the Swazi king Mbandzeni. He was successful, and for several years was heavily involved in affairs in Swaziland. He was accompanied by another Isandlwana survivor, his employee Jabez Molife. In the event, Henderson sold most of his holdings in Swaziland and in 1889 left for Johannesburg, where he married a widow, Penelope Smith.

He returned to Natal on the death of his father in 1899. With the outbreak of the Anglo-Boer War, he served with the Field Intelligence Unit, commanding scouts from the Edendale community, including Molife. He was awarded the CMG for his services. After the war he farmed near the Mooi River. In 1906, he served again as a Leader of Reserves with the Helpmekaar Field Force during the Poll Tax Rebellion. He died at Mooi River on 21 July 1927.

Longcast, Henry William

Longcast was born in 1850. His father William Longcast was apparently Irish, an early settler to Natal who ran a small inn in Pietermaritzburg which catered largely to men of the British garrison at Fort Napier. Both William Longcast and his wife Mary died young, and Henry Longcast and his younger sister Matilda were taken in by a Pietermaritzburg orphanage. They were then adopted by Robert Robertson and his wife, who were destined to become prominent Zululand missionaries. In 1850 the Robertsons began work at the Umlazi mission in Natal. Most mission societies were keen to evangelize across the border in Zululand, and in 1857, and largely for political reasons, King Mpande allowed the Anglican Church to establish a station at KwaMagwaza. The Robertsons were given the post, and moved to Zululand with their adopted children. They had to build the mission from scratch, and young Henry Longcast grew up self-reliant, practical, and fluent in isiZulu. He regularly accompanied Robertson on journeys to the royal courts of Zululand, and knew both Mpande and his successor personally. In 1870 Henry Longcast married, his wife Alice apparently being a Zulu Christian convert.

Robertson was a great advocate of armed intervention in Zululand, believing that Christian evangelism could only proceed once King Cetshwayo's administration had been overthrown. This made his position vulnerable as tension between the British and Zulus increased, and he abandoned the KwaMagwaza mission in August 1877. Longcast stayed on until war was imminent and only crossed into Natal in October 1878.

In Natal Longcast found large numbers of British troops massing on the border, and he applied for a position with the troops. Lord Chelmsford soon recognized the value of Longcast's excellent language skills and his knowledge of Zulu affairs, and appointed him as his personal interpreter. Longcast joined Chelmsford's staff shortly before the invasion of January 1879, was present with him throughout the Isandlwana campaign, and indeed throughout the entire war. By the time British troops reached the heart of Zululand in June 1879, Longcast was able to offer personal advice on the topography and routes for advance. After the Battle of Ulundi, Chelmsford paid tribute to Longcast who 'has proved of the greatest value to me'.

When Lord Chelmsford resigned his command, Longcast secured the equivalent post on the staff of his successor, Sir Garnet Wolseley. On 13 August Longcast accompanied a major sweep through central Zululand in pursuit of the fugitive King Cetshwayo; when the British dispersed into smaller groups,

Longcast accompanied the party commanded by Lord Gifford that narrowly failed to capture the king. Nevertheless, Longcast's contribution during the search was widely acknowledged. Cetshwayo was finally captured on 28 August by Major Marter of the 1st Dragoon Guards. He was taken to Wolseley's camp at oNdini, where it was agreed that Longcast should accompany the king into exile at the Cape. Longcast remained with King Cetshwayo at Cape Castle until January 1881; it is apparently he who stands, leaning on a gun carriage, in a famous photograph of Cetshwayo, his jailor Major Poole and his attendants, taken at this time.

On leaving King Cetshwayo, Longcast returned to KwaMagwaza, where the mission – destroyed by the Zulus during the war – had been rebuilt. When King Cetshwayo was restored in early 1883, he granted Longcast a tract of land near the mission in recognition of his services during his exile. Longcast continued to visit the king, and indeed had only just returned from oNdini to KwaMagwasa when *inkosi* Zibhebhu attacked Cetshwayo in July 1883.

The civil war of 1883 and the intervention of the Boers ultimately spelt ruin for Longcast. He and his family – by this time he had several children by Alice – remained precariously at KwaMagwaza until, in the aftermath of the combined Boer/Royalist victory over Zibhebhu at Tshaneni mountain, the whole of central Zululand seemed likely to be ceded to the Boers. Reluctant to acknowledge Boer authority, and uneasy at how his marriage might be regarded, Longcast moved into the British Reserve Territory. He settled with a number of other refugees from KwaMagwaza on the eThalaneni mission in the Nkandla district.

For much of the rest of his life, Longcast attempted to secure official recognition of the grant King Cetshwayo had given him. He did not succeed. The KwaMagwaza plot lay in the heart of territory disputed by the British and Boers, and although with the annexation of Zululand in 1887 it fell under British control, still his claim was refused, despite his service in 1879. Longcast and his family continued to live in poverty at eThalaneni. In 1906, when the area was at the epicentre of the 1906 disturbances in

Zululand, Longcast placed his most treasured possessions in the safe of the magistrate at Nkandla; they comprised his South Africa 1879 medal, and signed testimonials by Chelmsford, Wolseley and others. In 1908 Longcast became ill and was sent to the hospital at Eshowe for treatment. He asked to be allowed to return home, and on 13 January, while on the road, he died. His body was taken to eThalaneni for burial; the worldly possessions he left to Alice were assessed at a value of just over £7.

Lonsdale, Rupert LaTrobe

Rupert LaTrobe Lonsdale was born in Melbourne, Australia, in September 1849, into a family with extensive military connections. His father, William, was an officer in the 4th Regiment who had settled in Australia, and an uncle, James Faunce Lonsdale, had been a captain in the 27th Regiment and had been severely wounded by the Boers at the action at Congella, during the British occupation of Natal in 1842.

Rupert Lonsdale entered the Royal Military College at Sandhurst in 1867, and joined the 74th Regiment as an ensign by purchase in 1868. In 1874 he sold out of the Army; popular legend has it that he wished to marry but his colonel refused permission because of his insufficient means. Whether this was the case or not, he married Katherine Russell in November 1875. The following year the couple left for the Cape, settling at Keiskamma Hoek, close to King William's Town where James Faunce Lonsdale had spent his retirement, and where a number of his descendants then lived.

Lonsdale took up the post of magistrate at Keiskamma Hoek, and when the 9th Cape Frontier War (1877-78) broke out he volunteered to join the auxiliary units then being raised. He was given a command of a unit of amaMfengu ('Fingo') levies and served throughout the campaign, earning an enviable reputation both for his ability to inspire auxiliary troops, and for his personal courage and dynamism. Evelyn Wood wrote of him that he was 'Brave as a lion, agile as a deer and inflexible as iron, he is the best leader of Natives I have seen'. John Crealock thought that his 'face is redeemed by boyishness by the square jowl that tells of the determination which will make his name an unforgettable one as long as tales of this war are told'.

At the end of the Frontier campaign, with war looming against the Zulus, Lonsdale again offered his services as a leader of auxiliaries, and he was given command of the 3rd Regiment, Natal Native Contingent, which assembled at Sandspruit, near the Mzinyathi border, at the end of 1878. The regiment then moved forward to join the Centre Column, assembling at Helpmekaar, before advancing to the crossing at Rorke's Drift.

Here misfortune befell Lonsdale. With the date set for the invasion just days away, Lonsdale fell from his horse. Lieutenant Harford:

> ...saw the fall. He appeared to have struck his head and then, rolling over on his back, lay quite still with one of his arms projecting in the air at right angles to his body. I got off at once and ran to his assistance, only to find that he was unconscious, and rigidly stiff.

Lonsdale was badly concussed, and was unable to lead his men when the column crossed into Zululand on 11 January, nor during the attack on Sihayo's homestead the following day. He had, however, returned to his command before the 3rd Regiment was appointed to lead Lord Chelmsford's designated sweep through the Malakatha and Hlazakazi hills on 21 January, although he was apparently still suffering from the after-effects.

The reconnaissance of the 21st severely tested the newly formed NNC. They were required to march through miles of rugged hill-country in the baking heat, and that evening they were unnerved by the discovery of a Zulu force in the hills at the head of the Mangeni gorge. Required to bivouac in the open that night, they succumbed several times to false alarms. The following morning, they were reinforced by the arrival of Lord Chelmsford's force from Isandlwana, and spent the day skirmishing with small parties of warriors in the hills above Mangeni. Lonsdale himself gave chase to some mounted Zulu scouts, but failed to catch them.

These exertions seem to have exacerbated Lonsdale's recent concussion. The absence of a large Zulu force at Mangeni had been a disappointment to Lord Chelmsford, who now decided to move the camp forward from Isandlwana to join him. Lonsdale was ordered to return to the camp to ensure that rations were sent ahead for the NNC and, feeling unwell, rode ahead in the hope of snatching a few minutes sleep. It was now early afternoon, and in the blazing sun, Lonsdale, according to a version of the story he told an old friend from his Cape Frontier days:

... was very short of sleep, and awfully tired. When we were within a few miles of the camp under Isandlana Mountain, I asked the General (Lord Chelmsford) if I might ride on ahead, get back to camp and get a rest. This was granted and I rode on my way. I was shot at by a couple of natives as I went on, but I thought nothing of it, as I imagined they were my own Swazis [sic] who had made a mistake, and I did not discover they were Zulus until later. I approached the camp we had so lately left, but being three quarters asleep did not notice that anything was amiss until I was well inside it. The first thing that woke me up and put me on the *qui vive* was a Zulu coming at me with a stabbing assegai, already wet with blood, in his hand. I was wide-awake enough then, and on the alert in a moment. I glanced round me and became instantly fully alive to what had taken place, and that the camp had been captured by the Zulus. I saw in a flash dead bodies of both soldiers and Zulus all over the place, tents rent in fragments, bags of flour cut open and the contents strewn about, boxes of ammunition broken open, everything in fact smashed and done for. Last but not least, Zulus with assegais still reeking with blood sitting and wandering about in all this indescribable chaos. I saw it all in a flash, turned and fled. My horse was as tired as I was. Many Zulus, becoming alive to the fact that an enemy and a white man was among them, rushed after me yelling and firing at me. It was the most deadly, awful moment I have ever had in my life, and you know we've had some pretty tight fits together. I could only screw a very moderate canter out of my poor gee, and as you know old man, Kaffirs are uncommonly fleet of foot. It was two or three minutes before I was clear of those howling devils. It seemed to me like two or three hours. At length they all gave up the chase, and I went on my way to rejoin the column. By the bye,

59

I saw the two men who had shot at me an hour before, and took the liberty of sending one of them to his happy hunting grounds. When I rode up to the general and reported what I had seen I believe he thought I was mad ...

The same friend to whom Lonsdale told this story thought that he had been deeply traumatized by the experience, and 'never seemed to be the same again'. It was Lonsdale who ordered the arrest of Captain Stevenson and Lieutenant Higginson following their actions on the 23 January.

Nevertheless, after the 3rd NNC was disbanded following its poor performance in the Isandlwana campaign, Lonsdale was sent to the Cape to raise a unit of white irregular cavalry, generally known as Lonsdale's Horse. The recruiting needs of the irregular units had already heavily plundered colonial society at the Cape, and those who joined Lonsdale's Horse were generally considered the dregs that remained. These had reached Natal in time to join the troops assembling on the borders for the general advance of June 1879, and were attached to Major General H.H. Crealock's 1st Division. Once in the field, Lonsdale's energy produced surprisingly good results from the unpromising raw material, and they did good work patrolling ahead of the 1st Division, and later during the pacification operations after Ulundi.

Lonsdale was awarded the CMG for his services in Zululand, and returned to Keiskamma Hoek. When the BaSotho 'Gun War' broke out in 1880, he raised another unit of Lonsdale's Horse to serve there. After the rebellion had spluttered out in 1881, he joined the Colonial Office, and accepted a post on the staff of Sir Samuel Rowe, who had been commissioned to establish trade routes through to the Asante capital of Kumase, on the Gold Coast of West Africa.

The focus of Lonsdale's career now shifted to West Africa. He joined Rowe in late 1881, and remained there for seven years, ending his time as a Commissioner for Native Affairs on the Gold Coast.

By the beginning of 1888 he was back in England, perhaps because of the cumulative toll his adventures had taken on his health. On 28 February he died at the residence of a doctor in

Liverpool, the cause of death being given as 'acute spinal paralysis'.

Lonsdale was not the only member of his family to serve in the Isandlwana campaign. His cousin, James Faunce Lonsdale – son of the man of the same name who had served with the 27th Regiment and retired to King William's Town – was also a veteran of the 9th Frontier War, and had joined the 3rd NNC with the rank of captain. He commanded one of the companies left in the camp at Isandlwana on 21 January, and was killed in the battle the following day.

Molife, Hlubi kaMota

Hlubi was the *inkosi* of a section of the Sotho-speaking Tlokoa people who lived in the Kahlamba foothills in central Natal. The Tlokoa had been greatly disrupted by the upheavals in the first decades of the nineteenth century. At the beginning of the eighteenth century they were living in Natal, on the upper Mzinyathi valley, but they were driven across the mountains during the wars which marked the emergence of the Zulu power. Wandering the interior, they had achieved a formidable reputation under their Queen MaNthathisi. After MaNthathisi's death, her son, *inkosi* Sikonyela, had remained in the high veld, but a section under Sikonyela's brother, Mota (sometimes given as Mbunda, possibly the isiZulu version of a Sotho name) moved close to the mountains. At the beginning of the 1870s Mota's son, Hlubi, crossed the mountains and settled in Natal. His neighbours were the amaHlubi people, with whom Mota had cultivated contacts; Hlubi himself, who was born about 1835, had apparently been named by his father to celebrate this link. The Tlokoa were known among Natal Africans by the isiZulu version of their name, Hlongwane.

In 1873, during the 'rebellion' of *inkosi* Langalibalele kaMthimkhulu of the amaHlubi, the Tlokoa were asked by Theophilus Shepstone to raise a unit of volunteer horsemen to assist in blocking the mountain passes. Hlubi's acquiescence was achieved through the intermediary of his kinsman, Jabez Molife of the Christian Edendale settlement. Like most Sotho, the Tlokoa were accomplished horsemen accustomed to riding in the rugged hill country. They supplied a contingent of mounted men who were present when Major Anthony Durnford RE attempted to prevent *inkosi* Langalibalele's escape over the Kahlamba passes in November 1873. Hlubi acted as Durnford's personal guide, and was present at the action at Bushman's Pass on 4 November. Elijah Nkambule, a senior member of the Edendale community, also accompanied Durnford as interpreter, and was killed in the incident. In the chaotic retreat that followed, the Tlokoa men had largely retained their discipline while others had been on the verge of collapse. Durnford had been impressed by this, and when drawing up plans for an African auxiliary force late in 1878 to support the British invasion of Zululand, he asked both the Tlokoa and Edendale community to supply mounted contingents. The impact that Hlubi's men had made on the British and settler military in 1873 was such that in 1879 the British tended to refer to all mounted auxiliary units as 'BaSotho'.

Hlubi personally led his troop (fifty strong) which was attached to Durnford's No. 2 column. Initially based on the escarpment above the Middle Drift, it was moved to Rorke's Drift to support Lord Chelmsford's planned advance from Isandlwana, and arrived in the camp there on the morning of 22 January. When Durnford split his command to investigate the Zulu movements beyond the iNyoni ridge, Hlubi's men formed part of the force which accompanied Durnford in person. Having ridden about four miles from the camp, they encountered the Zulu left 'horn', and then retreated again to make a stand in a watercourse in front of the camp. Running low on ammunition and in danger of being outflanked on both sides, they were forced to abandon the stand there, and Durnford then dismissed them from the field. Mehlokazulu kaSihayo, who held a command in the Zulu iNgobamakhosi regiment, recalled years later that he personally chased Hlubi's troop into the Manzimnyama valley, behind Isandlwana, and nearly caught Hlubi himself. The Tlokoa and Edendale troops forced their way through the Zulu right horn, then separated. Hlubi's own account makes it clear that, while the Edendale men went to Sothondose's ('Fugitives') Drift, his troop went to Rorke's Drift. They crossed at Rorke's old drift, and then dismounted to rest; theirs was the troop which reported to the senior officer at the Rorke's Drift mission, Lieutenant Chard RE, shortly before the battle began. Exhausted, demoralized and largely out of ammunition, they waited only to fire a few shots at the approaching Zulus before retreating.

In the aftermath of Isandlwana, the auxiliary units were re-organized. The Tlokoa and Edendale men had remained at Helpmekaar, patrolling the Mzinyathi border, but were then ordered to join Colonel Wood's Left Flank Column. They arrived at Wood's base at Khambula at the beginning of March, and took part in several patrols in the area. On 28 March both units were attached to Colonel J.C. Russell's section for the attack on Hlobane Mountain. Because Russell's part in the assault was largely unsuccessful, they escaped the heavy casualties which befell the other assault party led by Lieutenant Colonel Buller.

The following day Hlubi's men and the Edendale contingent were both heavily engaged when Wood's camp at Khambula was attacked by the main Zulu army. They formed part of the mounted probe that was sent out to provoke the Zulu right 'horn' into an unsupported attack on the camp. Although most of the mounted men then retired to the safety of the British wagon-laager, a number of Tlokoa and Edendale men refused to do so. Instead, they remained outside the laager, fighting in the open, hovering on the flank of the Zulu right and inflicting casualties from a distance. When the Zulus at last began to retire, the two African troops joined the white Irregular units in inflicting heavy casualties upon them.

Hlubi's men remained with Wood's column – re-designated the Flying Column – during the march on oNdini. They took part in a number of patrols and raids, and were present in the skirmish at eZungeni on 5 June when Lieutenant Frith of the 17th Lancers was killed. Together with the Edendale troop, they also formed part of Buller's cavalry reconnaissance across the White Mfolozi on 3 January. This reconnaissance almost came to grief in the face of a well-executed ambush and, in the general retreat that followed, the Edendale and Tlokoa men were almost cut off.

On 4 July Hlubi's men were part of Lord Chelmsford's final advance on oNdini. At the beginning of the battle, they harassed Zulu troops advancing from the direction of oNdini itself; they then retreated inside the British square. Once the Zulu attack had been largely destroyed by the firepower of the square, the mounted men – including Hlubi's – rode out to chase the Zulus from the field.

In the aftermath of Ulundi, at the end of July, the Sotho and Edendale troops were sent back to Pietermaritzburg to be paid off and dismissed. Hlubi initially returned to his old home in the mountain foothills, but the post-war settlement of Zululand held a pleasant surprise for him. Chelmsford's successor, and the man charged with implementing a post-war settlement of Zululand, Sir Garnet Wolseley, had resolved to divide the country into thirteen separate districts, to be ruled over by appointees of the British. Most of these appointees were representatives of senior Zulu lines who were either thought to be hostile to the Zulu Royal House, or sympathetic to the British. However, it was considered a strategic imperative that a buffer zone be created along the Zulu side of the Natal border which was firmly in the hands of *amakhosi* whose status was entirely dependant upon the British. In the event, part of this buffer zone was given to the 'white Zulu' *inkosi* John Dunn; the other part was offered to Hlubi. This consisted of a stretch of land running along the left bank of the Mzinyathi River, opposite Rorke's Drift; ironically, it included part of the original territory from which the Tlokoa had been driven more than half a century before.

Hlubi and his followers arrived in his new territory in October 1879. He built a homestead in the Batshe valley, not far from the ruins of *inkosi* Sihayo's old homestead. He was acutely aware that his Sotho group was isolated from the Zulu community among whom they lived – many of whom had fought ardently for the Zulu cause in 1879 – and who they now ruled. Hlubi therefore cultivated his links with the European world upon which his power was based – he befriended local missionaries and magistrates – while at the same time he tried not to antagonize representatives of the former administration. His main problem – local loyalties to Sihayo, who returned to the district at the end of the war – was largely resolved by a decision by *inkosi* Mnyamana Buthelezi to levy a heavy fine of cattle upon Sihayo for his part in provoking the British ultimatum. Thus impoverished and humiliated, Sihayo was largely powerless to resist Hlubi's directive that he leave the Batshe valley and live on the fringes of Hlubi's territory.

Throughout the troubled 1880s, Hlubi's followers proved a ready source of support for British military activities. Although – as Wolseley had intended – the border areas remained largely aloof from the growing tensions between royalist and anti-royalist supporters in 1880 and 1881, numbers of royalists left Hlubi's area to join the general mobilization of the king's supporters which took place after Cetshwayo's restoration in 1883. The same agreement which had seen the king restored had also led to Hlubi and Dunn being lumped together under direct British control as the Reserve Territory. When Cetshwayo's restoration provoked an open and catastrophic civil war, the Zulu populations in the Reserve came under pressure to ally themselves with one side or another and British troops were moved into southern Zululand as a precaution. When the royalist abaQulusi threatened to advance into the northern reserve, Hlubi's followers were mobilized to intercept them. In the event, this threat collapsed, but violent clashes along the middle Thukela led Hlubi to turn about and attack the homesteads of several prominent royalists in the region. By 1884, in the aftermath of King Cetshwayo's death and the subsequent intervention of the Transvaal Boers in Zululand, a new British garrison was established at Fort Northampton, squarely in Hlubi's district on the Zulu bank at Rorke's Drift. Together these provided a powerful deterrent to the escalating violence which was spreading across the country.

In 1887, after acting to curb Boer ambitions in Zululand, the British government formally annexed the remainder of the country. This, however, provoked King Cetshwayo's son and heir, Prince Dinuzulu, into a last-ditch attempt to restore his rapidly disappearing inheritance by force. Hlubi was again instructed to arm his followers, and personally took to the field at the head of over 300 mounted men. These were dispersed between British concentrations in northern and southern Zululand. Some 140 Tlokoa were present when British troops broke up a concentration of royalist supporters, commanded by Prince Shingana kaMpande, at Hlopekhulu, near oNdini, on 2 July 1888. During the battle, the Tlokoa supported an advance by Zululand Police against the Zulu centre on Hlopekhulu Mountain which effectively broke the Zulu defensive position. Hlubi himself, with a further 180 of his followers, was attached to a British column operating around Eshowe, which first attacked the homesteads of local royalists, then embarked on a protracted sweep up through the coastal flats and up the Black Mfolozi valley and back again. The campaign ended with the surrender of Dinuzulu and his uncles, the Princes Shingana and Ndabuko, towards the end of 1888.

All in all, Hlubi kaMota had proved a consistently loyal supporter of the British interests in Zululand upon which he was dependent, and his followers, in all their campaigns, earned considerable respect from the British military. Yet the rewards can hardly have been as Hlubi had hoped. The imposition of direct British control inevitably led to a reduction of the largely independent status he had enjoyed in the immediate aftermath of the invasion of 1879, and Hlubi's authority became increasingly limited to the area settled by his own followers in the Batshe valley. Ironically, he had discovered a hard truth underlying the progress of European rule across southern Africa; that it ultimately undermined the power and prestige of all traditional African leaders, whether collaborators or no.

Hlubi became ill in 1897, displaying signs of mental instability that may have been the result of long-term exposure to malaria. He died in October 1902. He was succeeded as *inkosi* of his section of the Tlokoa by Isaak Lenega, his son by his great wife Mamentjie, but in the 1940s much of the vestigial power Isaak enjoyed was removed by the South African government, and the political influence of the Tlokoa in the Rorke's Drift area largely came to an end. There remain, however, a number of Sotho speakers in the Nquthu and Nondweni areas who trace their descent directly to Hlubi's followers.

Molife, Jabez

Jabez Molife was a member of the Edendale Christian community established by the Methodist missionary, James Allison, near Pietermaritzburg in 1851. Molife was apparently a Sotho, a member of the Molife family who led the Tlokoa community in the Kahlamba foothills. Theophilus Shepstone, Natal's Secretary for Native Affairs, drew upon the services of the Edendale community, who were largely westernized and therefore regarded as progressive and natural supporters of the colonial administration, as intermediaries in his management of traditional *amakhosi*. In 1873, Jabez Molife accompanied Shepstone in the expectation to 'crown' King Cetshwayo in Zululand, and in 1874, on the outbreak of the 'rebellion' of the Natal *inkosi* Langalibalele kaMthimkhulu, Shepstone asked Molife to act as intermediary to his kinsman, the Tlokoa *inkosi* Hlubi kaMota, to persuade him to raise a force of auxiliaries to suppress the rebellion. The support of the Tlokoa and Edendale communities on that occasion led Colonel A.W. Durnford to ask that they raise further auxiliary units to take part in the invasion of Zululand in 1879. Jabez Molife served as the junior sergeant major (the senior one was Simeon Nkambule) with the Edendale contingent, which was attached to Durnford's No. 2 Column, and fought at Isandlwana. Molife later left an account of the battle, and his description of Durnford's behaviour at the height of the battle has deservedly become a classic of the literature of the battle:

> The Colonel rode up and down the line continually encouraging us all, he was very calm and cheerful, talking and even laughing with us, 'Fire, my boys! Well done, my boys!', he cried, some of us did not like him exposing himself so much to the enemy, and wanted him to keep back behind us, but he laughed at us and said, 'Alright, nonsense!' … one of the men brought his gun with the old cartridge sticking so he dismounted, and taking the gun between his knees, because of only having one hand with strength in it, he pulled the cartridge out and gave back the gun ..

When Durnford's stand in the Nyogane donga collapsed, he directed the Edendale and Tlokoa troops to leave the battlefield. The Edendale men, running low on ammunition, paused to gather a few dropped rounds in the camp, then made their way towards Sothondose's Drift. During the retreat, Nkambule took a colonial trooper up behind his saddle, Molife holding Nkambule's carbine while he did so. The Edendale men were the only body of troops to make it across the Mzinyathi in good order, and they paused for a while on the Natal bank to cover the retreat of other survivors.

After Isandlwana the mounted auxiliary units were reorganized, and Molife fought throughout the rest of the war, and was probably present at Ulundi on 4 July. In March 1880 Molife accompanied, as interpreter, a party led by Major Henry Stabb who erected a monument on the spot in the Tshotosi valley where Prince Louis Napoleon had been killed during the war. On 12 October 1880, it was Molife who was tasked with exhuming Durnford's body, hastily buried on the field of Isandlwana, for re-interment in Pietermaritzburg.

Molife was a prominent member of the Edendale community throughout the 1880s, and was a prosperous smallholder there. He was interested in politics, and was a member of an organization formed to give voice to the aspirations and grievances of black Christians in Natal. In 1886 he accompanied Alfred Henderson – another Isandlwana survivor – to Swaziland, when Henderson secured a concession from the Swazi king, Mbandzeni. His association with Henderson continued into the Anglo-Boer War, and when Henderson was directed to organize a unit of African scouts, Molife became his sergeant major. Both men served during the siege of Ladysmith. After the war, the British Government refused to recognize the services of the Edendale men by the issue of campaign medals; Molife was among those who signed a petition of protest. They were eventually awarded bronze, rather than silver, medals.

A number of photographs of Molife exist, taken during Stabb's expedition and at the turn of the century, when Molife was an elder at Edendale. He died in the 1920s.

Mossop, George Joseph

George Joseph 'Chops' Mossop was born near Durban on 10 October 1861. His father, James Mossop, had arrived in Natal with two brothers, Joseph and George Mossop, from Cockermouth, Cumberland, in May 1849. James married Ann Upjohn in August 1854, and settled initially on the Berea ridge overlooking Durban harbour. The couple had nine children and later moved to Greytown, closer to the Natal/Zulu border. Here George Mossop grew up and attended school 'when I could not sneak out of it'. In his own words, 'wanderlust was in my bones', and at the age of fourteen George Mossop ran away to the Transvaal Republic. Here he joined a band of professional Boer hunters who made their living shooting game in the eastern Transvaal; it was the twilight of the golden age of the hunter for, as Mossop observed, the great herds of game which had once roamed the high veld 'were at their last gasp, and were making their final stand'. Under the pragmatic tutelage of the Boers, Mossop learned the skills necessary to survive in the bush – to be self-reliant, to ride in wilderness terrain, and to shoot at moving targets from the saddle. Towards the end of 1878, with British troops assembling on the Zulu borders, Mossop was prompted by a yearning for a different sort of adventure to volunteer for one of the irregular mounted units then recruiting:

> My ambition was to join the Frontier Light Horse. The name appealed to me; there was something grand about it, and the Corps had been fighting Sekhukhuni in the north. Because I could ride and shoot, I reckoned that I could become a member of that famous Corps by simply going and joining it. I had not the remotest idea of what life in the F.L.H. meant, but I found out alright in time.

Riding alone to the border, Mossop overtook the FLH as they crossed the Ncome River into Zululand with Colonel Wood's column on 6 January. He was taken before Redvers Buller and, embellishing his age, was allowed to enlist as a trooper. The FLH had started its career with an impressive uniform of braided corduroy, but after prolonged service on the Cape Frontier and in the Transvaal the supply of replacement uniforms was long gone, and the only outward sign of Mossop's new allegiance to the military was a red rag wound around his hat.

> It was a hard life for the F.L.H. at this time – always on patrol, wet to the skin for days on end. We had no overcoats or raincoats, and only one blanket, strapped to the saddle, in

which we wrapped ourselves; and in long rows, closely packed together for warmth, we would sleep, with the rain pouring down on us ... Such a life soon hardened me, and I was able to endure it all as well as the toughest man in the corps.

On 28 March Mossop took part in the attack on the Zulu positions on the Hlobane Mountain. His account of the battle – of the nightmarish ascent through the cliffs during a dawn thunderstorm, of the skirmishing across the undulating summit of the plateau, and of the terrible descent of the so-called 'Devil's Pass' – is deservedly regarded as one of the most eloquent and vivid eyewitness descriptions to emerge from an ordinary soldier throughout the war:

> I ... looked down, and my blood turned cold.
>
> The pass was steep and narrow, and choked with boulders. About twenty yards from where we were standing was free of horsemen, or, rather, of men leading their horses, for no one could sit a horse in such a place. Below that was a complete jam.
>
> Zulus, crawling over the huge rocks on either side, were jabbing at the men and horses. Some of the men were shooting, and some were using clubbed rifles and fighting their way down.
>
> Owing to the rocks on either side the Zulus could not charge. The intervening space was almost filled with dead horses and dead men, white and black ...

Mossop threw himself over the edge, scrambling down through the rocks, only to be sent back at the bottom by Buller, who ordered him to retrieve his horse, a BaSotho pony named Warrior. Cut off from the main retreat, Mossop managed to elude parties of pursuing warriors through Warrior's exertions, and returned to the camp at Khambula that evening. The following morning, to Mossop's dismay, Warrior died from exhaustion and the injuries he had sustained during the retreat. Stiff, bruised and sore, Mossop rejoined his unit and was issued with a horse far too big for him. By this time, a fresh battle was imminent, for the Zulu army – which had arrived from oNdini in time to join the defence of Hlobane the previous day – was now deploying to attack Khambula. Mossop was among those sent out to provoke the Zulu right horn into launching an uncoordinated assault on the defended camp. The experience nearly cost him his life for a second time; the FLH dismounted to fire a volley, and the sudden war cry it brought forth from the Zulus so startled Mossop's horse that he could not mount. Only the intervention of Captain Oldham, who saw his plight and slowed Mossop's horse long enough for him to scramble into the saddle, saved him; by the time Mossop rode back to the camp the British artillery had opened fire, and 'I expected each moment that one of the shrieking rockets would snip my head off'. When the Zulu army was subsequently repulsed, Mossop took part in the British pursuit, pausing long enough to dismount and snatch a fine snuff-horn from around the neck of one of the dead warriors; to his surprise, as he tugged on the cord, the warrior's body tensed reflexively, causing a leg to spasm – and Mossop got a severe fright 'from being kicked by a dead man!'

Mossop served with the FLH throughout the remainder of the war, patrolling on occasion with Louis Napoleon, the French Prince Imperial. He took part in both the skirmish on the plain before oNdini on 3 July and in the Battle of Ulundi the following day. Taking his discharge at Landman's Drift when the FLH were disbanded, Mossop rode to Utrecht. Although his accumulated pay amounted to a tolerable sum, his clothes were worn out by the rigours of campaigning, and on his first night in the town was refused a room at the hotel because of his disreputable appearance, 'and all my boyish dreams of returning a "warrior bold" melted with the frost on my clothes'.

Mossop took work briefly as an assistant at a trading store, but when the Transvaal broke into revolt against British administration in December 1880, he volunteered to serve as a guide to the British forces assembling in Natal. He witnessed the Battles of Laing's Nek and Majuba from the camp at Fort Prospect, but the experience left him disillusioned with the attitudes of the British military.

After the war, he worked as a transport rider, escorting wagons

71

loaded with goods from Durban to Johannesburg, and from Johannesburg on the fever-ridden road to Delagoa Bay in Mozambique. By that time, civil war had broken out in Zululand between royalist and anti-royalist factions and when, in 1884, the royalists appealed to the Transvaal Boers for military assistance, offering farms to those who responded, Mossop enlisted. Although Mossop did not take part in the decisive Battle of Tshaneni on 5 June 1884, he nonetheless received his reward. In August over a million hectares of northern and central Zululand were ceded to the Boers, who declared it to be a *Nieue Republiek* – New Republic – and laid out the capital at Vryheid ('freedom'), close to Hlobane. Mossop himself acquired a farm on the southern slopes of the mountain of Hlobane, close to the route by which the FLH had ascended during the battle in 1879.

Like many frontiersmen, Mossop made his living in peacetime by combining farming with hunting, trading and transport riding. In 1885 he married a childhood friend, a widow, Matilda Flood Cutbush Archer, who bore him two sons, James and Robert. During the Anglo-Boer War, he again served in an intelligence capacity with the British, and his farm was destroyed during his absence. Disillusioned by British policy during the war, Mossop returned to the wilderness. Lured by 'the sound of the elephant's trump and the low, deep "wuff-wuff" of the lion, where the buffalo live in deep ravines; and as the sun sinks behind the mountains in the west, the long, loud, melancholy "hoo-hoo" of the hyena welcomes the dawn of his day', he acquired a farm in Macequece in what was then Portuguese East Africa (now Mozambique) in 1914. It was there during the 1930s that he drafted his memoirs – *Running the Gauntlet* - which records both his military experiences and something of his frontier adventures. He wrote a second book which was never published. He died at Umtali on 22 May 1938 aged seventy-seven. Some of his descendents still live at Vryheid, in sight of Hlobane.

Mthonga kaMpande Zulu, Prince

Mthonga was the son of King Mpande kaSenzangakhona by his wife Nomantshali, and was born in 1847. In later life, grieving for the loss of so many of his sons during the succession dispute of

72

1856, King Mpande became particularly attached to Nomantshali, and according to some accounts forsook his other wives for her. This led Prince Cetshwayo to suspect that Prince Mthonga was being groomed to be Mpande's successor. Mpande, who had skilfully played the ambitions of his sons off against one another to protect his own position, did little to discourage the view. In March 1861, when Mthonga was fourteen, Cetshwayo attempted to remove him as a threat. He sent an *impi* to kill both Nomantshali and Mthonga in secret, but the plan misfired. Mthonga and his brother Mgidlana managed to escape, although the warriors managed to detain another of Mpande's young sons, Mpoyiyana. Frustrated, the *impi* took him to King Mpande's residence at Nodwengu, and demanded that Mpande surrender Queen Nomantshali. Since she was absent, he could not, and Cetshwayo's men killed Mpoyiyana; they later tracked down Nomantshali, who gave herself up to her death.

Mthonga and Mgidlana fled by way of Khambula into the Transvaal. When he heard of this Cetshwayo hurried to the border with a force and demanded that the Boers surrender them. They did so, later claiming that Cetshwayo had recognized their territorial claims along the Ncome River in return, a fact which Cetshwayo vehemently denied. As a sop to the Boers' consciences, Cetshwayo had promised not to harm either of his rivals, but this proved a political mistake for Mthonga slipped away again, crossing this time into Natal. He was taken under the protection of Natal's Secretary of State for Native Affairs, Theophilus Shepstone, who housed him with his own chief *induna*, Ngoza kaLudaba. Mthonga later spent some time under the tutelage of Bishop Colenso who hoped that through him the Zulu Royal House might be converted to Christianity. Shepstone had no scruples about using the presence of the various princes in Natal as a tool to influence affairs in Zululand. This was a constant irritation to Cetshwayo, who could not be assured of an uncontested succession while they were at large. In October 1868 all three princes – Mthonga, Mkhungo and Sikhotha – moved to the Zulu border, rousing fears in Zululand that they were preparing an invasion, and causing Cetshwayo to mobilize his followers. With panic rife among Natal's settlers, Shepstone removed the princes further into Natal. Nevertheless, it is clear that Mthonga and Mkhungo harboured very real ambitions, and in 1872 they made a dangerous visit to their ailing father in the hope that he might publicly support them; when Cetshwayo heard of their presence at kwaNodwengu he sent an *impi* to intercept them, and they only just managed to escape back across the border.

The youngest and perhaps most ambitious of the exiled princes, Mthonga moved between Natal and the Wakerstroom district of the Transvaal, hoping to exploit the different political aspirations of the two colonial states to his advantage. With the coming of war in 1879, he saw a chance to gain influence by the British intervention, and attached himself briefly to the staff of Colonel H. E. Wood, who commanded the British No. 4 Column, operating on the Transvaal border. Wood records that on 27 March, he set off with his staff and escort to observe the planned attack on the abaQulusi stronghold on Hlobane mountain, accompanied by 'seven mounted Zulus under Umtonga, a half-brother of Cetewayo's, whom his father, Umpande, had originally designated to succeed him'. When, during the ascent of the mountain the following day, Wood came under fire and two of his staff, Campbell and Lloyd, were killed, it was Mthonga's men who dug a hurried grave with their spears. Wood then retired from the mountain with his escort, leaving the assault in progress behind him; 'When we were under the centre of the mountain, Umtonga, whom I had sent out to a ridge on our danger flank, gesticulated excitedly, explaining by signs that there was a large army near us.'

Wood rode up to see the main Zulu army, which had marched from oNdini to attack Khambula and had arrived at the height of the battle on Hlobane, deploying a wing to attack. Wood only just managed to retire ahead of them; many of those on the mountain were trapped and killed. That evening, back at Khambula, most of Wood's African auxiliaries dispersed to protect their homes, Mthonga apparently among them.

If Mthonga had hoped to be rewarded by a place in the new order in Zululand at the end of the war, he was to be disappointed. The British realized that his long absence from the country, his relative youth, and the jealousy with which his mother,

Nomantshali, had been regarded had left him with little support among the Zulus. When, in May 1880, Evelyn Wood again passed through the Utrecht area, escorting the Empress Eugenie on her pilgrimage to the spot where her son, the Prince Imperial, was killed, Mthonga paid him a visit. Under the guise of paying his respects, Prince Mthonga appealed for a greater recognition of his support during the invasion; as far as the British were concerned, he had nothing to offer in return, and he left Wood empty-handed.

Prince Mthonga married a total of nineteen wives, among them a daughter of *inkosi* Pakhade of the amaChunu (whose followers had fought with the 3rd NNC at Isandlwana), and fathered a number of children. Towards the end on the century, he returned to Zululand, and took up residence in the Eshowe district. During the 1906 disturbances, he supplied a number of his followers to serve Government forces as levies. He remained involved on the periphery of the politics of the post-colonial Royal House; as late as 1915 his name appears on a list of prominent Zulus proposed by King Solomon kaDinuzulu to join a delegation to meet with the Union government in Pretoria in an attempt to delineate the role of the Zulu king.

Nkambule, Simeon

Simeon Nkambule (often spelt Kambule) was the son of Elijah Nkambule, a member of the Edendale Christian community, founded outside Pietermaritzburg by the Methodist Reverend James Allison in 1851. The community later acquired property at Diefontein, north of Ladysmith. Many of the converts who were originally attracted to this community were Sotho or Swazi speakers (The name Nkambule is Swazi in origin) – few were Zulu-speakers. The community as a whole aspired to western concepts of civilization and progress, and rejected traditional belief-systems, clothing and farming methods. They were therefore regarded by the colonial administration as progressive and natural supporters of colonial policy. In 1873 Elijah Nkambule had served as interpreter to (then) Major A.W. Durnford on Durnford's expedition to seal the Kahlamba passes during the 'rebellion' of *inkosi* Langalibalele kaMthimkhulu.

During the skirmish at Bushman's Pass on 4 November, Elijah had been at Durnford's side when the shooting began. Elijah's horse was hit, but as Durnford attempted to pull him onto his own horse, Elijah was shot through the head and killed. Although the Langalibalele expedition was a debacle, Durnford was impressed by the performance of his African auxiliaries and, charged with raising an African force to assist in the rebellion in 1879, he again turned to the Edendale community. Daniel Msingmang, one of the community elders, responded that:

> We have sat under the shadow of the Great White Queen for many years in security and peace. We have greatly prospered, and some have grown rich. We enjoy great religious privileges, and have brought up our sons and daughters to honour God, and walk in his ways ... Shall we not gladly obey her, when she calls for the services of her dark children?

Fifty-four men responded to the request. Although one of the elders, John Zulu Mtimkulu, was appointed leader, practical command fell to Simeon Nkambule, who was a younger man. At that point Nkambule was one of the largest landowners at Edendale. He was given the rank of sergeant major. Jabez Molife was also made sergeant major, and one John Gama served as the unit's religious leader. The Edendale men took pains about their appearance and equipment and, on being told that as Africans they would be granted no different rations to the auxiliaries drawn from traditional communities, they decided to pay for their own food.

The Edendale troop was attached to Durnford's No. 2 Column, and was present at Isandlwana, where it was part of the force led out of the camp by Durnford himself. When Durnford encountered the Zulu left 'horn', he retired to the Nyogane donga, where he made a stand. When their ammunition ran low, and his men were in danger of being outflanked on both sides, Durnford ordered them to leave the field. Nkambule kept the Edendale men together, and in the camp they attempted to find fresh supplies of ammunition. One wagon stacked with boxes was guarded by a drummer of the 24th, who refused to allow the Edendale men to take any. Instead, they gathered up loose rounds dropped around in the grass. Nkambule attempted to persuade the drummer to leave with them, but he would not abandon his post. The Edendale troop was able to force its way through the Zulu right 'horn' in the valley behind Isandlwana, and apparently led the way towards the crossing at Sothondose's Drift, which Nkambule knew. During the retreat Nkambule saved the life of a colonial trooper by taking him up behind his saddle. At the Drift, the men crossed in relatively good order and rallied on the Natal bank, firing several volleys across the river to discourage Zulus from pursuing the survivors.

In the aftermath of the disaster, the Edendale men camped near Helpmekaar, and patrolled the border area. When the auxiliary units were then reorganized, they were attached to Colonel Wood's column, where they arrived at the beginning of March. They took part in the foray against the abaQulusi stronghold at Hlobane on 28 March as part of Colonel J.C. Russell's force, which attacked the western end of the mountain but withdrew before the arrival of the main Zulu army. During the Battle of Khambula the following day, the Edendale men were part of the mounted detachment which harassed the Zulu right horn into making an unsupported attack on the British positions. A number of Edendale men remained outside the British laager and harassed the Zulus from a distance; they then took part in the ruthless pursuit. The Battle of Khambula was a turning point in the war which both severely damaged the Zulu army, and allowed Lord Chelmsford time to regroup for a fresh invasion of Zululand. When, during May 1879, British troops again assembled on the Mzinyathi and Ncome Rivers, the Edendale troop was extensively employed in scouting across the border. When the new offensive began, from 1 June, they continued to provide a cavalry screen for the general advance, harassing Zulu patrols and destroying homesteads.

By the beginning of June, Lord Chelmsford had reached the White Mfolozi River, the last geographical barrier before oNdini. On 3 July a mounted detachment under Lieutenant Colonel Redvers Buller was sent across the river to scout the vicinity of the royal homestead of kwaNodwengu. Here it was very nearly drawn into a skilful Zulu ambush and only just extricated itself.

Here Simeon Nkambule again saved the life of a man during the retreat, and this time his gallantry was recognized by the award of a Distinguished Conduct Medal. According to the citation:

> This non-commissioned officer has also set an excellent example to the men of the Troop, of courage and ready obedience under fire. At the White Umvolozi River on the occasion of Lieut. Colonel Buller's reconnaissance towards "Ondine", the day before the Battle of Nodwengo, Simeon Kambula saved the life of an officer of the Frontier Light Horse, by bringing him out of a very heavy fire behind him on his horse. He was present at "Sandhlwana", "Hlobane", "Kambula" and "Nodwengo", besides many smaller actions, and has taken part in every patrol of the mounted Troops of the Flying Column, since 14 March 1879.

The following day, the Edendale troop took part in the Battle of Ulundi, first feeling out the Zulu positions to draw them on, then, at the end of the battle, pursuing them in retreat.

The battle marked the end of the active phase of the war, and it was decided that the Edendale contingent was not needed for pacification and patrolling operations. In the middle of July they returned to Pietermaritzburg, where the settlement's elders greeted their return. Although their actions were widely commended, and drew praise from the Methodist mission community in general, there is just a trace of disillusion in the Revd. Owen Watkins' comment that had Nkambule 'been a white man, he would have received the Victoria Cross'. Nevertheless, in 1881 Sir Evelyn Wood instigated the presentation of a Colour to the Edendale Contingent in commemoration of their service.

Simeon Nkambule returned to play a leading roll in the life of the community. During the Anglo-Boer the Edendale Horse were again called upon, and they took part as scouts during the siege of Ladysmith, again led by Nkambule. At the end of the war, however, the Edendale men were denied the silver campaign medal issued by the British government; after considerable protest, they were issued a cheaper bronze version.

Simeon Nkambule appears in a number of group photographs of Edendale elders.

O'Toole, Edmund, VC

The story of Edmund O'Toole's life in many respects typifies the largely anonymous experience of the men who fought in the various irregular corps in 1879, many of whom, like O'Toole, rose briefly from obscurity to distinguish themselves, and then sank back again. Few reliable details have yet emerged about Edmund O'Toole. By common agreement he was of Irish stock, and he may have been born at Grahamstown, on the Eastern Cape. It is thought that he joined one of the irregular units that operated there during the Eighth Frontier War, and in December 1877 he transferred to the Frontier Light Horse. It is popularly held that he was a friend of Cecil D'Arcy and that they enrolled together; in fact, the official record of their service suggests they joined a week apart and any friendship between them may date only to their service together. O'Toole served with the FLH throughout the last stages of the Frontier War, the abortive Sekhukhune campaign of 1878, and the invasion of Zululand. By 1879 he had attained the rank of sergeant. He was present in the action at Hlobane and the Battle of Khambula, and on both occasions his gallantry, in assisting unhorsed troopers, was noted.

On 3 July 1879 O'Toole was present with the irregular force under Buller which crossed the White Mfolozi to scout out the Ulundi plain. Buller's men were ambushed by Zulus concealed in the long grass, and several men were unhorsed by a sudden volley. One, a Sergeant Fitzmaurice of the 24th Regiment (serving with the Mounted Infantry) was trapped under his horse, and Lord William Beresford returned to rescue him. Fitzmaurice was badly stunned by the fall and Beresford had difficulty persuading him to mount. With the Zulus rushing towards them, O'Toole at first took up a position between Beresford and the Zulus and tried to keep them at bay, but, becoming frustrated at the delay, threw down his carbine and dismounted to help Beresford heave Fitzmaurice into the saddle. By the time O'Toole regained his own horse, the Zulus were just yards away.

The skirmish brought VC awards for Beresford, D'Arcy and O'Toole. O'Toole was presented with the medal by Major-General Clifford in a ceremony on 16 January 1880, on the same occasion that Commissary James Dalton received the decoration.

With the end of the Zulu campaign the Cape authorities sought recruits from among the men of the recently disbanded irregular corps for units being raised to combat the 'rebellion' of Chief Moorosi of the baPuthi, who lived on the western side of the Kahlamba (Drakensberg) mountains. A number of ex-FLH men were recruited into Herschel's Native Contingent, and O'Toole signed up with the rank of captain. The regiment was present during the final storming of Moorosi's mountain stronghold in November 1879. Otherwise, little has survived about O'Toole's career in the 1880s, although in 1890 his name appears on the roll of Cecil Rhodes' Pioneer Column troops who occupied Mashonaland in modern Zimbabwe. After that, his life is the subject of little more than rumour. One story has it that he took part in the Matabele and Mashona campaigns of 1893 and 1896, another that he died in Salisbury (now Harare) in 1891. In 1900, however, he was listed in a newspaper report as then living at the Cape, and he may have spent part of his life in America. No reliable record of the date and circumstances of his death have yet emerged.

O'Toole posed for a famous portrait standing beside Cecil D'Arcy, both men wearing uniforms and their VCs. The picture presumably dates to the early part of 1880. A similar photograph exists showing D'Arcy and another man in the same pose, wearing civilian dress; the similarity between the two studies invites comparison and suggests that the standing man may also be O'Toole. It is difficult to be certain however, as in one picture he wears heavy side-whiskers, and in the other he does not. It has been suggested that the civilian photograph was taken before enlistment, and has been taken as proof of the pre-existing friend-ship between the two men; in fact their ages in both photographs appear similar, and they may have been taken within weeks of each other – with the civilian study intended to reflect their return to civilian life at the end of the Anglo-Zulu War.

Raaff, Pieter Johannes

Pieter Raaf was born in Bloemfontein, the capital of the Orange Free State, in 1849. His father had been an official in British service during the short-lived Orange River Colony, and Raaff's family were 'Hollanders' – a contemporary term used to describe those who were recently descended from Dutch immigrants, rather than long-standing Afrikaner or 'Boer' settlers – whose education and interests inclined them politically towards the British. They had little sympathy for the parochial political aspirations of the rural Boers, and indeed apparently refused to recognize the Afrikaans language in their home. Raaff sometimes spelt his Christian name in Anglicized form, 'Peter'. Although the most slightly built of his siblings, – in adulthood he was just 5 feet 4 inches tall – Pieter Johannes Raaff was destined to become a frontiersman of note whose military career was characterized by a marked loyalty towards the British Empire. He was a noted horseman in his youth – a family anecdote recalls how he once snatched up a running hare at the gallop and presented it to a visiting British prince – and his adventurous disposition had led to him volunteer for service in the Free State/BaSotho War of 1865 when, aged only sixteen, he had been wounded. After trying unsuccessfully to make his fortune at the newly opened diamond fields, Raaff joined the Boer commandos in their disastrous campaign against King Sekhukhune's baPedi on the north-eastern Transvaal border. Following the British annexation of the Transvaal in 1877, Raaff volunteered to raise his own irregular unit, Raaff's Transvaal Rangers, which took part in Colonel Hugh Rowlands' scarcely more successful Pedi campaign in 1878. Three men from the corps were killed early in the campaign, and several wounded.

In November 1878, with the Zulu crisis brewing, Raaff went to the Kimberley diamond fields to raise fresh recruits. Promising them a share of any booty looted in Zululand, Raaff managed to raise a force of 150 men, 100 Europeans and 50 of mixed descent. The tough appearance of his men aroused widespread comment, a Kimberley newspaper describing them as 'Kimberley Riff-Raaff'. Lieutenant Tomasson, an officer who served with both the Frontier Light Horse and Baker's Horse – two irregular units who raised their own fair share of eyebrows – thought of Raaff's men that 'a more forbidding lot of mixed Hottentots and scum of the Diamonds Fields was never collected together outside a prison wall'. Raaff himself was only twenty-eight when the war began.

Raaff's Transvaal Rangers were attached to Colonel Rowlands' column, which assembled on the northern Transvaal/Swazi/Zulu border. On 15 February they took part in the attack on Talaku Mountain, when Rowlands sought to deprive the local Zulus of a rallying point. At the end of the month, however, Raaff was transferred to Colonel Wood's command, and the Rangers were redeployed to Khambula. On 28 March Raaff and some of his men took part in the attack on Hlobane mountain; the following morning, it was a small patrol under Raaff which first spotted the Zulu army advancing towards Khambula camp from their overnight bivouac along the amaGoda stream (outside the present town of Vryheid). During the subsequent battle Raaff's men took part in the fierce pursuit which turned the Zulu retreat into a rout. When Wood's column was re-designated the Flying Column, the Transvaal Rangers remained attached to it, and took part in the second invasion of Zululand. On 2 June Raaff and a handful of his men accompanied the cavalry expedition which recovered the body of Louis Napoleon, the Prince Imperial of France. On 3 July Raaff's men made up part of the command, under Redvers Buller, which scouted the plain north of the White Mfolozi River, where King Cetshwayo's royal homesteads were concentrated; in the ensuing skirmish two of the Rangers were wounded. They were also present at the decisive Battle at Ulundi (oNdini) the following day. During the pacification operations, Raaff's men were attached to Colonel Baker Russell's column operating in northern Zululand. The Rangers were finally disbanded in September.

Raaff had emerged from the Anglo-Zulu War with his reputation enhanced, and for his services he was made a Commander of the Order of St Michael and St George. Nevertheless, his campaign medal was apparently withheld due to financial irregularities in the administration of his unit. He returned to the Transvaal and at the end of 1880 – with Republican discontent spilling into open rebellion – he was appointed court messenger and field-cornet at Potchefstroom by the British Administrator. When the British garrison at Potchefstroom was attacked and besieged by the Boers in December 1880, Raaff quickly raised a new unit, the second incarnation of Raaff's Rangers, to defend the town. He played a conspicuous part in the defence of one of the outlying buildings, the Landrost's Office. The roof of the building was set on fire, and the defenders forced to surrender; Raaff was kept in handcuffs for more than two months. His Dutch ancestry made him the subject of considerable animosity from the Boers – who resented his loyalty to the British – and Raaff was tried for treason and sentenced to death. Paul Kruger, one of the principle republican leaders, intervened on his behalf and ordered a retrial, which found him not guilty. The Boer rebellion was successful and the Transvaal was returned to Boer government, leading to considerable hardship among those who had supported the British cause, including Raaff. He apparently returned to the Free State and opened a butchery business in Kroonstad; he expressed his disillusion by hanging a sign over the door which read 'Peter Raaff, C.M.G., Butcher'.

In 1891 Raaff joined the Bechuanaland Border Police and became a resident magistrate in Bechuanaland. When, in 1893, Cecil Rhodes' British South Africa Company invaded the Matabele kingdom, in modern Zimbabwe, with limited official support, Raaff volunteered for a third time to raise Raaff's Rangers, this time mostly from the mining population of Johannesburg. This unit served alongside the Bechuanaland Border Police in the column which advanced into southern Matabeleland. After the capture of the Matabele capital, Bulawayo, in November 1893, a column was organized to capture the fugitive Matabele king, Lobengula kaMzilikazi, who had fled along the valley of the Shangani River towards the Limpopo. The column was under the command of a former regular officer, Major Patrick Forbes, and Raaff and some of his men were attached to it. The column was under-strength, the expedition poorly planned; food was in short supply and the weather turned wet. The relationship between Forbes and his fellow officers, including Raaff, deteriorated. Forbes pursued Lobengula to the Shangani, but on 4 December a detachment of thirty-four men under Major Allan Wilson were cut off by the Matabele on the far side of the river and killed. Forbes' party then came under attack and were forced to retreat to Bulawayo. By this time Forbes' relationship with Raaff was poor, although

Raaff's considerable experience was credited by many as the means of the column's survival. Raaff had not long been back in Bulawayo when, on 26 December 1893, he was taken suddenly ill and died. Although the controversy surrounding the 'Shangani Patrol' has led to lingering speculation that his death was due to foul play, Raaff's family were adamant that he died of ptomaine poisoning brought about by a heavy meal. During the expedition, when most of the troops had resorted to eating horsemeat, Raaff had survived by eating roots and berries; the temptation afforded by the plentiful food supplies to be found on his return to Bulawayo had apparently proved fatal.

Robertson, Reverend Robert

Robert Robertson was a prominent missionary in Zululand. He was born in Scotland in 1830 and offered his services to Bishop Grey, the Bishop of Cape Town, as an Anglican missionary. In 1854 Robertson accompanied Grey and Bishop Colenso on a visit to Natal; he was later ordained by Bishop Colenso. In 1855 he married a widow, Mrs Woodrow, who ran an orphanage in Pietermaritzburg, and shortly afterwards established the Umlazi mission outside Durban. Most mission societies were anxious to evangelize in Zululand, but the Zulu kings remained largely unwilling to grant permission to establish missions there. In the aftermath of the Battle of Ndondakusuka in 1856, and the dreadful loss of life among the Princes of the Zulu Royal House, King Mpande agreed to allow a number of missions to be established largely for political reasons; he hoped to exploit the contacts with the white world the missions afforded, to offset the ambitions of his son Prince Cetshwayo. In 1860, under the aegis of the Society for the Propagation of the Christian Gospel, the Robertsons moved to KwaMagwaza. Here they had to build the mission buildings from nothing, cutting their own timber and baking their own bricks.

For the most part, the Zulu missions won few converts. The Zulus were attached to their traditional spiritual beliefs and wary of the cultural baggage Christianity brought with it, while Prince Cetshwayo, well aware that his father was using the missionaries as political pawns, was wary of them. Nonetheless Robert

Robertson created a marked impression in the vicinity of KwaMagwaza, partly because of his willingness to intervene to save people accused of witchcraft.

Nevertheless, his time at KwaMagwaza was to prove an unhappy – indeed, tragic – one. In 1864 a wagon overturned and, shedding its load, crushed Mrs Robertson to death. Robertson laboured on, and in 1869 married again. His second wife died in 1874, however, and ushered in a prolonged breakdown for Robertson. He took to consoling himself in his loneliness with drink and Zulu girls whom, his detractors insisted, he 'bought' rather in the manner of a Zulu *isigodlo*, attracting them to KwaMagwaza by offering their fathers compensation. On one occasion a visiting missionary arrived to find Robertson badly the worse for drink, and only his reputation as Zululand's leading Anglican activist saved him from dismissal.

Initially Robertson had placed high hopes in the young Prince Cetshwayo, in whose intelligence and ambition he saw the chance of concessions to Christianity. Yet Cetshwayo was an ardent Zulu traditionalist, and after his succession in 1874 he remained opposed to further evangelism. Disillusioned, Robertson then began to campaign for British intervention in Zululand, arguing that the Christian cause could only advance there once Cetshwayo's opposition had been forcibly removed. He wrote anonymous letters to the Natal press to that effect, spreading stories of the persecution of Christian converts and of daily executions at Cetshwayo's court, and sought to influence the policies of administrators like Shepstone and Frere. His tone is best summed up in one letter to the Natal press in which he likened Zululand to 'a tree with rotten roots, it needs only a blast to lay it low'.

With the British annexation of the Transvaal and the heightened tension between Natal and Zululand, the missionary community – not only vulnerable but keen to make their vulnerability apparent – abandoned Zululand in August 1877. Robertson declared that he intended to return to Zululand as a volunteer chaplain with the British forces, and he was as good as his word. He resigned his post with the SPG and attached himself as Anglican chaplain to Pearson's coastal column. He was present when Pearson crossed the border and during the Battle of Nyezane on 22 January. This he found a sobering experience – 'a battle is all very well to read about at a distance', he wrote, 'it is another thing to be in one, and hear the bullets whistling past, to see the dead and wounded carried in, and to know that you may, at any moment, be in eternity' – and a description by a British officer suggests that it brought to the fore the doubts which had plagued him over the previous few years:

> I found him ... with a rifle across his knees, a faint specimen of the Church Militant. He told me that he now considered he had never really made a Zulu a true Christian. His faithful driver (a zealous convert) said he had just come in, covered with blood and had stated that he found his own brother among the wounded Zulus and so killed him. Scarcely a Christian act.

Robertson remained with Pearson throughout the siege at Eshowe, and found plenty to keep him occupied:

> We had parade and service every Sunday, and so much was that appreciated that when Sunday happened to be wet, it was held on Monday instead. I also had a Bible meeting four times a week ... These meetings were, as a rule, well attended, and were very interesting. I used also, about once a week, to deliver a lecture on Zulu history, which interested both officers and men much. You would have been astonished to find how little all of them knew about the people they were fighting, or why they were fighting ...

Indeed, so useful was Robertson's knowledge that Pearson came to rely on him increasingly as an unofficial political agent for the column.

After Eshowe was relieved and the war was over, Robertson and the KwaMagwaza community returned to their old station. It had, of course, been destroyed by the Zulus during their absence, and Robertson was forced to rebuild everything. He noted with some satisfaction that over the following months a number of items looted from the complex during the war were returned to him by Zulus living locally.

Although the Zulu people remained reluctant to accept Christianity, and the post-war period was a turbulent one for white civilians caught up in successive wars and rebellions, Robertson was indeed correct in that the removal of King Cetshwayo and the assertion of British force allowed for the expansion of mission activities. There was a significant increase in Anglican activity in the 1880s with the establishment of a number of new missions (including St Vincent's at Isandlwana). In the aftermath of the war between Dinuzulu and Zibhebhu in 1884 – when Robertson was again forced to flee KwaMagwaza – it was decided to open a new mission at eThalaneni, in the Nkandla district. Robertson himself supervised the building of the mission, which was dedicated in 1888. Robertson remained concerned to extend Anglican influence across Zululand, and at the end of 1891 began work on a new site at Nhlwati, north of the Black Mfolozi River, on a spur of the Lebombo Mountains, west of the coastal flats of Tsongaland. Here he continued to work until old age and a hard life overtook him, and he died on 9 November 1897 at the age of sixty-seven. In a final touch, entirely appropriate to the beliefs that had shaped his life, one of his last wishes was that he be buried in his vestments and wrapped in a Union Flag.

Rorke, James Alfred

James Alfred Rorke was the son of James Rorke, one of three brothers from County Galway in Ireland (the others being Michael and Thomas) who emigrated to the Cape in 1823. It is not entirely clear whether the three brothers were soldiers – which is entirely possible, given the involvement of the British Army in the Eastern Cape frontier, and the high proportion of Irishmen then in the ranks – or whether they were following in the wake of the 1820 settlers. James Rorke acquired a property at the village of Blinkwater on the Eastern Cape; his son James Alfred Rorke was born in South Africa in 1827. In 1849 James Alfred Rorke moved to Natal, which had only recently become a British colony, and acquired a farm of 1,000 acres on the middle-Mzinyathi River. Quite why James Alfred left the Cape is unknown – his father lived until 1859 – and the possible causes range from a family quarrel to wanderlust, a yearning to explore new lands and the opportunities which came with an expanding Imperial frontier. Rorke's farm abutted the Zulu border and included a good ford across the Mzinyathi which became known as Rorke's Drift. Rorke built a dwelling and a store at the foot of the Shiyane hill, and which commanded a fine view of the Biggarsberg escarpment looking across the Mzinyathi valley. Like many frontier farmers, he derived his income from a variety of economic activities; he offered a canteen to passing traders, traded across the border, raised cattle and hunted the last of the big game to be found in the region. His nearest neighbours were Voortrekkers – the Vermaak family at Helpmekaar – and Rorke was on friendly terms with the Afrikaner community. Rorke married Sara Johanna Stydom and had two children, James Michael and Louisa. As the white community grew slowly along the Mzinyathi frontier, Rorke became a valuable member of the fledgling colonial society. He became a lieutenant in the Buffalo Border Guard – a volunteer unit formed in 1873 to protect the settlers in the aftermath of the Langalibalele 'rebellion' – and a Border Agent for the Natal administration, using his network of contacts to report regularly on events in Zululand. Despite an occasionally fierce temper and attitudes typical of frontier life at the time, Rorke was widely known and respected among the African community, who knew his store as 'KwaJim' (or 'Jimu') – Jim's place. Although by local standards he had prospered, life on the Zulu border remained harsh, and Rorke died on 24 October 1875 at the age of forty-eight.

Local legend has it that he bought consignments of gin from Greytown and had them carried by wagon to the frontier; when one such shipment was delayed on the road, Rorke shot himself. Whether this was a result of a fit of depression brought about by the deprivation of his favourite tipple, or whether the consignment was stock and the loss had a financial implication, the rumour does not specify. Rorke was buried behind his old store at the foot of Shiyane hill. His widow Sara sold the farm to John Surtees, who occupied it only briefly before selling it to the Swedish missionary Otto Witt.

Rorke, James Michael

James Michael Rorke was the son of James Alfred Rorke – of Rorke's Drift fame – and his wife Sara. He was born in the 1850s, and seems to have moved across the border into the Zulu kingdom even before his father's death in 1875. He lived at Ngome in northern Zululand and, together with Herbert Nunn and a Mr Calverley, attached himself to Prince Hamu kaNzibe as an adviser on European affairs, and trading agent, fulfilling much the same role as John Dunn did with Cetshwayo. It is possible that James Michael Rorke had married a European woman before moving to Zululand, but the evidence is confused; what is more certain is that he subsequently took more than one Zulu wife. When the war began in 1879, Rorke, Nunn and Calverley all remained in Zululand, and Rorke acted as Prince Hamu's secretary, signing several letters on his behalf during the negotiations which culminated in Hamu's surrender to the British. All three white men accompanied Hamu and his followers when they placed themselves under British protection; Rorke may have been present when Hamu's warriors fought for the British at the Battle of Hlobane on 28 March, and indeed Calverley was killed on that occasion. After the war, the British confirmed Prince Hamu as ruler of a tract of northern Zululand, and Rorke returned to live near him at Ngome. He died in 1934 leaving at least three children by his Zulu wives.

Schiess, Christian Ferdinand VC

Few careers are more illustrative of the largely anonymous lives of the itinerant white wanderers and adventurers who were enlisted into the British auxiliary units than that of Christian Ferdinand Schiess. Little is known about his life for certain; he was apparently born on 7 April 1856 in Bergdorf, Canton Berne, Switzerland; his father Nicklaus Schiess, was a stone-cutter. He is believed to have enlisted, probably under a false name and certainly under-age, in the French Army and fought in the Franco-Prussian War of 1870-1871. He sailed for the Cape from Hamburg on 9 June 1877 as part of a scheme sponsored by the Cape government to recruit Swiss artisans and farmers. He arrived on the Eastern Cape Frontier in August 1877 and took part in the 9th Cape Frontier War, although details of his service there remain unknown. He was presumably among those disbanded irregulars recruited in late 1878 to join the newly-formed Natal Native Contingent, although his name does not appear on lists of those transferred from the Cape to Natal for the purpose. Of his physical appearance equally few details remain – Lieutenant Harford, who met him, wrote that he was short and dark, and that he may have once been a sailor and wore an earring. At the beginning of the Anglo-Zulu campaign he was a corporal in the 3rd Regiment NNC which was attached to the No. 3 (Centre) Column. He was present at the action at *inkosi* Sihayo's homestead on 12 January, and at some point thereafter was admitted to the field hospital at Rorke's Drift suffering from acute blisters. When news of the attack on the column's camp reached Rorke's Drift, Schiess was considered well enough to leave the hospital and take part in the defence. During the later stages of the battle he was one of a party who held the exposed angle between the biscuit-box barricade and the front wall; most of this party were injured and Schiess himself was slightly wounded by a musket-ball in the ankle. The defenders were troubled by Zulus who, under cover of the abandoned front barricade and the rocky ledge below it, were able to approach close to the British line without being seen, and who could then shoot at the defenders at close range. According to Chaplain George Smith:

> One fellow fired at Corporal Scheiss of the N.N.C. (a Swiss by birth, who was a hospital patient), the charge blowing his hat off; but he instantly jumped upon the parapet and bayoneted the man, regained his place and shot another, and then repeating his former exploit, climbed up the sacks and bayoneted a third; a bullet struck him in the instep early in the fight, but he would not allow that his wound was sufficient reason for his leaving his post, yet he has suffered most acutely from it since...

The 3rd Regiment NNC was disbanded in the aftermath of its poor performance in the Isandlwana campaign and Schiess, once he had recovered, joined Lonsdale's Horse as a corporal and apparently served throughout the final stages of the war. Although his gallantry at Rorke's Drift was mentioned by several participants his recommendation for the Victoria Cross was apparently made only after considerable lobbying on the part of the Colonial authorities who were keen that a colonial soldier's contribution should be recognized. The award was gazetted on 27 November 1879 and Schiess was presented with the medal by Sir Garnet Wolseley in the Market Square, Pietermaritzburg, on 3 February 1880.

After the war, however, Schiess' fortunes declined rapidly. He found work for a time in the telegraph office in Durban but by 1884 he was unemployed and destitute. His plight aroused some public sympathy and the Royal Navy agreed to ship him to England while his food was funded by public subscription. In early December 1884 he set sail on HMS *Serapis* but his health was poor and he succumbed to pneumonia at sea on 14 December 1884. He was buried off the coast of West Africa; his death certificate gives his age as 'not known – about 36', an indication of the hard times he had endured; he was in fact twenty-eight years old.

Schermbrucker, Frederick Xavier

Frederick Xavier Schermbrucker was born in Bavaria in 1832, and in 1850 joined the Bavarian Army. In 1856, however, Britain – reviving the tradition of Hanoverian connections which they had been able to exploit for recruiting purposes during the Napoleonic Wars – raised a German Legion to fight in the Crimea. Schermbrucker enlisted, but by the time the Legion arrived in England the Russian war was over. Instead, men of the Legion were offered land in southern Africa, the intention being to bolster the volatile Eastern Cape Frontier with settlers with military training. Over 2,000 members of the Legion arrived at the Cape in 1857, establishing a number of villages with German names in the King William's Town district. Frederick Schermbrucker was one of them. In fact, the scheme was not a great success, and many of the German settlers either drifted away or enlisted in the volunteer corps which served in the wars which marked British progress across southern Africa.

Schermbrucker showed an early interest in local politics – in 1868 he was returned to the Cape House of Assembly as a representative for King William's Town – but by the 1870s he had moved to Bloemfontein in the Free State, where he edited one of the first Afrikaans-language newspapers, *De Express*. With the outbreak of the 9th Cape Frontier War, however, Schermbrucker returned to the Cape and was offered a command in the local forces. During the early stages of the Ciskei campaign, he was in charge of a volunteer force operating in the Xhosa stronghold of the AmaThole Mountains. When Sandile, head of the amaNgqika section of the Xhosa was killed in a skirmish in May 1878, Schermbrucker was in charge of organizing the funeral. Sandile was buried at Isidenge on 9 June, Schermbrucker commenting that the ceremony was proper 'but without any military consideration'. Sandile was buried between the graves of two white volunteers who had been killed earlier in the fighting; this was Schermbrucker's choice, and he commented 'that will keep the Blackguard quiet'.

About this time Lieutenant Colonel J.N. Crealock, of Chelmsford's staff, described Schermbrucker as 'an erect well-made man with a figure telling of former military training. His rapid gestures and vivacious descriptions soon put us au fait as to the points of interest around us'.

At the end of the Frontier war he was appointed to a post on the civilian administration at King William's Town, but in October 1878 Lord Chelmsford asked him to raise a force from among the German settlers for service against the Zulus. The result was the Kaffrarian Rifles (sometimes called Kaffrarian Vanguard), over 100 strong, who arrived at Durban a month later. They were marched up to Colonel Wood's base at Utrecht with the intention of employing them to protect the vulnerable German-speaking settlement at Lüneburg. This they did for two months, but towards the end of February it was decided to reorganize them as a mounted unit, and they marched to Wood's base at Khambula to receive their horses. Over the next few days they patrolled the border between Khambula and Lüneburg, but on 27 March they were appointed to join Wood's attack on the Hlobane mountain complex.

About seventy-five men of the Kaffrarian Rifles took part in the battle under Schermbrucker's leadership. They were part of Lieutenant Colonel J.C. Russell's force, which ascended the complex by the Ntendeka Mountain to the west. Russell judged it impossible to climb to the main plateau by the steep staircase of rock later known as the 'Devil's Pass', and when informed of the approach of the main Zulu army – which, coincidentally, had been dispatched to attack Khambula – he withdrew from the mountain without being seriously engaged.

Late the following morning the Zulu army attacked Khambula, and was driven off after hours of heavy fighting. The Kaffriarian Rifles spent this part of the battle manning the north-western face of the main British laager, lying 'under the wagons, pointing our rifles over the sod wall'. When the Zulus began to retire, Schermbrucker himself commanded one of three columns of mounted men sent out by Wood to turn the Zulu retreat into a rout, and his account of the slaughter is one of the most vivid descriptions of the ruthlessness of the British pursuit:

> For fully seven miles I traced two columns of the enemy. They fairly ran like bucks, but I was after them like the whirlwind and shooting incessantly into the thick of the column, which could not have been less than 5,000 strong. They became exhausted, and shooting them down would have taken too much time; so we took the assegais from the dead men, and rushed among the living ones, stabbing them right and left with fearful revenge for the misfortune of the 28th inst. No quarter was given.

At the end of April, the period of service for which the men of the Kaffrarian Rifles had enlisted expired, and most of the men returned to the Cape. Schermbrucker himself stayed at the front, together with about twenty-five men who elected to re-enlist. The unit continued to patrol the Khambula/Lüneburg sector, and on 18 May Schermbrucker himself had a narrow escape. He was patrolling near Lüneburg with Major Moore of the 4th Regiment, and an orderly, Trooper Larsen. Only a few miles from the settlement, they were ambushed by Zulus as they rode through long grass, and Schermbrucker's horse was killed. He promptly commandeered Larsen's horse, ordering the trooper up behind him, but 'the horse refused the double load'. Larsen was a good runner, and set off on foot. By this time, the Zulus were quite close, and a shot hit and killed Major Moore's horse, forcing him to mount behind Schermbrucker. Schermbrucker and Moore escaped to Lüneburg but Larsen did not return, and his body was found in a donga some months later.

The Kaffrarian Rifles was finally disbanded in September, at the end of the hostilities. Schermbrucker returned to King William's Town, but with the outbreak of the BaSotho 'Gun War' in 1880, he again volunteered, organizing and commanding a unit of BaSotho Police. When the rebellion ended, he returned to politics and for the next ten years was returned to the Cape parliament in one capacity or another, representing both King William's Town and Uppington, in the Northern Cape. From 1884 he was the Commissioner for Crown Lands and Public Works for Uppington. He died in April 1904.

Shepstone, George

George Shepstone was born in June 1849, a few years after his father Theophilus moved the Shepstone family to Natal. Like his brothers, George Shepstone grew up fluent in isiZulu, a good shot and excellent horseman. In 1873 he accompanied his father and elder brother Henrique on the expedition to 'crown' King Cetshwayo. Also accompanying the expedition was Major Anthony Durnford RE, and it is likely that he and George first met during this time. Shortly after the expedition's return to Natal, the *inkosi* of the amaHlubi people, Langalibalele ka Mthimkhulu, attempted to cross the Kahlamba Mountains into BaSotholand in an attempt to escape an entanglement with the colonial authorities. Durnford was ordered to block the antici-pated escape route, and George Shepstone volunteered to lead a unit of African auxiliaries that was raised to counter the crisis. Durnford's mission faltered badly in a skirmish on top of the Bushman's Pass on 4 November 1873, and in the aftermath it was Shepstone who collected and buried the colonial dead on the summit. Although much of settler society in Natal was critical of Durnford's conduct, Shepstone nevertheless offered to join

Durnford again when the latter was charged with organizing auxiliaries for the invasion of Zululand in 1879. Shepstone's father,
Theophilus, was troubled by his son's decision:

> It is strange but true that when I heard he had been appointed
> to serve with Colonel Durnford, I felt as if I had heard his
> death warrant. I had no confidence in Durnford's prudence or
> capacity to suit himself to the circumstances in which he
> might be suddenly placed.

Durnford himself was given command of No. 2 Column, which
originally consisted largely of auxiliary troops and which was
placed on the escarpment overlooking the Middle Drift on the
Thukela. George Shepstone was appointed as Durnford's Political
Agent, to serve as his adviser on African politics and affairs, a
position which effectively made him Durnford's senior staff
officer.

Once the invasion began on 11 January 1879, Durnford was
ordered to move to Rorke's Drift to support the advance led by
Lord Chelmsford himself at the head of the Centre Column.
Durnford took with him the most mobile element of his
command – his mounted units and an attached RA rocket battery.
He crossed the Mzinyathi on the 20th and camped at Rorke's
Drift.

Chelmsford had advanced to Isandlwana that same day, and on
the 21st had ordered a probe into the hills further along his line
of advance. This probe encountered some resistance on the
evening of the 21st, and before dawn on the 22nd Chelmsford
moved out to support it. Before leaving he ordered Durnford to
move to Isandlwana, without specifying what he was to do on
arrival there.

Durnford, accompanied by Shepstone, reached the camp at
about 10.30 a.m. on the 22nd. A significant enemy presence had
been reported on the iNyoni heights nearby, and in the absence of
any specific orders from Chelmsford Durnford decided to clear
the heights with his own troops. He sent two detachments onto
the hills, accompanied by George Shepstone; Durnford himself
took the rest of his command along the foot of the hills in what
he clearly hoped would be a pincer movement.

The men with Shepstone stumbled across the Zulu army concealed in the Ngwebeni valley at about noon. The Zulus responded with an immediate attack, and Shepstone rode back to warn the troops in the camp. He arrived somewhat breathless at the foot of the escarpment, and Lieutenant Colonel Henry Pulleine seemed at first undecided how best to react to his report. Memorably, Shepstone replied 'I am not an alarmist, sir, but the enemy are in such black masses over there, such long black lines, that you will have to give us all the assistance you can. They are fast driving our men this way.'

Pulleine promptly began to deploy his troops, and shortly after Shepstone's men spilled down the escarpment with the Zulus in pursuit. After that, there are only snatched references to the part played by George Shepstone; he apparently rejoined his men, but after the British line began to crumble he was heard to say that he must find Durnford. It is unlikely that he did. The British collapse, when it came, happened quickly, and with the men retiring on the camp, pursued by the Zulus, everything dissolved in confusion.

George Shepstone's body was found on a rocky outcrop below the southern peak of Isandlwana, on a spot which overlooks the approach from the Manzimnyama valley. It is surrounded today by a cluster of cairns which suggests that a determined stand was made there, perhaps in the hope of holding back the Zulu right horn, or of covering the flight of survivors by the road. Quite who died with Shepstone remains undetermined; it is possible they were auxiliaries, and neither British nor Colonial burial details claimed them as their own. According to the Zulu boy Muziwento:

We were also told that there was present a son of Somseu [Theophilus Shepstone]. He fought very bravely. He killed our people. The others feared to approach him. Suddenly there dashed in our brother Umtweni before he could load and killed him. But that young fellow died at Hlobane ...

Today Shepstone's grave is one of the few which is individually marked on the Isandlwana battlefield.

Shepstone, John Wesley

A younger brother of Theophilus Shepstone, born at the Cape in 1827, John Wesley Shepstone was intimately involved in his brother's dealings with African peoples. He accompanied Theophilus to Natal in 1845, and between 1846 and 1896 filled a number of different administrative posts in the colony, often standing in for his brother. In 1857 Theophilus sent John in command of a patrol of colonial troops to interview the Sithole *inkosi*, Matshana kaMondise, regarding allegations that members of the *inkosi*'s family had been killed on charges of witchcraft. John Shepstone lured Matshana to a meeting on the promise that he was unarmed; at a critical moment Shepstone produced a gun. Matshana managed to escape – ultimately to Zululand – but several of his men were killed in the ensuing skirmish. When Theophilus went to the Transvaal as Administrator, in the wake of the British annexation of April 1877, John took over his old role as Acting Secretary for Native Affairs. It was John Shepstone who read Frere's ultimatum to the Zulu representatives at the meeting at the Lower Thukela Drift in December 1878. At the end of the war, Shepstone was one of Sir Garnet Wolseley's principle advisers in deciding the post-war settlement. Although Wolseley had himself decided to divide the country, he leaned heavily on Shepstone for advice regarding the appointment of the *amakhosi*. It was Shepstone who argued that by favouring historic lineages within the country, a pre-Shakan order could be re-established which would undermine the Zulu Royal House. When the settlement subsequently led to friction, many reports and deputations from Zululand passed through Shepstone's hands, still acting as he was as his brother's stand-in in the office of Native Affairs. He used his influence to reinforce the settlement and check the aspirations of the Royal House. In 1883, on the restoration of Cetshwayo to Zululand, Shepstone was appointed British Resident in that portion of the country placed under direct British control (his nephew Henrique took over as Secretary for Native Affairs in Natal). Shepstone failed to draw any distinction between the interests of the Natal administration and the welfare of Zululand's British subjects, and he remained opposed to the royalist party. The settlement collapsed following Cetshwayo's defeat by *inkosi* Zibhebhu in July 1883. He remained influential within Natal on the subject of African affairs and, together with his nephews Henrique and Theophilus Jnr., provided evidence to the South African Native Affairs Commission as late as 1904, arguing against the African franchise.

He died in 1916.

Shepstone, Henrique

Shepstone was the eldest son of Theophilus Shepstone, and was born at Fort Peddie in the Cape Colony on 18 January 1840. He accompanied his family to Natal in 1845, grew up fluent in isiZulu, and assumed many of his father's attitudes. He was a leading member of Shepstone's dynasty, trusted as his father's representative in his political dealings with African peoples.

In 1873 Henrique accompanied Shepstone on the expedition to 'crown' King Cetshwayo; in 1877 he again accompanied his father to Pretoria for the annexation of the Transvaal. He became the Secretary for Native Affairs in the new colony, and as such was part of the Transvaal deputation which met at Rorke's Drift in March 1878 to consider the fate of the border territory whose ownership was disputed between the Transvaal and Zulu kingdom. Henrique Shepstone complained that the commission was too even-handed in its deliberations, and placed too much weight upon Zulu testimony; in the event the award of the commission's report was delayed until Sir Bartle Frere had incorporated it into his 'ultimatum' demands of December 1878. Shepstone's post in the Transvaal came to an end with the retrocession that followed the revolt of 1881, and he returned to Natal.

In July 1882 he accompanied King Cetshwayo on his journey to London. When his father retired as Natal's Secretary for Native Affairs in 1884, Henrique succeeded him. He held this post until his retirement in 1893, acting largely within the framework of policies implemented by his father. During the 1880s, he supported the official British position in Zululand, which was to reduce the influence of the Zulu Royal House by bolstering that of its opponents. In 1907 he was one of three judges appointed to try King Dinuzulu kaCetshwayo on charges of treason connected with the Poll Tax uprising. Henrique Shepstone died in Durban in October 1917.

Shepstone, Theophilus

For thirty years, Theophilus Shepstone dominated the policies of the colony of Natal with regard not only to its own indigenous population but in its relationship with its independent neighbours as well. Shepstone was the architect of the system of government which controlled Natal's African population – the so-called 'Shepstone System' – and, through his complex dealings with the Zulu kingdom, greatly influenced the decision of the British to invade in 1879.

Shepstone was born at Westbury, near Bristol, on 8 January 1817. When he was three years old his father, the Revd. William Shepstone, sailed to the Cape as one of the '1820 settlers' and took up a missionary post on the Eastern Frontier. Young Shepstone was educated at mission schools and grew up fluent in the Xhosa language. From an early age he took an interest in the politics of Anglo-African interaction on the Frontier which created in him a life-long commitment to the cause of British Imperialism and an unquestioning belief in Christian values and western concepts of civilization and progress. During the 6th Frontier War (1834-35) he served as an interpreter on the staff of the British Governor, Sir Benjamin D'Urban, and on the cessation of hostilities he took up a post as Resident Agent among the amaMfengu people. In 1838, he accompanied the first British military expedition to Natal when a small force was sent to isolate Port Natal from the control of the Boer Voortrekkers. Although this force was soon withdrawn, Britain later seized Natal from the Voortrekker Republic and in 1846 Shepstone returned as Diplomatic Agent to the Native Tribes. He brought with him his wife Maria (née Palmer, whom he had married in 1833), his brother John and his own sons. Together the Shepstones would provide a powerful clique whose influence dominated Natal's African policy beyond the end of the nineteenth century.

Shepstone was, of course, faced with a difficult task on arrival in the country. The African population had been greatly disrupted by the rise of the Zulu kingdom under King Shaka and by the brief interregnum of the Voortrekkers but nonetheless outnumbered the fledging white community. Although Shepstone had, in theory, the full might of the British Empire to back him up, the resources actually at his command were painfully small since the Imperial garrison within the colony was tiny and he had only a handful of staff at his disposal. It was in these days that he adopted a pragmatic approach which largely remained his hallmark throughout his career. Land was apportioned to the African population in reserves known as 'locations' which reflected the existing settlement patterns where they did not conflict with settler demand for farmland. Shepstone acknowledged the authority of existing chiefs but grafted over it a superstructure of colonial administration. The right of the *amakhosi* to govern their own people according to traditional administration was recognized but was subject to supervision from white magistrates who were ultimately responsible to Shepstone. Thus the *amakhosi* became an important prop of the colonial administration and their authority was subverted to the cause of Imperial control. Where Shepstone could discern no hereditary *amakhosi* within a particular fragmented group, he simply created a new artificial chiefdom and appointed one himself. The practical administration of the people was administered through 'native law', which ultimately depended on Shepstone's interpretation of customary practice. Well aware that his ability to enforce his authority was actually limited, Shepstone created something of a mystique about his own persona; he interpreted his African name, Somsewu, to mean 'white father' and allowed the widespread belief that he had an unparalled and mystical understanding of 'the native mind'. He also maintained a widespread and effective intelligence system, which gave him a remarkable degree of knowledge of affairs both within and outside the colony, and in his manner was taciturn, giving away few of his thoughts. Sir Bartle Frere once described him as 'a singular type of Afrikaner Tallyrand, shrewd, observant, silent, self-controlled, immobile'. When, on occasion, the contradictions inherent in the 'Shepstone system' provoked African resistance, Shepstone could be ruthless. In 1857 an *inkosi* in southern Natal,

Sidoi, overstepped the bounds of acceptable behaviour and attacked a neighbour; Shepstone broke up the chiefdom, destroyed homes and confiscated property. That same year the Sithole *inkosi* Matshana kaMondise was accused of ordering deaths among his people on charges of witchcraft, an act which usurped the supreme authority of Shepstone's office. Shepstone sent his younger brother John to remonstrate with Matshana. John Shepstone invited Matshana to an ostensibly unarmed meeting, then produced weapons and tried to arrest him; Matshana only just managed to slip away to Zululand, and several of his followers were killed. In 1873 the *inkosi* of the amaHlubi people living in the Kahlamba foothills, Langalibalele kaMthimkulu, learned the hard way of the dilemma which the 'Shepstone system' posed to traditional authority. Many young amaHlubi had ventured to work in the Kimberly diamond field and returned home with firearms as wages. Langalibalele was ordered by the authorities to confiscate them; caught between the reluctance of his followers to surrender their weapons and the threatening manner of the authorities, Langalibalele fled across the mountains. He was later arrested and Shepstone ordered his people to be dispossessed.

Shepstone's outlook was essentially expansionist. With the growth of the settler economy he considered that much of the African population would be surplus to its requirements, and he sought outlets in which to relocate them. In 1854 he attempted to expand Natal's control into Pondoland, to the south, and across the mountains into BaSotholand. The territory he considered most useful for the long-term expansion of Natal, however, was the strip of land running north of the Ncome River, the ownership of which was disputed between the Zulu kingdom and the Boer republic of the Transvaal. Not only did this sparsely populated area offer potential as a location which could soak up thousands of Africans resettled from Natal, but it commanded the route to the interior. Shepstone's imperial vision saw the port of Durban as a gateway to Africa which would extend Natal's influence across the continent, bringing prosperity to its white settler population in return.

For this reason Shepstone sought to influence the internal

affairs of the Zulu kingdom. Following the succession dispute of 1856, Shepstone harboured Prince Cetshwayo's rivals who sought refuge in Natal. Once it became clear, however, that the Prince would succeed his father Mpande as king, Shepstone attempted to establish some control over Cetshwayo's policies. He was effectively given that opportunity by Cetshwayo's invitation to attend the coronation ceremonies which marked his accession in 1873. Cetshwayo himself remained insecure and wary of internal challenges, and had invited Shepstone's participation in the hope that a show of support from Colonial Natal would intimidate his rivals. In the event, the coronation expedition was largely farcical, as a powerful Zulu faction within the country insisted that Cetshwayo undergo the necessary traditional ceremonies before Shepstone arrived. Shepstone attempted to overawe the Zulus with bluster and by relying on the mystique of his reputation, and the subtle power struggles which underpinned the expedition are best summed up in an incident of high farce which took place when two praise singers, representing Shepstone and Prince Cetshwayo, attempted to shout each other down in front of the assembled crowds. The enduring legacy of the expedition was the speech in which Shepstone outlined a series of points for the good government of Zululand. His motives – typically – appear to have been ambiguous, and while Cetshwayo interpreted these as a reinforcement of his authority, the British later claimed they were conditions upon which their support had rested.

In the aftermath of the expedition Shepstone became a firm advocate of the Confederation policy, which aimed to subordinate regional differences within southern Africa to the interests of British Imperialism. With little sign that King Cetshwayo would prove compliant, Shepstone began to work for the armed overthrow of the Zulu kingdom. In April 1876 – the same year in which Shepstone was knighted – he was appointed Administrator of the Transvaal, and was responsible for annexing the republic to the British Crown. He held the post for four years, during which he worked to further his Imperial vision for the region. Now directly involved with the disputed territory issue, he met with senior Zulu representatives at Conference Hill, on the

Ncome River, on 18 November 1877. Shepstone's high-handed manner at this meeting greatly irritated the Zulus, and contemporary Zulu opinion held that the meeting was the first step on the road to war. The Zulus struggled to understand Shepstone's shifting attitudes, but in fact he was entirely consistent with his basic aim – the triumph of British influence – and had merely altered his policies to suit the changed situation following annexation.

Following the meeting at Conference Hill Shepstone worked to persuade the new British high Commissioner at the Cape, Sir Bartle Frere, of the need to overthrow Cetshwayo's administration. Although no longer directly involved in Natal affairs, his influence was immense, not least because members of his family still occupied key positions in the administration. When Frere finally presented an ultimatum to Cetshwayo's envoys on 11 December 1878, it was Shepstone's brother John, Natal's Acting Secretary for Native Affairs, who actually read it.

In the ensuing conflict, several of Shepstone's sons took part; his son George, serving as Political Agent to Colonel Durnford, was killed at Isandlwana.

At the end of the Zulu war, it was Shepstone who largely influenced Sir Garnet Wolseley's decision to split Zululand into thirteen component parts, supposedly representing the chiefdoms which had dominated before Shaka's day. By 1880, however, the Confederation policy was largely discredited by the cost of the British victory – and in particular by the Zulu success at Isandlwana – and by stirring republican discontent in the Transvaal, and Shepstone decided to retire from public life. He returned to live in Pietermaritzburg.

Ironically, he was lured out of retirement in early 1883 to supervise the restoration of King Cetshwayo – the second time he had participated in ceremonies to install the Zulu king. He remained ideologically opposed to the influence of the Zulu Royal House, and through those members of his family who remained active in Zulu affairs sought to reduce its influence. These policies contributed significantly to the outbreak of the Zulu civil war and the defeat of King Cetshwayo by Zibhebhu at oNdini on 21 July 1883, and to the frustration of Zulu royalists which found expression in Dinuzulu's rebellion in 1888

Shepstone died on 23 June 1893 in Pietermaritzburg. The system of African administration he had created survived him, despite the disturbances in 1906 which were to some extent the result of its shortcomings. It continued to influence government policy in Natal into the 1920s.

Shepstone, Theophilus Jnr.

Known as 'Offy', Shepstone was the third son of Sir Theophilus Shepstone. He was born at Fort Peddie in the Cape Colony in 1843, and came to Natal with his family in 1845. Like many settlers raised in the colony, he grew up to speak isiZulu fluently, was a good horseman, and largely inherited his father's attitudes towards African peoples. As a young man he entered the Natal colonial administration, and in 1865 he became secretary to the acting Lieutenant Governor of Natal, Colonel John Bisset, whose daughter Helen he was later to marry. Shepstone was a devout Anglican, a factor which would involve him both with the life of the Bishop of Natal, John Colenso, and the Christian African communities at Edendale and elsewhere.

Shepstone enlisted in the Natal Carbineers, whose members were recruited from among the settler gentry in the Natal midlands, and who were arguably the most fashionable of the Natal Volunteer Corps. He commanded the unit between 1872 and 1881. With the mobilization of Natal troops which preceded the invasion of Zululand, the Carbineers were attached to the Centre Column, which assembled on the Helpmekaar heights in late 1878. On 6 January – five days before war officially began – Shepstone led a patrol of Carbineers across the Mzinyathi River where they arrested the inhabitants of a Zulu homestead as spies, and took them back across the border. On 11 January the invasion began; on the 12th the Carbineers were present in the attack on *inkosi* Sihayo's homestead.

When Lord Chelmsford initiated the foray into the Malakatha and Hlazakazi hills on 21 January, Shepstone led the Carbineers in the party directly commanded by Major Dartnell. On the 22nd, in skirmishes between the Magogo and Phindo hills, Shepstone spotted and recognized a Zulu *inkosi* on horseback. He was

Matshana kaMondise of the Sithole people, whom Shepstone's uncle, John, had attempted unsuccessfully to arrest in 1857. Theophilus Shepstone gave chase, but Matshana escaped by jumping off his horse and scrambling down a steep incline, where Shepstone could not follow. Later that day, when Chelmsford's command returned to the devastated camp at Isandlwana, Shepstone searched unsuccessfully for the body of his younger brother George, who had been killed in the battle having been Lieutenant Colonel Anthony Durnford's political agent.

Shepstone was present during the first burial expedition to Isandlwana on 21 May 1879, during the course of which he found Durnford's body. He removed a ring from the finger to send to Durnford's family, an incident which later led to accusations that he had also removed papers from the corpse which might have proved damaging to Lord Chelmsford's reputation.

When auxiliary forces were reorganized in the aftermath of Isandlwana, a new mounted unit was raised to make good the loss of those who had dispersed after the battle. In May Shepstone took command of this unit, who were variously known as 'Shepstone's Horse' or 'Shepstone's BaSotho', despite the fact they were mostly amaNgwane men from the Kahlamba foothills or Edendale Christians, and none were Sotho. This unit was attached to the 2nd Division during the advance on oNdini. On 4 July, Shepstone commanded the unit when they first attempted to draw the Zulu right into attacking the British square at oNdini; later, when the Zulus began to retreat, Shepstone's Horse took a vigorous part in the ruthless pursuit.

Shepstone's Horse was disbanded on 30 July 1879, and Shepstone himself received the CMG for his services.

From 1884 Shepstone became increasingly involved in the affairs of the Swazi kingdom. The Swazi king, Mbandzeni waMswati, was beset by Europeans seeking concessions to exploit the mineral resources which were believed to lie under Swazi soil, and he had approached the Shepstone family asking for a representative to assist him. With his father's approval, Shepstone went to Swaziland to act as an intermediary between the Swazi and the white concessionaries. This proved to be an influential post at a time when Swaziland was not only under such economic pressure from the whites but increasingly trapped between competing British and Boer Imperial visions. Shepstone eventually formed a committee of white concessionaires to regulate their activities, although his own increasing financial involvement in the country – he secured concessions himself – meant that he was highly partisan. The historian Huw Jones has judged that he was 'greedy and unscrupulous in his dealings with the Swazi ... [and] failed to represent their interests during the eight years in which they had relied upon him for advice and guidance. Largely through his interest in personal aggrandizement, the Swazi had effectively lost their independence'. At the height of the intrigues surrounding the Swazi concessionaries, Shepstone often turned to drink. His African name, Mhlakuvane, represents a plant whose seeds pop when ripe, and is said to reflect Shepstone's temper; Robert Baden-Powell thought him clever, but apt to be flippant. Others thought his vision was limited by his personal ambitions. Shepstone's influence in Swaziland came to an end amidst allegations of financial irregularities after the Transvaal Republic assumed responsibility for the white settlers in the kingdom in 1895. He died of cancer in Johannesburg in March 1907.

Shepstone, William Edward

A son of Theophilus Shepstone, William Shepstone was born at Fort Peddie in the Eastern Cape in September 1841. He grew up in Natal, and later studied law at Cape Town. After trying his luck unsuccessfully in the diamond fields, Shepstone established a successful law practice in Durban. He was a noted horseman and it was said would ride any troublesome horse for a wager. He was also an excellent shot and an enthusiastic member of the Natal Volunteer movement. In 1874, as a member of the Durban Mounted Rifles, he won the trophy for best shot in a competition between Durban and Pietermaritzburg Volunteer units. In 1879 he took to the field as a captain commanding the Durban Mounted Rifles, who were attached to Colonel Pearson's Right Flank Column. On 22 January, when a Zulu force under the command of Godide kaNdlela attempted to halt Pearson's advance on the Nyezane River, the DMR were escorting wagons at the rear of the column, and so missed the action. When news of Isandlwana reached Pearson at Eshowe he decided to reduce the size of his command, and the Volunteer units including Shepstone and the DMR, were sent back to the Thukela. They patrolled the lower border for the remainder of the war.

After the war Shepstone returned to his law practice. He resigned from the DMR on 28 March 1881, and died in 1892.

Shervington, Charles St Leger

Shervington was born in June 1852 into a family with a long military tradition. His great-grandfather had served in the 41st Regiment, his grandfather in the 11th Regiment in the Peninsula War, and his father, also Charles, had served in the Crimea as an officer in the 41st Regiment. From an early age Charles Shervington had displayed an adventurous disposition. As a teenager he had joined a Royal Navy training ship and passed out 6th of 104 cadets before entering an Army 'crammer'. He developed a sudden interest in electrical telegraphy and postponed his studies to travel to the West Indies where he worked laying cables. On his return he failed his Army entrance exam, but, declaring to his father 'it was all my fault; I won't cost you another shilling', he enlisted as a trooper in the 11th Hussars. Within six months he had risen to the rank of lance sergeant, but his father bought him out and he took a course in land-surveying instead. He went to Asia to work as a coffee planter, and sought diversion from the routine in big-game hunting. Standing on a wall one day directing attempts to put out a fire, his knee was badly injured when the wall collapsed. He was sent back to England where the general medical opinion was that he might never recover, but on hearing of the outbreak of the 9th Cape Frontier War in southern Africa in 1877 he immediately decided to volunteer. Shervington was twenty-five years old at the time, and together with his younger brother Tom, set sail for the Cape. Their father was in Hong Kong at the time, and they did not seek his permission, fearing his objection and worrying that the fighting would be over before they could get there. They arrived in Africa in August 1877 and Charles joined Pulleine's Rangers – an irregular unit formed by Colonel Henry Pulleine of the 1/24th

Regiment – and Tom the Frontier Armed and Mounted Police. With his usual energy Charles had been promoted to the rank of captain by the beginning of 1878.

At the end of the Cape campaign, both men volunteered for the auxiliary units being assembled for the invasion of Zululand and joined the 2nd Regiment NNC, Charles as a captain and Tom as a lieutenant. The 2nd NNC was attached to Colonel Pearson's column, and Charles joined the main body during the advance while Tom remained on garrison duty at Fort Pearson. Charles was present during the early stages of the invasion, including the action at Nyezane on 22 January. Shortly after Pearson had reached his first objective, the deserted mission station at Eshowe, he received the news of Isandlwana, and decided to reduce his command. Most of the NNC were sent back to Natal. A few of their officers and NCOs volunteered to stay, including Shervington. Since Pearson had also sent most of his mounted troops back to the Thukela, the column was critically short of cavalry for scouting and patrolling duties. Captain Shervington suggested raising a small scratch force from volunteers among the various units left at the fort who could ride, and mounting them on officers' horses, or horses left behind by the departing Natal troops. This force took to calling itself 'the Uhlans', an ironic reference to their decidedly mixed appearance. They provided a regular chain of vedettes on the high ground around Eshowe, and frequently skirmished with Zulu patrols. In particular, the Zulus several times attempted to ambush a vedette post on a hill known as mBombotshane, and it was left to Shervington to decide a response. With six volunteers from his 'Uhlans', he set out before dawn and lay in wait in the darkness on the approaches to mBombotshane; at first light, a party of Zulus was seen picking its way up the hill to set an ambush. Shervington's men sprang up and fired a volley, scattering the Zulus back down the hill. Thereafter the mBombotshane post remained secure.

Other vedettes remained in danger. On the morning of 11 March, Shervington was placing his outposts as usual when suddenly:

...about 30 Zulus jumped up out of the long grass and fired a volley into us. Two of the men's horses took fright, turned

108

straight round and bolted, the third man, Pte. Brooks 99th, was thrown from his horse and his foot caught in the stirrup. The Zulus who had fired into us had retired immediately afterwards but another party on a hill across a kloof about 300 yards distant shouted out there is a man down. About 12 men immediately returned to assegai Pte. Brooks who could not yet get his foot free. I had been sitting on my horse which was very fidgety waiting for Pte. Brooks to mount when I saw these men return, they were only a few yards (5 or 6) from him (it being impossible to see them before owing to the length of the grass). When I charged in among them and drove them back, I put Pte. Brooks on my horse as he was a good deal shaken by being dragged about. After placing him under cover I returned and picked up his rifle and helmet, and shortly afterwards more mounted men came up, the party of Zulus on the hilltop ceased firing and retired.

Shervington remained at Eshowe until the end of the siege. On his return to Fort Pearson, he was surprised to discover another brother, Will Shervington, had followed him to Africa and enlisted in Lonsdale's Horse. After the war, Shervington's mother wrote to Colonel Pearson suggesting that her son's action might be worthy of the award of the Victoria Cross. Certainly, a number of VCs had been won in the campaign in similar circumstances, and Pearson agreed that Shervington had done 'right good service'. Pearson passed on the suggestion to Lord Chelmsford, but the initiative faltered on a point of protocol, since Shervington's actions had not been witnessed by a senior officer. Neither Chelmsford nor Pearson seemed interested enough to pursue the matter, for the siege of Eshowe had not attracted public glamour like other more dramatic incidents in the war, and Shervington's gallantry was destined to be overlooked. He remained, however, the only man to be considered for the award during the Eshowe campaign.

The remainder of his career was typically adventurous. In 1880 he joined the Cape Mounted Rifles and took an active part in the BaSotho Gun War, where he was wounded – 'a blow on the inside of my knee from a spent ball' – at the storming of Lerothodi's Stronghold. With the return of peace he married but soon became bored, and in 1884 he accepted an offer to assist the army of Madagascar, then an independent African kingdom under threat of French occupation. Shervington was given the rank of colonel and appointed second in command, and received a concession to exploit gold deposits on the island. In 1895, France invaded Madagascar, the Malagasy army was defeated, and Shervington returned to England disillusioned and impoverished by the experience. The French confiscated his property on the island and his health was undermined by bouts of fever. One day in April 1898 his father received a letter from Shervington that read 'it is all up'. Hurrying round to the hotel where Charles was staying, he found his son lying dead on the floor of his room, a bullet wound in his left temple and the gun still in his hand.

Charles St Leger Shervington was forty-five at the time of his death and was buried in Brompton Cemetery, London.

Sikhotha kaMpande Zulu, Prince

Prince Sikhotha was a son of King Mpande kaSenzangakhona by his wife Queen Masala. He was born about 1838, and enrolled as a cadet in the iNsundu section of the uDloko regiment. The uDloko did not pass from cadets to be formed into a proper regiment until 1858, and Prince Sikhotha had already left Zululand by that time. The succession crisis of 1856 split Mpande's sons; although Sikhotha, still only a youth, did not fight in the war between the rival princes Cetshwayo and Mbuyazi, his position was made insecure with Cetshwayo's victory at the Battle of 'Ndondakusuka. Cetshwayo began to eliminate surviving potential rivals within Zululand, and in 1857 Sikhotha fled to Natal. He was settled on land near the Bushman's River in the Weenen district. This area became a focus for political refugees fleeing from Zululand, most of whom were known by the name given to Cetshwayo's rival faction, the iziGqoza. Sikhotha was soon joined by his brother Prince Mkhungo kaMpande, who was widely regarded as a pretender to the Zulu throne. As late as 1878 members of the iNdluyengwe *ibutho*, alienated by feuds originating with Cetshwayo's reinstatement of regimental marriage laws, left Zululand and placed themselves under Mkhungo. When Lord Chelmsford planned his

invasion of Zululand in 1878, he was keen to secure the participation of Mkhungo and Sikhotha since the presence of members
of the Zulu Royal House within his command legitimized the
pretence that the British invasion was directed specifically against
King Cetshwayo's administration. Prince Mkhungo was directed
to provide 300 men to join the 3rd Regiment, Natal Native
Contingent; in fact rather more turned out, motivated by the
desire to settle old scores. Mkhungo himself was beyond the
demands of active service, but sent one of his sons and his brother,
Prince Sikhotha, to represent him. Henry Harford thought
Sikhotha 'a very fine specimen, and very like his father in
features', and he was attached to the regimental staff.
Commandant Lonsdale presented Sikhotha with a shirt; he was
delighted with it but, being rather larger than Lonsdale, struggled
to get it on. Once on, however, he wore it with evident satisfaction for several days.

Prince Sikhotha was present with the NNC companies left for
piquet duties at Isandlwana. He was with his men in the firing line
during the Zulu attack; when the line collapsed, however, and the
24th companies withdrew towards the tents, Sikhotha fled the
field. A charming account by the Zulu boy Muziwento – whose
father was told the story by Sikhotha himself – recalls how
Sikhotha turned to another senior member of the NNC,
Gabangaye kaPakhade of the amaChunu people, and said, as the
Zulus began their final assault:

'O! Not for me! I'm off! I know those fellows over there. It is
just "coming, come" [i.e. no stopping] with them. They are
not to be turned aside by any man, and here are we sitting still
for all the world like a lot of turkeys!' He then called ...
'Away! Lets's away Ungabangaye, let's make a run for it!' Said
Ungabangaye, 'Oh stop a moment just till I see them tackled
by the white men!' 'O!' cried Usikota, 'A pleasant stay to
you!' He seized his horse and bolted. He escaped through the
'neck' before the *impi* encircled the [camp]. Up came the Zulu
army and made an end of Ungabangaye...

Prince Sikhota reached Sothondose's Drift on the Mzinyathi, and
managed to cross in the company of a handful of men from the

NNC, some African wagon drivers and 'also some white men who had got across'. They were attracting the attention of a number of Zulus when the *induna* Vumandaba kaNthati intervened, reminding the Zulus of King Cetshwayo's instructions not to cross the border. 'We were saved by that alone', said one of the wagon drivers, 'for if they had come across, we should just have been killed, being utterly exhausted.'

In the aftermath of Isandlwana the 3rd Regiment NNC was disbanded. Prince Sikhotha claimed to be willing to serve in the field again, but Mkhungo – no doubt influenced by Sikhotha's experiences – voiced a number of complaints about the way the regiment had been organized and handled. In the event, when the NNC was later reorganized, the iziGqoza were given a largely defensive role. Prince Sikhotha did not fight on Zulu soil again.

After King Cetshwayo's defeat, Prince Sikhotha remained in Natal, and his close alliance with Prince Mkhungo continued. Although married, Prince Mkhungo had no children of his own; according to Zulu custom, he gave two members of his female household, the *isigodlo*, to his brother Sikhotha to father children on his behalf. One of them, a daughter of the amaNgwane *inkosi* Zikhali kaMatiwane – whose followers also fought at Isandlwana as the Zikhali Horse – produced a son who duly succeeded to Prince Mkhungo's estate.

Uys, Petrus Lefras ('Piet')

Petrus Lefras Uys was born into an extensive family who arrived at the Cape from Holland at the beginning of the eighteenth century. Uys was born on the farm Braakfontein, on the Kroome River in the Swellendam district, on 1 September 1827. His father – also Petrus Lefras – led one of the 'commission treks' in 1835 to explore the possibility of emigration from the British-held Cape into the interior, and also served commando duty in the closing stages of the 6th Cape Frontier War (1835-6). The Uys family joined the Trek movement in 1836, and was heavily involved in the events surrounding the war with King Dingane's Zulus in 1838. Petrus Lefras Uys Snr. was killed by the Zulus at the Battle of eThaleni on 11 April 1838; in an incident which became part of Afrikaner folklore, Uys' eldest son Dirkie (Piet

Uys' brother) went to his father's aid and died at his side.

The surviving members of the Uys clan secured farms in Natal in the aftermath of King Dingane's defeat. In 1842, however, British troops arrived to occupy Port Natal and fighting broke out which brought an end to the short-lived Boer republic of Natalia, and led to Natal being officially adopted as a British colony. Many Boers with strong republican sentiments left Natal and moved instead to the interior, but a number of families secured permission from the Zulu King Dingane in 1847 to settle in the Drakensberg foothills along the upper Mzinyathi River. Among them was Piet Uys Jnr. This area was claimed by the Transvaal, and a small settlement sprang up at Utrecht. The gradual expansion of these Boer groups into Zulu territory was the origin of the 'disputed territory', which with the British annexation of the Transvaal in 1877 became one of the causes of the Anglo-Zulu War. Piet Uys owned a number of farms outside Utrecht. In 1848, at the age of twenty, he married Maria van Niekerk, with whom he duly had a large number of children.

The annexation of the Transvaal in 1877 hardened Boer attitudes towards the British. With war against the Zulu kingdom looming, Colonel Evelyn Wood – whose column was based at Utrecht – attempted to raise a burgher force to assist the British troops, but found most Boers unwilling to serve. Piet Uys was an exception. While Uys shared the general wariness of British intentions, he was concerned for the future of the Utrecht district, for the safety of his own farm – which lay exposed on the border – and was influenced, too, by a sense of unfinished family business with the Zulus. Uys was the only Boer leader of note to support the invasion, and the forty or so men who rode with him into Wood's camp included four of Uys own sons (Cornelius, Dirks, Johannes and 'Vaal Piet') and many of his extended family and friends. A number of them had apparently been further tempted by the prospect of looted Zulu cattle.

Uys made a good impression on Wood who admitted him to his close-knit staff coterie, and relied on him heavily for advice. Wood's commander of mounted troops, Lieutenant Colonel Redvers Buller later claimed that he had relied heavily on Uys' advance in perfecting his tactics. With Wood's advance across the

Ncome River, a few days before the British ultimatum expired, Uys' commando was extensively employed in scouting, particularly towards the Zungwini and Hlobane mountains, which were the centre of Zulu (abaQulusi) resistance. In the last week of January, Wood, operating well in advance of his base at Fort Thinta, cleared the Zulus off Zungwini, and was in the process of driving across the foot of Hlobane when news of the disaster at Isandlwana caused him to disengage.

Wood then moved his camp to a more secure position at Khambula, and Uys continued to assist Buller's long-range strikes into Zululand. On 27 March, encouraged by orders from Lord Chelmsford to launch diversionary attacks along the border, Wood set out with his mounted troops and auxiliaries to assault Hlobane Mountain. The attack was designed as a pincer movement, with British parties assaulting the mountain at either end; Uys' commando was attached to Buller's party, which, before dawn on 28 March, ascended the far (eastern) end of the mountain.

The attack initially appeared to be going well, and Buller's men rounded up a large herd of cattle which the abaQulusi had driven up onto the summit for safety. Once they were up, however, the abaQulusi began extending round the cliffs at the base of the summit, cutting off their line of retreat, before pressing up onto the plateau in large numbers. Buller's men were driven westwards, and their position became critical when a large Zulu army – advancing by coincidence to attack Khambula – came into view in the valleys to the south. Buller's men then attempted to get off the mountain as quickly as possible and, under growing Zulu pressure, descended by a broken staircase of rock at the western end.

The retreat down the so-called 'Devil's Pass' became something of a rout, Buller and his officers striving to retain what order they could. Piet Uys and his sons apparently remained on the summit until the end, until most of the men had descended. They then began to pick their way down, running the gauntlet of warriors who were among the rocks all around them. Uys had apparently reached the bottom when someone called to him that his eldest son, 'Vaal Piet', who was behind him, was in danger. In an ironic

. James Brickhill in the late 1880s.
(Talana Museum)

2. Sir Henry Bulwer.
(SB Bourquin Collection)

. George Hamilton Browne, c.1881.

4. Agnes Colenso.

5. Frances Ellen Colenso. *(Bodlian Library)*

6. Harriette Colenso.

7. John William Colenso.
   (Ron Sheeley Collection)

8. Cecil D'Arcy (left) and Edmund
   O'Toole, c.1880.

9. John Dartnell, 1879.

10. John Dunn.

11. Henry Francis Fynn Jnr., c.1880.

12. Alfred Fairlie Henderson, c.1890.

13. Rupert Lonsdale, c.1872.
    (Regimental HQ, Royal Fusiliers)

14. George Mossop, c.1885.

15. An interesting slice of frontier life reflecting the changing order of the 1880s. In the centre of this group is Hlubi kaMota Molife; sitting on the left of him is Prince Ndabuko kaMpande and on the right Prince Shingana kaMpande.

16. Two members of the Zulu Royal House c.1883, tentatively identified as Prince Mkhungo kaMpande (left) and Prince Mthonga kaMpande.

18. Robert Robertson c.1877.

17. Pieter Johannes Raaff, c.1880.

19. James Alfred Rorke; Rorke of Rorke's Drift.

20. A group of members of the Edendale Christian community, photographed c.1902. Th[e] big man in the centre of the back row is Simeon Nkambule; next to him, left, is Jabez Molife. *Inkosi* Stephen Mini is sitting on the end of the row left.

21. Friedrich Schermbrucker, c. 1878.
(Killie Campbell Collections)

22. George Shepstone.
(Killie Campbell Collectio[n)

23. John Wesley Shepstone.

24. Theophilus Shepstone Snr.
(Ron Sheeley Collection)

25. Theophilus Shepstone Jnr. sketched in
the uniform of the Natal Carbineers,
Zululand 1879. *(National Army Museum)*

26. Charles Shervington, 1877.

27. Prince Sikhotha kaMpande (centre), one of his wives and his *induna*.

28. Janet Wells. R. R. C.

29. Petrus Lefras Uys (centre) photographed in the field in 1879, surrounded by his sor
left to right, Cornelius Lucas, Dirk Cornelius, Jacobus Johannes and Petrus Lefras Jn

30. Frederick
    Augustus
    Weatherley.
    *(Royal Archives,
    Windsor Castle)*

31. Otto Witt, c.1885.

32. King Cetshwayo kaMpande, photographed on his visit to London in 1882.
(Ron Sheeley Collection)

33. Prince Hamu kaNzibe, photographed
during his time in Utrecht, 1879.

34. King Cetshwayo photographed in captivity in Cape Town. On the left is his jailor,
Major Poole RA; then Mkhosana kaSangqana and the interpreter, Henry William
Longcast.

35. *left:* Prince Dabulamanzi kaMpande, photographed with his attendants at King Cetshwayo's 'coronation', 1873.

36. *below:* Mehlokazulu kaSihayo, photographed after his arrest in September 1879.

37. *Below:* Mkhosana kaSangqana Zungu, photographed in London when he accompanied King Cetshwayo in 1882. *(Ron Sheeley Collection)*

38. *Right:* Prince Mbilini waMswati (right). *(SB Bourquin Collection)*

39. No authenticated portrait of inkosi Mnyamana Ngqengelele has yet been traced; he was sketched among this group of important Zulu negotiating with Sir Garnet Wolseley at oNdini in August 1879. The artist has distinguished him as the man leaning forward, left of the man with the stick (centre).

40. Prince Ndabuko kaMpande, 1888. He was apparently not married – and therefore unhead-ringed – in 1879.

1. This is generally accepted to be a photo of Ntshingwayo kaMahole.

2. Ntshingwayo kaSikhonyana and his sons, c.1890. Images of Ntshingwayo kaSikhonyana have often been mistaken for those of his kinsman, Ntshingwayo kaMahole.

43. Sigcelegcwele kaMhlekehleke, photographed at King Cetshwayo's 'coronation' in 187 *(SB Bourquin Collection)*

44. Somopho kaZikala.

45. Sitshitshili kaMnqandi, c.1906.

. Zulu envoys listening to the British ultimatum, 11 December 1878. Vumandaba kaNthathi sits front row, second from the right. *(SB Bourquin Collection)*

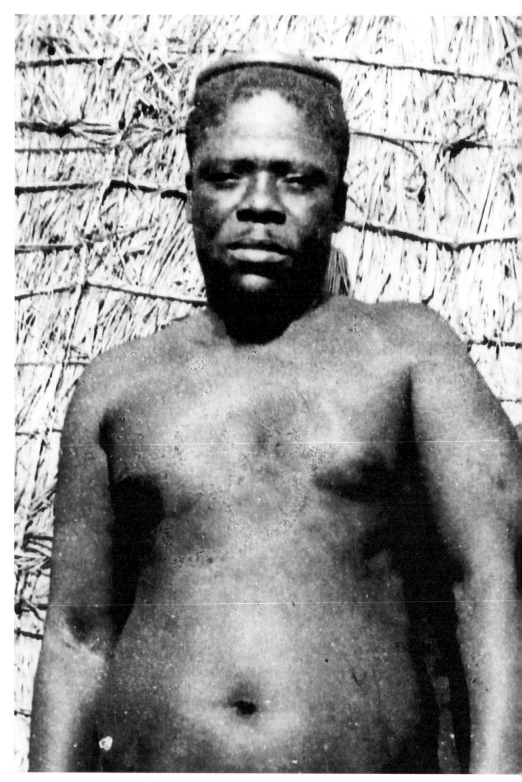

47. Zibhebhu kaMaphitha, c.1883.

reversal of the circumstances of his father's death, Uys turned back to rescue his son, driving the Zulus away who threatened him. At the very foot of the pass, a warrior, picking his way over the boulders, stabbed Uys in the back.

Uys' body was left on the field as the remainder of Buller's command fled onto the level ground below. His four sons all survived. The following morning, before the attack on Khambula, most of Uys' followers, concerned for the vulnerability of their farms in the light of the Zulu offensive, abandoned Wood's camp and went home.

In July 1879, Uys' brother Cornelius 'Cripple Koos' Uys, together with Uys's son Dirks and Cornelius' son, also Cornelius, rode to the foot of the Devil's Pass, and identified Piet Uys' remains by a knapsack lying beside them, and by his waistcoat. The bones were collected and taken to Piet Uys' farm Wydgelegen, near Utrecht, for burial.

Wood greatly regretted his loss, and made good his promise to secure the future of Uys' family by granting them farms on the Zulu border. Wood himself instigated a memorial to Piet Uys' memory at Utrecht. In November 1988 Piet Uys' remains were moved from his farm and re-interred at Utrecht. The Uys family erected a memorial on the spot at Hlobane where he was killed, although, despite its remote location, it has repeatedly been damaged over the years – possibly by herd boys, conceivably by lightning and definitely, in recent times, in deference to a wide-spread belief that such monuments mark the site of treasure buried by Europeans in their march across Zululand.

Vijn, Cornelius

Cornelius Vijn was born in Hoorn, Holland, c.1856, and travelled to Natal in 1874. Here he set up as a trader, taking blankets, picks, knives and beads by wagon into Zululand to exchange for cattle and hides. He made several trips into Zululand in 1878, undaunted by the rising tension between the kingdom and colonial Natal. He began his final trip at the end of October, crossing into Zululand at the Lower Thukela Drift on 1 November. He found the country alive with rumours of an impending conflict with the British but paid them no great heed because 'the Zulus were very friendly towards me, and trade was unusually good'. He was reassured by the presence of John Dunn – who had not yet abandoned the country – and by the manner of the important men of the kingdom, including Prince Dabulamanzi who, Vijn noted nevertheless, was confidant of a Zulu victory in the event of war because 'according to his ideas, since they had now as good weapons as the whites, they would be stronger than the English'. Vijn travelled northwards through the valley of the Black Mfolozi towards Prince Hamu's district where he befriended Hamu's white adviser, James Michael Rorke. The war had by this time begun, however, and Rorke expressed his concern for the safety of white men within the country. Shortly afterwards, Vijn was plundered of his cattle and wagons by the orders of *inkosi* Zibhebhu kaMaphitha. Vijn sent messengers to appeal to King Cetshwayo for protection, and was duly fetched by royal *izinduna* and placed under care in one of the royal home-steads near oNdini. His plundered goods were restored for him. Here he lived for several months, well treated and witnessing at first hand the effect of the war on Zulu society.

He first heard news of Isandlwana three days after the battle when he encountered a group of mourners bewailing the loss of a family member in the battle. On several occasions, groups of passing warriors threatened to vent their anger upon him, but each time he was saved by the intervention of the king's *izinduna*. After the Battle of Khambula (29 March) he noted that strange rumours swept the country, attributing the British victory to their supernatural prowess. At the beginning of June, he was taken under escort to the royal homestead of kwaMbonambi, where King Cetshwayo was then residing, and asked to translate a letter which had been sent to the king by Lord Chelmsford. Thereafter Vijn acted as the king's occasional secretary, translating and explaining messages from the British and writing out the king's response. Towards the end of June, the royal court returned to oNdini, and Vijn with it. By this time, British troops were descending from the Mthonjaneni heights into the valley of the White Mfolozi, and a final confrontation appeared imminent. A last flurry of exchanges took place at the beginning of July, during which Vijn took the chance to scribble a message of his own on one of King Cetshwayo's replies, warning Chelmsford that the Zulu army had once more assembled. On 4 July Vijn watched the Battle of Ulundi in the company of several of the king's brothers from a distant hillside; in the confusion which followed the Zulu defeat, Vijn attempted to return to the king, but it was some days before he found him, living in a homestead on the Black Mfolozi.

King Cetshwayo was uncertain how to react to the catastrophe, and wary of surrendering to the British for fear of being killed. Vijn eventually agreed to visit the British camp and ask what terms for surrender were offered. Vijn found that the newly arrived Sir Garnet Wolseley had recently established a camp near the ruins of oNdini. Wolseley offered Vijn £250 if he could persuade Cetshwayo to surrender; Vijn agreed and returned to the king, but found Cetshwayo still suspicious. He returned to Wolseley and agreed to accompany a large patrol led by Major Percy Barrow in an attempt to capture the king. The patrol found the country too rugged for rapid progress and Barrow lost patience with Vijn, whose concept of the distances involved was hazy. In the event, Vijn led Barrow to the homestead where King Cetshwayo had been staying, but the king had already left. Barrow's patrol returned to oNdini amidst some acrimony over the reasons for its failure. Nevertheless, Wolseley offered Vijn a post as interpreter; he accepted and accompanied further patrols into Zibhebhu's territory and into the Black Mfolozi bush. He was not present, however, when King Cetshwayo was finally captured by Major Marter's party of Dragoons on 28 August.

Vijn was largely unimpressed by his experience of the British military, especially as Wolseley only paid him £50 of the promised £250 on the grounds that he had failed to secure King Cetshwayo's surrender. Vijn himself was outspoken in defence of Cetshwayo's conduct throughout the war. He wrote the story of his adventures in Dutch, which Bishop J. W. Colenso translated and published in 1880 as *Cetshwayo's Dutchman*. Colenso added a series of notes to the text expanding his own view that the war was unjustly forced on the Zulu people. The book provides a unique insight into conditions within the country as the war progressed. Vijn himself disappeared from history thereafter, declaring only that the post-war settlement of Zululand made life impossible for traders such as himself, and that he intended instead to move his operations to Swaziland.

Weatherley, Frederick Augustus

Weatherley was born in Newcastle-upon-Tyne in 1830, the son of a ship owner. A number of Weatherley's family had military connections, and Weatherley was educated for four years at the renowned military academy in Dresden. He then secured a commission in the Austrian army as a cavalry lieutenant, and saw action at the end of the First War of Italian independence. He returned to Britain and secured a command in the Tower Hamlets Militia. With the outbreak of the Crimean War, Weatherley used his influence – including the support of Lord Cardigan – to gain a commission in a regular regiment, the 4th Light Dragoons. This regiment was dispatched to the Crimea, arriving in August 1855, and Weatherley took part in the actions on the Tchernaya and the siege of Sevastopol. Weatherley then eloped with a rich heiress, Maria Louisa Martyn, daughter of a colonel of the Life Guards, and returned to England to marry her at Windsor. With the outbreak of mutiny in India, Weatherley again transferred regiments, this time to the 6th Dragoon Guards, with whom he served in the later stages of the mutiny. He sold his commission in 1868, returning to England to settle in Brighton, and in 1875 he was given a command in the Sussex Artillery Volunteers with the rank of lieutenant colonel.

In 1872, Weatherley invested in a company set up to exploit gold in the Zoutpasberg district of the Transvaal Republic. Four years later, having poured much of his capital into the project with decidedly uneven prospects of a return, Weatherley, his wife and sons set out for southern Africa to assess the situation for himself. On his arrival, he found the Republic engaged in a protracted struggle with the neighbouring Pedi kingdom of King Sekhukhune woaSekwati. Recognizing that military experience was sorely needed, Weatherley volunteered to join the Transvaal forces. The subsequent campaign was a fiasco, and Weatherley abandoned the remote Zoutpasberg to move to Pretoria. Here, with British intervention in Transvaal affairs imminent, he became a vocal supporter of annexation.

In fact, the British annexation of the Transvaal in April 1877 merely added to Weatherley's growing difficulties. After advising Theophilus Shepstone's staff on the possibilities of raising auxiliary forces for local defence, Weatherley expected to be given a prominent military post, and resigned his command in the Sussex Volunteer Artillery. In the event, no post was forthcoming, and Weatherley was convinced that Shepstone had personally excluded him. Indignant at the implied slur on his reputation, he became a bitter opponent of Shepstone's administration. This led him into the curious company of one Charles Grant Murray Somerset Seymour Stuart Gunn, commonly known as the Gunn of Gunn. The Gunn was an amiable and plausible charlatan who was also no friend of Shepstone, and when a petition orchestrated by the Gunn and demanding that Shepstone be replaced as Administrator by Weatherley was proved to be made up almost entirely of forged signatures, Weatherley's standing plummeted still further. Things got even worse for Weatherley when it emerged that his wife Maria was having an affair with the Gunn, and Weatherley was forced to issue a very public suit for divorce. Realizing that he had been duped, Weatherley had little choice but to make a humiliating apology to Shepstone.

By 1878 Weatherley was approaching late middle age, his successful military career a thing of the past, his marriage a failure, his reputation in tatters, and his finances precarious. The imminent military activity – the British campaign against Sekhukhune, and the projected invasion of Zululand – offered him a way out. Weatherley suggested to Lord Chelmsford that he raise a unit of mounted auxiliaries from among the white population of the Transvaal, and Chelmsford agreed. In November 1878 Weatherley officially formed a unit of 150 men initially known as 'Weatherley's Border Lances' (not Lancers, as has often been misquoted), commonly called the Border Horse.

At the beginning of March 1879 the Border Horse was attached to Colonel Wood's column at his camp at Khambula. It had seen little active service, but on 28 March was attached to Lieutenant Colonel Redvers Buller's detachment of the expedition designated to attack the abaQulusi stronghold at Hlobane Mountain. Weatherley had with him his fourteen year-old son Rupert. They moved out of Khambula with the rest of Buller's force, and bivouacked south of the Zungwini Mountain. It was Buller's intention, however, to move camp after dark to deceive Zulu scouts as to their intended line of attack, but when Buller's men moved off from the Zungwini bivouac, Weatherley delayed the Border Horse. The reasons for this remain controversial, but Weatherley may have been waiting for a personal order from Buller, while Buller assumed the Border Horse would respond to the general call 'boots and saddles'. It was dark by the time the Border Horse moved off, and a mist and heavy drizzle came on. Weatherley started in Buller's direction, but then became lost, and indeed at one point, according to the survivor Captain Dennison, spotted distant fires which they guessed belonged to a large Zulu army. By dawn they were close to the southern approaches of Hlobane Mountain, and could see the flashes of gunfire which they took to be Buller's party ascending. They rode towards them, and not far from the line of cliffs that surround the summit, they encountered Wood and his staff. Dennison says that he reported the presence of the large Zulu army, but that Wood dismissed the idea. By this time they were coming under fire from Zulus concealed among the fallen boulders at the foot of the cliffs. Wood's interpretor, Llewellwyn Lloyd, was shot and mortally wounded.

Wood was unnerved by Lloyd's death, and what happened next is a matter of controversy. According to Wood, he ordered the Border Horse forward but they refused to obey, and in irritation Wood's staff officer, Captain Ronald Campbell, rushed forward with Wood's personal escort. Campbell himself was promptly shot dead, but the escort cleared the nearest Zulu from among the rocks. According to Dennison, however, Wood ordered the Border Horse off the track to the summit and sent them into the rocks. They were skirmishing among the rocks, having taken several casualties, when Campbell suddenly ran past, and was killed. Men of the Border Horse then helped carry the body further down the slope, where Wood supervised Prince Mthonga's followers in digging a hasty grave for both Campbell and Lloyd. Wood then left the battlefield, and as he passed along the southern slopes of Hlobane his attention was drawn to the large Zulu army which was indeed approaching.

Wood's version of events of course excused his own misjudgement of the situation, and effectively laid the blame for the deaths on Weatherley's failure to advance.

And Weatherley would not be able to defend himself. After Wood's departure, the Border Horse followed the track to the summit, only to find that the abaQulusi had gathered in large numbers, and were driving Buller's men westwards. With the Zulus occupying the tracks behind them the Border Horse were in danger of being cut off, and they met a troop of the Frontier Light Horse coming in the other direction with an order from Buller saying that the mountain was surrounded and they were to make their way off it. Both the Border Horse and the FLH successfully descended the mountain, fighting their way through the cordon of warriors among the rocks. On the open ground beyond, they suddenly ran into the vanguard of the uKhandempemvu regiment, dispatched from the main army to intercept them. Under heavy fire, they turned about and rode onto the Ityenka Nek at the eastern foot of Hlobane. By now discipline was in danger of breaking down, as the abaQulusi lined the heights ahead of them and the uKhandempemvu followed behind. Over the Nek, they found the descent on the far side was cut off by a line of cliffs falling away below them. Here the Zulus caught them and a running fight broke out; several men and horses fell over the cliffs. Dennison managed to keep a group of men together and they found a steep path down through the rocks to the right of the Nek. Dennison says that Weatherley had almost reached the foot of the slope, leading his horse with one hand and his son with the other, when a group of Zulus overtook them, and they were killed.

Dennison survived the battle, the only officer of the Border Horse to do so; Barton and a number of men from the FLH also descended through the rocks, but were killed on the flats beyond.

Weatherley's death was the final catastrophe in the chain of misfortune that had dogged him since he first became involved in southern African affairs, and in a last irony it robbed him of his reputation in posterity. Wood's version of the encounter on the southern slopes of Hlobane early on the morning of the battle has

121

only recently been challenged.

Witt, Peter Otto Holger

Otto Witt was born in Malmo, Sweden, in August 1840; his father, Holger Witt, was a pastor in the Lutheran Church of Sweden. Witt grew up against a deeply religious background and was educated in Malmo and at the University of Lund. Although he excelled in mathematics and classical languages and intended originally to seek a career as a teacher, Witt followed his father into the Church of Sweden. He became a pastor in 1875, and the same year married Elin Pallin. According to the historian Frederick Hale, Witt's career would prove him a 'restless and spiritually unstable soul', prone to crises of conscience which shaped his calling. It was apparently one such crisis that decided him to become a missionary, at a time when the Church of Sweden was preparing to enter the mission field in southern Africa. Witt applied and was accepted as a missionary – the first to be sent to Natal by the Church of Sweden. He and his wife left Europe early in 1876 and arrived at Durban on 19 April. Initially, Witt forged a relationship with the Norwegian Mission Society under Bishop Schreuder, which was already active in Natal and Zululand, and went to work at Schreuder's mission at Ntunjambili (Kranskop). In late 1876 the Witts' first child, a daughter, was born – the first of six. The needs of the emergent Swedish mission were not entirely in accord with those of the Norwegians, and Witt decided to look for his own property at which to establish a mission. In January 1878 he purchased on behalf of the Church of Sweden the farm Shiyane – Rorke's Drift – from the trader John Surtees, who had bought it not long before from James Rorke's widow. Witt's family moved to the site shortly afterwards, turning Rorke's barn-like storehouse into a church and making themselves as comfortable as they could in his old house. Witt named the mission Oscarsberg, in honour of the King of Sweden.

Over the following year Witt struggled to convert both the Africans living on the farm property, and those across the Mzinyathi River in Zululand proper. He was largely unsuccessful in this – one report suggests that while his services were well

122

attended by those who were in effect his tenants, he had converted only four individuals before the Anglo-Zulu War began. Like many missionaries working in the Zulu field, Witt became convinced that the destruction of King Cetshwayo's administration was an essential precursor to widespread conversion to Christianity. He greeted the prospect of the British invasion with optimism; 'with God's help', he wrote, 'Cetshwayo's power has been or will soon be broken'.

The selection of Rorke's Drift as a starting point for the British invasion was problematic for Witt. Once the imminence of the conflict had become obvious, the Swedish Government had asked the British to offer the Oscarsberg mission some protection, exposed as it was at one of the most strategically significant crossings on the border. Paradoxically, however, any military presence at the post was in turn likely to increase the risk of attack. In the event, Witt was to find himself in the front line whether he liked it or not. By the end of December 1878 large numbers of British troops had concentrated at nearby Helpmekaar, and during the first week of January 1879 they began to move down to the crossing at Rorke's Drift. The British commander, Lieutenant General Lord Chelmsford, was keen to utilize Witt's buildings as a supply depot, since permanent structures – needed to keep food supplies out of the elements – were in short supply on the border. Witt agreed to rent his church to the Army as a storehouse, and his house as a field hospital, although he remained on the premises to ensure they were safeguarded.

With the commencement of hostilities, Witt dispatched his family to the relative safety of the Gordon Memorial Mission at Msinga, some miles away from the border. He was, however, present when, about noon on the 22 January, the garrison at Rorke's Drift heard firing from the direction of the distant British base at Isandlwana. Witt, together with Surgeon James Reynolds and volunteer chaplain George Smith, climbed to the top of Shiyane hill, above the mission. Here Witt claimed to have seen something of the Battle of Isandlwana unfold. Although later ridiculed in the press for his account, it is perfectly possible that the party witnessed the final stages of the battle, which took place in the valley of the Manzimnyama, and which is clearly visible from the summit of Shiyane. They watched a long column of African troops moving towards the river, under the impression they were British auxiliaries. Only once the warriors had crossed the river did the party recognize them as Zulus, coming to attack the post. They hurried down from the hill, and Witt decided that, as a missionary, it was not his place to join the battle. Together with an unnamed Swedish friend, who happened to be visiting him, and a sick officer of the NNC, Witt rode away from the post about 4.30 p.m. just as the Zulu attack began. From the road he looked back and saw the first Zulu skirmishers attacking the makeshift barricades.

Witt parted from the NNC officer – who rode to Helpmekaar – and he and his companion made for the Gordon Memorial Mission, but lost their way in the evening gloom. At some point they were overtaken by an African who later met Mrs Witt, and told her that he had seen Otto killed in the fight. Mrs Witt hurried away from Msinga with her family, and when Otto finally arrived there he found them already gone. He continued to Pietermaritzburg where, to their mutual delight, he encountered his family.

When news reached Pietermaritzburg of the fighting, and of the destruction of Oscarsberg, Witt decided to leave for Sweden. The family left Natal on 11 February, but when their ship docked in England Witt found his story was in great demand. He gave a number of press interviews and was later persuaded to give public lectures in London. He is described at the time as 'a short, spare man, with a light beard and moustache'. While he certainly exaggerated his account of the battles for dramatic effect, his account largely concurs with other sources. A number of remarks he made expressing sympathy for ordinary Zulus defending their homeland, coupled with criticism of the Natal settlers' attitudes towards African employees, incurred the wrath of settler society. The Witts stayed in England for just two weeks before continuing their journey to Sweden, where they remained until the war was over.

After some deliberation among his superiors, it was decided to return Witt to Oscarsberg, and he left Sweden in the middle of 1880. On his arrival in Durban, he found himself a controversial and unpopular figure, and the family was compelled to take a circuitous route back to Rorke's Drift to avoid settlements along the way where feeling ran high against them. They arrived at Oscarsberg on 21 August. Their house – used by the military as a hospital – had been completely destroyed during the battle, and the surviving storehouse had been converted into a fort. Witt tried to secure compensation from the British Government for the damage done to his property but was largely unsuccessful, since the Government argued that while British troops had indeed occupied the post this was by the owner's consent, while the actual destruction of the buildings was the result of Zulu – not British – action. The financial burden of rebuilding the post was therefore returned to the Church of Sweden. Witt decided to demolish the existing structures and rebuild a new purpose-built mission on the foundations; his church and home are still standing today, and form part of the modern battlefield complex. When they were complete Witt threw himself back into mission work but the reluctance of the African population to accept Christianity lingered.

In June 1885 Witt underwent a spiritual crisis that caused him to doubt elements of Lutheran practice. He became more evangelical in his approach, travelling into Zululand and preaching from homestead to homestead. Although this did not bring about an immediate rupture with the Church of Sweden, disagreements with colleagues and his occasionally prickly personality and wrangles over the cost of rebuilding the mission led to a steady deterioration in his relationship with the mission society that sponsored him. In August 1889 Witt met representatives of the Free East Africa Mission, a pan-Scandinavian non-denominational group who had recently arrived in Durban with the intention of establishing an evangelical mission in Natal. Witt found that his theological ideas were largely in step with theirs and he announced his intention of leaving the Lutheran church. The Witts left the Oscarsberg mission at Rorke's Drift in April 1890, and, despite the controversy which surrounded them, the loss of their first missionary in Natal was something of a blow for the Church of Sweden. For several months Witt preached among migrant workers in Durban in association with the Free East

Africa Mission, but in 1891 he decided to leave Natal altogether. Although he cited ill health on the part of his wife as the reason, he may well have become disillusioned with mission work for he never returned to Africa nor took part in missionary endeavour again.

The Witts returned to Sweden, and for the next thirty years Witt continued his ministry based largely around Stockholm, although he occasionally undertook evangelist tours of Norway. From 1907 he became increasingly attracted to the Pentecostal movement which was then enjoying popularity in Scandinavia. With the outbreak of the First World War in 1914 he became more overtly pacifist. He retired to the town of Osthammar where, in 1922, he published his memoirs. He died on 25 August 1923.

The Zulus

Cetshwayo kaMpande, King

Cetshwayo was born at emLambongwenya, one of the royal homesteads of his father, Prince Mpande kaSenzangakhona, in 1832. The name Cetshwayo ironically means 'the slandered one' and if ever a man's history grew to suit his name it was Cetshwayo. The reason he was so-called is obscure, but it is thought to reflect an intrigue within the Zulu Royal House, for the kingdom had not yet recovered from the assassination of the legendary King Shaka, only four years before. Shaka had been succeeded by his brother and assassin, Dingane kaSenzangakhona, who was sensitive to any potential threats within his family, and indeed had steadily eliminated a number of his brothers on various pretexts. Prince Mpande had survived largely by assuming a role of indolence and lack of ambition. In dismissing the threat posed by Mpande, King Dingane made a serious political error. In 1838 Dingane became embroiled in a brutal war against the Boer Voortrekkers, who, having left the British-dominated Cape, were seeking land in Natal in which to establish themselves. The first phase of the war was essentially a stalemate, ending in the Boer victory at Ncome (Blood River) in December 1838. With King Dingane's position weakened, Prince Mpande took the opportunity to break free of his authority. In 1839 Mpande and several thousand of his followers crossed the Thukela River and offered their allegiance to the Boers; this was a decisive split within the Royal House, and was remembered as 'the breaking of the rope' which bound the nation together.

Prince Cetshwayo, then only a boy, accompanied his father. The

Boers, while keen to exploit divisions within the Royal House, were also seeking to secure a long-term influence over the Zulus, and as a condition of their protection demanded that Mpande identify his heir. At that point Cetshwayo was the obvious choice; he was the son of his father's senior wife, Queen Ngumbazi, and when Mpande had married, King Shaka himself had paid Ngqumbazi's father the *ilibolo* 'bride price'. When Mpande pointed Cetshwayo out, the Boers clipped a small piece from his ear to identify him, as if he were a prize heifer. Despite this, Mpande's alliance with the Boers proved a significant one, for in 1840 he invaded Zululand, with Boer support, and drove out Dingane. In February 1840 the Boers proclaimed Mpande the new king of the Zulu.

Mpande established his principle residence, kwaNodwengu, north of the White Mfolozi River. Of all the great Zulu kings, his reign was to be the longest, lasting for more than thirty years until ended peacefully by old age in 1872. An astute political survivor, his reign was characterized by a patient programme to restore the central authority of the Zulu state in the aftermath of the damaging conflicts of 1838-40, and to limit the corrosive effects of European economic penetration.

Cetshwayo himself spent much of his youth at another of his father's homesteads, oNdini, which was then sited near the coast. About 1850 he was enrolled as a cadet in what would later become the uThulwana *ibutho*. The uThulwana was regarded with particular affection by King Mpande because a number of his sons were enrolled in it. Unlike his predecessors – who had been careful not to father children for fear of raising rivals within their own household – Mpande took many wives and fathered twenty-nine sons and twenty-three daughters. Despite recognized criteria for the selection of an heir, the presence of so many possible contenders inevitably created political insecurity as they grew to manhood. Mpande's solution to this was to reinforce his own position by playing the aspirations of his sons against one another. For Cetshwayo – quite literally marked out in early boyhood – this situation became intolerable.

In 1852 the uThulwana were given their first taste of military action. Although not yet formally enrolled, and still carrying mats for their elders, they were attached to an army dispatched by Mpande to raid southern Swaziland. Although the Swazis retired before their advance, taking refuge in natural strongholds, there was considerable skirmishing, during which Cetshwayo himself is said to have killed an enemy warrior. The campaign gave much-needed experience to the king's younger regiments and enhanced Cetshwayo's prestige. Two years later the uThulwana were formally enrolled as a regiment.

By this stage Cetshwayo had begun to accrue considerable support within the country. Worried, however, that he might prove a threat, King Mpande went as close as he dared to repudiate his original selection of Cetshwayo as heir. Instead, he began to favour another of his sons, Mbuyazi, whose mother had been given to Mpande from Shaka's *isigodlo*. Mpande therefore let it be known that, despite the otherwise inferior status of his mother, Mbuyazi had a claim to kingship by virtue of being an heir to Shaka's estate. In response, Cetshwayo began to gather a circle of close supporters around him who took the name uSuthu, from a drinking boast that they were as plentiful as the Sotho cattle Mpande had plundered during his raiding. Mbuyazi's own followers took the name iziGqoza.

Despite Mpande's obvious favouritism, Cetshwayo's support grew steadily throughout 1855. Many Zulus were unimpressed by Mbuyazi's claim, and by his arrogant, overbearing personality. By the middle of 1856 it was clear that Cetshwayo's followers far outnumbered their rivals and, worried for Mbuyazi's safety, Mpande urged him to cross the Thukela into Natal, as Mpande had once done, and secure the support of the whites. Mbuyazi delayed too long, and when he finally gathered his supporters in November 1856, the rains had begun and the rivers were swollen. By the time he reached the Thukela, with 7,000 fighting men and 13,000 dependants, the river was impassable. Mbuyazi could do little beyond appeal for the Natal authorities to intervene – they refused – and awaited the arrival of the uSuthu.

They came on a raw, drizzling morning on 2 December, as many as 20,000 of them, and commanded by Prince Cetshwayo himself. At first Mbuyazi's warriors tried to make a low stand on a ridge above the river but, disheartened when a sudden breeze cast down a feather from Mbuyazi's headdress, they soon collapsed under the uSuthu assault. As they retired back towards the river they became entangled with the non-combatants sheltering behind their lines and lost all formation. They were rolled up by the uSuthu and slaughtered in their thousands, the survivors streaming into the Thukela in panic, many of them only to be drowned or taken by crocodiles.

Mbuyazi himself was killed; and by his victory Cetshwayo secured the succession.

Prince Cetshwayo was not free to enjoy his victory entirely, Mpande still lived, and although many of the royal princes had perished in the battle, others remained who were neither allied to Cetshwayo nor reconciled to his succession. Several – Mthonga, Mkhungo, Sikhotha – placed themselves out of Cetshwayo's reach by fleeing to Natal, while Cetshwayo himself took steps to eliminate those who remained. Mpande, old, overweight and disillusioned, continued to remain the national figurehead, but throughout the 1860s Cetshwayo came to assume a greater influence in daily affairs. A more vigorous man than his father, a traditionalist with a genuine concern for the history and traditions of his people, he took a strong line on such sensitive international issues as the disputed territory with the Transvaal Republic while internally he attempted to revitalize the apparatus of state control, including the *amabutho* system.

King Mpande finally died in September or October 1872, the only one of *inkosi* Senzangakhona's sons to pass away of old age. An official period of mourning lasted for nearly a year and it was not until August 1873 that Cetshwayo felt able to proceed with his inauguration. He remained wary of a potential challenge, even at this late stage, and in order to bolster his position he invited the Natal authorities to send a deputation to the coronation ceremonies, an act which amounted to international recognition of his standing. Natal's Secretary for Native Affairs, Theophilus Shepstone, accepted the invitation, but his presence irritated a powerful traditionalist lobby within Zululand who felt that they did not need outside interference to crown their own king. In fact, the crucial traditional ceremonies were completed before Shepstone's arrival. Prince Hamu's Ngenetsheni and *inkosi*

Zibhebhu's Mandlakazi attended without mishap. Shepstone's contribution mounted to placing a theatrical crown on Cetshwayo's head and delivering an ambiguous lecture on good government. Only later would the new king discover that the invitation had been a crucial blunder; he had effectively given Natal the right to interfere in Zulu affairs.

The ceremonies over, Cetshwayo began the construction of a new royal homestead close to the site of his father's kwaNodwengu. The complex was variously known as oNdini or Ulundi, from the common root 'undi', meaning a high place. It contained as many as 1,400 huts and was widely regarded as one of the most impressive settlements in the kingdom's history.

King Cetshwayo was in the prime of life and self-confidence, secure at last in his birthright. Yet his was a troubled inheritance for he was beset by pressures externally and problems within. The long-standing dispute with the Transvaal settlers over the western border was unresolved, the country was awash with white traders, the national herds were under threat from contagious diseases and the state apparatus in need of renewal. When, in 1875, Cetshwayo allowed members of the iNdlondlo *ibutho* to marry, and directed that they take brides from a female guild known as the iNgcugce, he was astonished to find that many of the girls refused. They had taken lovers among younger regiments and were not prepared to forsake them for the older iNdlondlo. The king insisted, and finally lost patience, ordering out detachments of his regiments to guard the borders against girls fleeing the country, and to kill any members of the iNgcugce who had defied the edict. The loss of life was not heavy but rumours of the killings, deliberately exaggerated by the missionary community, spread to Natal, inflaming a sense of nervousness there among the settler community. The incident had repercussions, too, at the annual *umKhosi* (harvest) ceremonies in December 1878 when tension between the *amabutho*, fuelled by lingering resentments over the iNgcugce affair, led to a brawl – which cost the lives of more than sixty men.

It became increasingly obvious too, throughout 1877, that the relationship with colonial Natal was going sour. King Cetshwayo was astute enough to recognize the fact but had little idea that the underlying cause was the British decision to adopt the Confederation policy. In April the Transvaal Republic was annexed to the Crown, and the boundary dispute now became a British affair. In addressing it, Theophilus Shepstone adopted such a high-handed manner that many influential Zulus were outraged. King Cetshwayo eagerly seized upon the suggestion of a boundary commission, supervised by the nominally impartial Natal authorities, but throughout 1878 tension continued to build. Although the king regarded the border incidents of July 1878 as of little importance – and was prepared to offer the British an apology and compensation in cattle – the incident was seized upon by Frere. When the findings of the boundary commission were finally presented to the king's representatives on 11 December 1878, tagged onto them were a series of demands, prompted by the border incidents, which amounted to an ultimatum.

The king and his councillors were appalled. Some of his advisers urged him to surrender the sons of the border *inkosi* Sihayo, named in the ultimatum, but King Cetshwayo was reluctant to abandon a favourite, and neither he nor the council could in any case agree to the fundamental British demand that the *amabutho* system be disbanded. The king could do little more than wait and see whether the British were in earnest; once it became clear in the first week of January that they were massing on his borders, he orders that his army assemble at oNdini.

Although the king listened attentively to his military advisers – and in particular his commanders-in-chief *inkosi* Mnyamana kaNqgengelele and Ntshingwayo kaMahole – the final choice of Zulu strategy was his. When news arrived that the British had crossed the border, and that the Centre Column was targeting royal favourites on the Rorke's Drift border, King Cetshwayo decided to dispatch his main striking arm to oppose that column. A small detachment was sent to reinforce warriors who had remained in the coastal districts to contest Pearson's advance. Once the army left the vicinity of oNdini on 17 January, the king allowed his generals full scope, beyond a suggestion that they should be sure the British were in earnest before committing themselves to action. In the event, both armies were engaged on the 22nd, but while the coastal forces were dispersed at Nyezane, the main army decisively defeated the Centre Column at Isandlwana. Yet the victory would prove double-edged for the Zulu losses were staggering and the king had little option but to allow the regiments to disperse once they had undergone their post-combat purification rituals. King Cetshwayo was certainly committed to pursuing a defensive strategy, of fighting the invaders on his soil, but even had he wanted, the state of his army at the end of January was such that he could not have followed up with an attack on Natal. And in his failure to do so, the king allowed the initiative to slip steadily back to the British.

Towards the end of March it became clear that a new wave of fighting was imminent. The British were once again massing on the borders. King Cetshwayo reassembled his army, and this time decided to direct it against the northern column commanded by Colonel Wood. The choice was motivated by the realization, not only that Wood's column was then the most aggressive British force left in Zululand but, that it blocked any potential Zulu retreat towards the Swazi border. When it marched out, the army was accompanied by *inkosi* Mnyamana himself, a token of the importance the king placed on the expedition. Yet despite Cetshwayo's instructions that it should not attack defensive positions – 'do not put your faces into the lair of the wild beast', he is said to have warned, 'for you will be clawed' – the army dashed itself to pieces against Wood's fortifications at Khambula on 29 March.

The defeat was undoubtedly a turning point in the war, and King Cetshwayo himself came increasingly to doubt that the British invasion could be resisted by military means. He intensified his efforts to open negotiations with the British but Chelmsford, with the tide of war swinging inexorably in his favour, rebuffed him. By the beginning of June the king had largely lost control of the southern part of the country – occupied by the British 1st Division – and of the north-western borders, which were now controlled by the massing 2nd Division and Flying Column. The king recognized that his army had scarcely enough resources for one more major confrontation but, while he refused to contest the British advance until the last minute, many ordinary Zulus attached to *amakhosi* living along the lines of the British advance continued to harass their movements.

By the end of June the British had reached the White Mfolozi River, just a few miles south of oNdini. They had ravaged the emaKhosini valley – resting-place of Shaka's ancestors – and in doing so had unwittingly destroyed the sacred *inkatha*, the coil of grass rope, impregnated with mystical substances, which was said to embody the nation's unity. On 3 July Chelmsford probed across the Mfolozi, and on the 4th he crossed it in force, forming some 5,000 men into a large square within plain sight of oNdini. The *amabutho* gathered for the last time to resist, but they could not penetrate the fearsome curtain of British fire and were driven away.

The king had anticipated the defeat and did not stay to witness it. He had abandoned oNdini, and, accompanied only by his personal attendants, had listened to the sound of battle from behind a nearby hill. When the first fleeing warriors passed him, he rose quietly up, and walked away. He made for the homestead of Mnyamana Buthelezi, and from there attempted to open negotiations with the British. They were prepared to offer him no terms, however, and he moved further north, into the remote Ngome forest. The British had dispatched several patrols to capture him, however, and here, on 28 August, he was surprised and taken by Major Marter's patrol of the 1st Dragoon Guards.

The king was taken to the camp of Chelmsford's successor, Wolseley, near the burned-out ruins of his oNdini homestead, where he was officially told that he was to be exiled from Zululand. He was then escorted to Port Durnford on the coast and taken aboard the steamer *Natal*. Here he posed for some rather pained photographs – only the second ever photo-session he had agreed to. Accompanied by his *induna* Mkhosana kaZangqana, some attendants and *isigodlo* girls, he was taken to Cape Town and lodged in apartments in the old Cape Castle. His kingdom had already been divided up among British appointees.

Once the initial shock of defeat and exile wore off, King Cetshwayo found himself not without influence on Zulu affairs. His celebrity was such that he received a string of visitors to his apartments, mostly passing British gentry, many of whom became sympathetic to his plight and were in a position to influence official attitudes. With the stability of Zululand collapsing, King Cetshwayo began increasingly to lobby to be allowed to return to his country, under British authority, to restore order. His personal circumstances improved when he was moved from the Castle to a farm, Oude Moulen, on the Cape flats. Finally, in August 1882, he was granted permission to visit London to argue his case. He arrived, smartly dressed in European clothes, to find that he was something of a celebrity, and that crowds gathered who were curious to see the victor of Isandlwana. On finding that his manner was dignified and regal, and not at all the scowling savage represented in the illustrated press, the London crowds cheered him through the streets. He was granted an audience with Queen Victoria at Osborne House on the Isle of Wight and, while the Queen herself was wary of the man who had damaged Lord Chelmsford's reputation and destroyed the 1/24th, she presented him with a large silver mug as a souvenir and ordered her court painter to paint his portrait.

Diplomatically, the mission was only a partial success. The Colonial Office agreed that the king might be restored to Zululand, but only to part of his old kingdom. Large tracts of the country were to be set aside for those Zulus who had ruled in his absence – and who could not be expected to welcome his return – and he would not be allowed to re-establish the *amabutho* system. Nor was his return announced to his countrymen; he arrived back on Zulu soil on 10 January 1883 to find only a few Zulus waiting to greet him. He was escorted to his old capital by Sir Theophilus Shepstone – who had 'crowned' him a decade before, and who had come out of retirement for the occasion. Once news of his return spread, his old supporters, *amakhosi*, *izinduna* and commoners alike flocked to renew their allegiance.

King Cetshwayo began rebuilding a new version of oNdini, not far from the complex destroyed in 1879. It was a smaller affair – perhaps just 1,000 huts – but still an impressive statement of his authority. He was, however, supervised by a British Resident, and he found the country deeply divided by several years of friction between his supporters and the appointees set up by the British. In particular, his followers bitterly resented the oppression they had suffered at the hands of his erstwhile general, *inkosi* Zibhebhu kaMaphitha, and they were keen to be avenged. Probably without king Cetshwayo's knowledge – and certainly without his sanction – a number of royalist supporters assembled an army in March to attack Zibhebhu. Zibhebhu was equal to the challenge and on the 30th he routed the royalists in the Msebe valley and destroyed them utterly.

The attack caused consternation at oNdini. King Cetshwayo assembled many of his most prominent advisers to discuss the crisis and, despite the British ban on the *amabutho*, summoned those who still recognized their old allegiances. Before he could react, however, Zibhebhu struck first. At dawn on 21 July 1883 one of the women serving at oNdini was gathering water from a stream when she noticed a line of warriors silhouetted against the dim sky, advancing rapidly. Zibhebhu had made a daring night march with 3,000 warriors and was advancing to attack oNdini itself. As soon as word spread, the royalist warriors hurried out of their huts but their commanders were still in agitated discussion with the king when Zibhebhu fell upon them. Urged to flee, King Cetshwayo replied 'Am I to run away from my dog?' Yet the royalist stand soon collapsed in confusion, and flight was the only option. Most of the young warriors were fit enough to run away, but many of the king's elderly councillors were overtaken and killed. King Cetshwayo was led away on horseback but not far from oNdini the horse stumbled. Taking refuge in a small thicket he was spotted by two young warriors from Zibhebhu's army who hurled spears at him, striking him in the thigh. Even under such circumstances he maintained his composure. 'Do you stab me, Halijana son of Somfula?' he asked, recognizing one of his assailants, 'I am your king!' Awestruck, the young warriors assisted him dressing the wounds and helped him on his way.

King Cetshwayo escaped the slaughter, and made his way to the territory of *inkosi* Sigananda kaSokufa, head of the Cube people, a staunch loyalist who lived in the rugged country above the Thukela River. Here he hid for a while in a cave at the head of the Mome stream until, in October, he surrendered himself to the British authorities in Eshowe. He was allowed to live in a small homestead away from the British Residency. From here, for a second time, he attempted to rebuild his fortunes, and he was visited by a trickle of leading royalists. In fact, his defeat had been comprehensive and local British officials, who had been wary in any case of his restoration, refused to assist him. Then, suddenly, on the morning of 8 February 1884 King Cetshwayo kaMpande collapsed and died. A British doctor examined the body but was refused permission to conduct an autopsy; he officially gave the cause of death as heart failure, but privately suggested Cetshwayo may have been poisoned.

The king's supporters were determined to lay his body to rest away from the malicious influence of both the British and anti-royalists. After the necessary rites – the body was wrapped in a fresh bull's hide and smothered in blankets and allowed to desiccate in the heat of a closed hut – his remains were taken by wagon back to *inkosi* Sigananda's territory and buried not far from the Mome Gorge. The wagon was left on the spot and allowed to decay; its remains can now be seen in the Zulu Cultural Museum at oNdini.

Ironically, after his death – which had resulted from powerful divisions within the country, unleashed by the British invasion – King Cetshwayo's image came increasingly to be seen as a unifying one. He was seen by Africans suffering under the reality of colonial rule as the representative of a golden age of power and independence. In 1906, when African discontent broke into violence over the issue of a newly implemented Poll Tax, the 'rebels' sought to draw on the mystique of King Cetshwayo's name to unify their movement. The king's grave was used as a rallying point for the rebellion and, in a final bitter irony; it was nearby, in the Mome Gorge, that colonial forces inflicted a crushing defeat on one of the last traditionalist armies raised in Zululand.

Dabulamanzi kaMpande, Prince

Prince Dabulamanzi achieved a level of fame among his British enemies in 1879 which was out of all proportion to his achievements, largely due to his much-publicized attack on Rorke's Drift. He was born shortly after his father, Prince Mpande, crossed into Natal in October 1839 to secure the support of the Boers in his coup against King Dingane. Dabulamanzi's name commemorated the event – it means 'divider of the waters'. Dabulamanzi was of the same house as his older brother, Prince Cetshwayo, and closest to him in age, and the two grew up to be firm friends. Indeed, Dabulamanzi's fortunes were entirely connected with those of his brother. Like all Zulu youths, he was enrolled in an *ibutho* – the uDloko, formed about 1858 – and he grew up a self-assertive and confidant young man. In the succession dispute of 1856, when he was still a cadet, Dabulamanzi supported Cetshwayo without question, and he may have been present at the Battle of Ndondakusuka in December of that year.

Dabulamanzi spent much of his youth in the coastal districts and became acquainted with the white trader, John Dunn, whom Cetshwayo had set up as an appointed *induna* there to supervise European traffic in the region. Under Dunn's encouragement, Dabulamanzi learned to ride, to appreciate fine guns and to shoot, and acquired a fondness for European clothes and alcohol. When Cetshwayo became king in 1873, he allowed the uDloko to marry and Dabulamanzi built two homesteads in the coastal area, *eZulwini,* the heights, near Eshowe and *eZiko,* the fire, in the hot lowlands. He was a regular port of call for passing traders, many of whom found that he was not in the least overawed by whites and drove a hard bargain. In 1880 the traveller Bertram Mitford described Dabulamanzi as:

> …a fine looking man … stoutly built and large-limbed like most of his royal brethren. He is light in colour even for a Zulu, and has a high, intellectual forehead, clear eyes and handsome, regular features, with jet-black beard and moustache.

King Cetshwayo appointed Dabulamanzi an officer in the eSiqwakeni royal homestead, not far from his eZulwini residence. He was not, however, a commander in the Zulu army. In the crisis of 1878 he urged that the king should comply where possible with the British demands of late 1878; once war became inevitable he committed himself wholeheartedly to its prosecution. He attended the general muster with his uDloko regiment, and took part in the great advance towards the British camp at Isandlwana.

On the morning of 22 January the uDloko were camped in the Ngwebeni valley together with other *amabutho* associated with the royal homestead at oNdini. When elements of Durnford's force stumbled upon them, they were held back from the general advance by the senior commander, Ntshingwayo kaMahole. They were formed in a circle and administered the last-minute protective rituals – the only element in the army to be properly doctored – and were dispatched to act as a reserve under the command of Zibhebhu kaMaphitha. They swung wide of the Zulu right horn, cutting the British line of retreat by the road to Rorke's Drift before extending in pursuit of routing British troops fleeing towards the Mzinyathi River. One section of the reserve, the iNdluyengwe *ibutho*, apparently under Zibhebhu's command, crossed upstream from the survivors. The rest of the reserve – the uThulwana, iNdlondlo and uDloko – crossed higher still. Although Dabulamanzi held no official command within the reserve, his status as a royal prince and his strong personality seems to have led him to assume control, the more so because Zibhebhu abandoned his command at the river.

King Cetshwayo had ordered his men not to cross into Natal and Dabulamanzi later admitted that he took his men across the Mzinyathi simply because 'he wanted to wash the spears of his boys'. This was probably a later rationalization of the simple fact that, having taken little part in the action at Isandlwana, the reserve was only too aware that the Natal border lay open before them. Once across the Mzinyathi, numbers of Zulus split away to loot deserted homesteads while the main body, perhaps 3,500 strong and led by Dabulamanzi on horseback, moved towards the supply depot at Rorke's Drift. They were probably expecting an easy victory, but in fact the tiny garrison of the outpost had heard of Isandlwana from passing survivors and had fortified it with sacks and crates of supplies.

The Zulu attack on Rorke's Drift showed no great tactical sophistication, no doubt reflecting the fact that no great thought had been given to assaulting it beforehand. The initial Zulu attack against the rear wall was repulsed and the Zulus extended into the bush at the front, trying to penetrate the defences in a series of rushes. They drove the defenders away from the hospital building then set it on fire. Dabulamanzi himself is said to have taken up a position on the slopes of the Shiyane hill, from whence Zulu marksmen fired into the British compound. As a known good shot himself, it is conceivable that he was responsible for some of the British casualties from that fire. In fact, the nature of the ground and the limited British front meant that the Zulus had few tactical options. Having driven the defenders back to an apparently impenetrable position in front of the storehouse, Dabulamanzi seems to have accepted the inevitability of defeat at about midnight and began to withdraw his exhausted men. Some of these – including Dabulamanzi himself – were retreating across the Isandlwana road the following morning when Lord Chelmsford passed in the opposite direction; the two forces watching each other go by.

Dabulamanzi's failure at Rorke's Drift earned him general disapproval across Zululand. Mehlokazulu kaSihayo declared that he 'was not a good general; he is too hasty', and the discomforted prince withdrew to his eZulwini homestead. Here he found that Colonel Pearson's column had occupied the Eshowe mission station nearby. Once King Cetshwayo had forgiven him for the attack on Rorke's Drift, Dabulamanzi was given command, with Mavumengwana kaNdlela, of the Zulu forces surrounding Pearson. He orchestrated the siege from his eZulwini homestead. Large numbers of warriors gathered at eSiqwakeni and other royal homesteads nearby and patrols watched the British movements daily. Whenever there was a chance for the British to be caught outside the fort in numbers, the patrols were hastily reinforced. Skirmishes were common, and in an attempt to disrupt the Zulu cordon Pearson made a foray against eSiqwakeni on 1 March. The British were able to shell the homestead itself but retired with the Zulus in hot pursuit. A Zulu *induna* seen directing the warriors from horseback was probably Prince Dabulamanzi.

At the end of March it became apparent that Lord Chelmsford was intending to march from the Thukela to relieve Eshowe, and fresh Zulu troops were assembled in the area to oppose him. Dabulamanzi commanded one wing of the army under the overall command of Somopho kaZikhala. On 2 April the Zulus attacked the relief column at its camp at kwaGingindlovu. Dabulamanzi, again on horseback, commanded the right horn which attacked the rear of the British square. The attacks were driven off and Dabulamanzi himself was wounded in the leg. He retired to eZulwini, but on 4 April Lord Chelmsford decided – as a final gesture before abandoning Eshowe – to attack Dabulamanzi's personal homestead. The raid took the Zulus by surprise and the homestead was put to the torch, but Dabulamanzi was recognized among a group of Zulus on a hilltop who traded shots with Chelmsford's staff.

The victory at kwaGingindlovu effectively ended Zulu resistance on the coast, and from May the area was occupied by British troops of the 1st Division in large numbers. Dabulamanzi remained in the area but the British victory at Ulundi on 4 July destroyed any hopes of a Zulu revival. On 12 July Dabulamanzi submitted to the officers of the 1st Division. He was riding a horse and wearing a European jacket and forage cap, and the British – who had imagined him the most daring and irreconcilable of Zulu commanders – were delighted.

The post-war settlement imposed by the British was designed to undermine the power of the Royal House, and Dabulamanzi, while he was allowed to live in his own area, found himself under the chieftainship of John Dunn, his erstwhile friend who had defected to the British. Dabulamanzi closely allied himself to the movement to have the exiled King Cetshwayo returned to Zululand and in May 1882 was one of a number of prominent Zulus from Dunn's districts who walked to Pietermaritzburg to appeal against the settlement. When King Cetshwayo was restored in January 1883, Dabulamanzi attended the ceremonies held on the Mthonjaneni heights, and took the opportunity to deliver a stinging rebuke on British policy to Sir Theophilus Shepstone. He remained in attendance upon King Cetshwayo as he rebuilt his oNdini homestead. The king's return, however, had provoked a crisis within the country, for his supporters were bitter at the indignities they had suffered under the British appointees during his absence. They particularly resented the actions of Zibhebhu kaMaphitha, the king's former general who had been given an independent territory by the British and who had consistently denied the authority of the Royal House. In May an army of royalist supporters marched to attack Zibhebhu but was ambushed and defeated in the Msebe valley. In the uproar that followed King Cetshwayo assembled his supporters at oNdini, and Dabulamanzi took a force north to check any possible counter-attack from Zibhebhu. In the event, however, Dabulamanzi's force refused to attack a smaller enemy force which gathered to oppose it and for the second time in his military career Dabulamanzi was forced to return to the king to report an ignominious failure.

Weeks later, on 21 July 1883, Zibhebhu caught the royalists by surprise and launched a surprise attack which destroyed oNdini. During the royalist rout Dabulamanzi's son, Mzingeli, trod on a thorn which pierced his foot and Dabulamanzi helped him away, commandeering a horse from a passing *induna*.

The sacking of oNdini was an irrecoverable blow to the king's fortunes. He fled to Eshowe and placed himself under British protection. Here a number of prominent royalists rallied to him, among them his brothers, including Dabulamanzi. King Cetshwayo appointed his fifteen year-old son Dinuzulu as his heir and instructed Dabulamanzi to be his guardian. Since Dabulamanzi was relatively junior among the surviving royal princes, this act caused some dissention and resentment.

On 8 February 1884 King Cetshwayo collapsed suddenly and died. Prince Dinizulu decided to request Boer support in the struggle against Zibhebhu, and while he moved north, with his uncles Ndabuko and Shingana, Dabulamanzi was instructed to muster royalist supporters in the Nkandla forest. This area was now under British control – the so-called Reserve Territory – and the British Resident immediately ordered Dabulamanzi to disperse his men. When he refused the Resident marched against him with a small force comprising locally recruited Police and auxiliaries. With typical audacity, Dabulamanzi decided to attack and before dawn on 10 May 1884 he swept down on the Resident's camp. The black Police were warned in time to deploy, and Dabulamanzi's men were driven off by heavy fire. Although little more than a skirmish, the incident was to prove Dabulamanzi's last fight – and in keeping with a career characterized entirely by gallant failure, it was a defeat.

Prince Dinuzulu's initiative to involve the Boers had resulted in a royalist victory, but the price to be paid was high. The Boers demanded a huge swathe of territory in payment and established a 'New Republic', with its capital at Vryheid. The extent of their claims alienated the Royal House, and Dabulamanzi was among those who vigorously argued on Dinuzulu's behalf. It was his prominence in this regard which led to his death. On 21 September 1886 Dabulamanzi was arrested with his son Mzingeli by the Boers on a trumped-up charge of cattle rustling and taken under the escort of two men, Wilhelm Joubert and Paul van der Berg, to Vryheid. When they passed through the Nondweni district – which was in British territory – the Prince asked to rest at a homestead and then refused to go on, claiming that the Boers had no jurisdiction there. There was a scuffle which ended with van der Berg shooting Dabulamanzi through the body. The Prince managed to run off and Mzingeli jumped on his horse but van der Berg fired at them again. Mzingeli was thrown from his horse while Dabulamanzi was hit in the arm and fell. The Boers then rode off and people emerged from the Zulu homestead to help. Dabulamanzi was mortally wounded and died early the next morning. His body was later taken to the site of his eZulwini homestead near Eshowe where it was buried.

Godide kaNdlela

The family of Godide of the Nthuli people had played an important role within the Zulu kingdom since its early days. The Nthuli had originally inhabited the western bank of the Thukela River in the vicinity of modern Msinga, but had been disrupted early in the cycle of wars which ravaged Natal and Zululand at the beginning of the nineteenth century to the extent that they had frequently resorted to cannibalism to survive. Some sections of the Nthuli were driven across the river into Zululand by their vengeful neighbours, and Godide's grandfather, Sompisi kaKuguqa, settled among the Zulu. He became a personal servant of *inkosi* Senzangakhona kaJama and was known by the praise name Nkobe, because he ground the grain, *izinkobe*, of Senzangakhona. Sompisi's son, Ndlela, was a distinguished warrior who became a great favourite of King Shaka. During Shaka's famous campaign against the Ndwandwe, which culminated in the Battle of Mhlatuze c.1818, Ndlela had been seriously wounded, and had recovered only with the aid of Shaka's personal doctors. After attacking the groups living on the eastern side of the middle reaches of the Thukela in the 1820s, Shaka appointed Ndlela his *induna* with authority over the survivors. These people became known as *abakwaNthuli*, 'those of Nthuli's place', and were regarded as a bastion of Royalist support opposite the crossing at Middle Drift. Under Shaka's successor, King Dingane, Ndlela rose to become a senior royal councillor and commander-in-chief of the Zulu army; he commanded the Zulu forces against the Voortrekkers at the Battle of Ncome (Blood River) in December 1838. The disastrous outcome of this war precipitated a split within the Zulu Royal House, and Prince Mpande began to negotiate with the Boers. When he heard of this, Dingane planned to assassinate Mpande, but Mpande was warned by Ndlela, and promptly fled to Natal with his followers, and placed himself under Boer protection. Ndlela remained loyal to Dingane, and commanded his army when Mpande attacked him at the Maqgonqo hills. Dingane was defeated, however, and had Ndlela killed as a punishment for his failure. Dingane was himself later assassinated.

When Mpande became king, he repaid his debt to Ndlela by supporting Ndlela's sons. Ndlela was succeeded as *inkosi* of the Nthuli by his eldest son, Godide, who was born in about 1808. He was enrolled in the iziNyosi *ibutho*, and as an adult established his own homestead, under Mpande's patronage, near Macala Mountain on the Nzuze River. Godide's younger brother Mavumengwana governed a section of the Ntuli living between the Thukela and amaTigulu rivers, and also became a commander of the Zulu army under Cetshwayo.

Godide had risen to become a high-ranking councillor, one of the *izikhulu*, the 'great ones' of the nation, in Mpande's time, and he continued to enjoy Cetshwayo's support after the latter's succession. He was the principle commanding officer of the uMxapho regiment. By the time of the outbreak of the Anglo-Zulu War, he was about seventy years of age, a tall, thin man with his father's dark complexion.

When the British invaded Zululand, King Cetshwayo concentrated all his senior advisers and the bulk of his warriors at oNdini; only a few thousand men, living locally, were left to watch for British movements along the borders. When Lord Chelmsford attack *inkosi* Sihayo's homestead opposite Rorke's Drift on 12 January, the king and advisers decided to concentrate their main response in that direction. A smaller force was, however, appointed to reinforce those men who had remained in the coastal district, to harass the advance of Colonel Pearson's column. The army left oNdini on 17 January; on the 18th those designated for the coastal sector split off and struck out towards the Thukela River. They were commanded by Godide kaNdlela, and consisted of the greater part of his own uMxapho regiment, together with several companies each from the uDlambedlu and izinGulube *amabutho*.

From the first, Godide's command was dogged with misfortune. Dysentery broke out among the men and they were forced to linger for an extra day in the vicinity of the abandoned kwaMagwaza mission. They slept out on the open heights, and a particularly cold, raw night added to their discomfort. On the 20th they advanced to the old oNdini royal homestead, north of Eshowe, where they joined up with the local contingents, which consisted of men from a number of different *amabutho*. Altogether Godide's forces numbered about 6,000 men.

Godide underestimated the speed of Pearson's advance. On the 21st he pushed forward to the kwaGingindlovu royal homestead, reaching it after dark only to find that Pearson had already passed by and set it on fire. The British remained camped nearby, and Godide seized the opportunity to surround them in the darkness. For both practical and spiritual reasons, however, the Zulu were reluctant to launch an attack in the dark, and the frequent shouts by Pearson's sentries convinced Godide that the British were prepared. Instead, he called off his men and retired north, across the Nyezane River. The British were astonished to wake up the following morning to find large swathes of grass trampled flat around the camp.

Godide's revised plan was to attack Pearson that morning (the

22nd) as he struggled to get his wagons across the narrow, high banks of the Nyezane. To that end, Godide concealed his army behind a range of hills rising above the northern bank. Prominent among these was Wombane, on the slopes of which *inkosi* Matshiya kaMshandu – who was present with the Zulu force – had his homestead (the British knew the spot as 'Majia's Hill').

Early on the morning of the 22nd, Pearson began to push his wagons across the Nyezane River. Godide's scouts watched him from the heights, and Pearson sent forward a detachment of NNC to drive them away. The scouts disappeared into the long grass on the slopes of Wombane, only to rise up again suddenly and fire a volley as the NNC drew close. Several officers and NCOs of the NNC were killed and their men fled down the hill. The sound of shooting brought the uMxapho forward from behind Wombane, and they began to stream in a long encircling horn towards Pearson's crossing site. Pearson reacted by sending his men up the track ahead, which ascended a lower spur facing Wombane, and forming them into a firing line. Meanwhile Godide attempted to marshal the rest of his force so as to block Pearson's line of advance. The Zulu centre appeared at the head of Pearson's spur, and occupied a deserted homestead there; Godide attempted to throw out a right horn to surround the British beyond the road.

Pearson's position was a secure one, separated from Wombane by a gully which was choked with bush. In addition to his infantry (men of the 3rd and 99th Regiments) Pearson had two 7-pounder guns, and a naval detachment which included rocket tubes and a Gatling gun. Despite a determined effort, the uMxapho were not able to close with Pearson's men, while a charge by the NNC and Naval Brigade dislodged the centre from the homestead. The right 'horn' never came into action. After about an hour and a half Godide's men began to withdraw. They left upwards of 300 dead on the field. The survivors regrouped later that day on a hill about four miles away; after he had buried his own dead, Pearson continued his advance, and occupied the deserted mission station at Eshowe the following day.

Once Pearson had established himself at Eshowe, he found himself effectively isolated by Lord Chelmsford's defeat at Isandlwana. A cordon of warriors – many of them men from

Godide's army – surrounded the post at a distance and prevented any communication with the British bases on the Thukela. Godide himself does not seem to have featured prominently in the siege of Eshowe and King Cetshwayo's apparent displeasure after the failure at Nyezane may well have been the cause. The king considered that the battle had been mismanaged and Godide retired to his homestead on the Nsuze, leaving management of the siege to his younger brother, Mavumengwana – who had been joint commander at Isandlwana – and Prince Dabulamanzi, who, despite his own failings at Rorke's Drift, remained high in the king's favour.

Godide seems to have remained isolated throughout the rest of the war. When King Cetshwayo called up his army again towards the end of March, large numbers of Nthuli men reported to their respective *amabutho*; Godide is said to have lost several sons during the attack on Khambula on 29 March, while Mavumengwana fought at kwaGingindlovu on 2 April.

On 20 May British forces based on the central Thukela mounted a raid across the river into Zulu territory. The Nthuli were caught by surprise and bore the brunt of the attack; a score of homesteads was burnt, the foodstores destroyed, and hundreds of cattle carried away. Among the huts destroyed were those belonging to Godide himself, and a fine herd of 150 cattle was rounded up and driven across the border. This incident further soured the relationship between Godide and the king when it transpired that the cattle belonged to King Cetshwayo.

The raid hardened the attitude of the Ntuli towards the British. No sooner had the British withdrawn than a small force of Ntuli warriors followed them up, crossed the border, and burnt some huts in retaliation. Over the following weeks, sniping and small-scale skirmishes along the river continued, and on 25 June a large Zulu force mounted a highly successful attack across the border, destroying homesteads and driving away cattle before the British troops garrisoned nearby could stop them. Godide's personal involvement in this incident is limited; indeed, it seems his younger, and perhaps more vigorous brother Mavumengwana may have been the instigator.

Nevertheless, in the aftermath of King Cetshwayo's defeat at oNdini on 4 July, Godide remained reluctant to surrender. Although he opened tentative negotiations with the British, he kept his men under arms and drove his cattle into the Nkandla forest, a sure sign that he intended to resist. Only the widespread submission of the coastal *amakhosi*, including Mavumengwana on 5 August, persuaded him to reconsider. He finally submitted on 15 August, surrendering a few firearms in accordance with British demands, including a carbine captured at the Battle of Hlobane. Even so, many young Nthuli men remained unreconciled to the Zulu defeat until Colonel Clarke's column, retiring from Zululand by way of Middle Drift, finally browbeat them into surrendering their weapons.

Under Wolseley's post-war settlement the area along the Zulu bank of the lower Thukela was given to John Dunn, who wisely made no attempt to interfere in existing local hierarchies; he allowed both Godide and Mavumengwana to retain their positions among the Nthuli.

Nevertheless, after Cetshwayo's capture and exile Godide remained an ardent royalist supporter. When Cetshwayo was restored in 1883, Godide rallied to him, and answered the call to the rebuilt oNdini in that July. Faced with the opposition of an anti-royalist coalition which had thrived in his absence, Cetshwayo attempted to reassemble his old *amabutho*. Godide resumed command of the survivors of his old uMxapho regiment. At dawn on 21 July, *inkosi* Zibhebhu kaMaphitha launched a surprise attack on oNdini. The royalist regiments were hurried out to meet them, but many were without their senior officers, who were in frantic consultation with the king. The royalist right broke in the face of a determined attack, leaving the centre – including the uMxapho – and left, to fall back in confusion. The retreat soon collapsed into a rout, and Zibhebhu's victorious warriors chased the royalists through oNdini and across the plain beyond.

Many senior royalists – elderly men no longer able to run fast – were overtaken and killed, and the death toll among men of the highest rank, councillors and commanders dating to Mpande's reign, was high. Among those slain was Godide kaNdlela; a tragic end to a family involvement with the Zulu Royal House which had lasted three generations, which predated the kingdom's rise – and perished in its fall.

Hamu kaNzibe, Prince

In 1828, during King Shaka's ill-fated campaign against the followers of *inkosi* Soshangane in modern Mozambique, one of Shaka's brothers, Prince Nzibe kaSenzangakhona, died. Prince Nzibe was regarded as a senior member of the Zulu Royal House as well as a warrior of note, and in accordance with a custom known as *ukungena*, one of Nzibe's widows, Nozibuko Nxumalo, was married into the household of Nzibe's brother, Prince Mpande kaSenzangakhona. In 1834 Prince Mpande fathered a child by Nozibuko to be heir to the house of Nzibe. Thus, although that child, Prince Hamu, was biologically the son of Mpande, he was considered to be heir not to Mpande's estate, but to Nzibe's.

In many respects, Prince Hamu's life was defined by his relationship to the senior ruling line. In 1828 King Shaka had been assassinated and succeeded by his brother, Prince Dingane, and in 1840, following a disastrous Zulu war against the Voortrekkers, Prince Mpande was instrumental in overthrowing Dingane. Three sons of the same man, *inkosi* Senzangakhona, were destined to rule the greater Zulu kingdom between them from about 1816 to 1872; unlike either Shaka or Dingane, however, King Mpande fathered a large number of children. During the latter part of his reign, in an effort to keep his own position secure, he played off the aspirations of his sons against one another, refusing to nominate an heir. In 1856, the leading contestants – the Princes Cetshwayo and Mbuyazi – sought to resolve the contest in battle, resulting in the death of Mbuyazi at the Battle of 'Ndondakusuka in December 1856.

Because of his status as head of a collateral branch of the Royal Family, Prince Hamu was not entitled to contest the succession as King Mpande's heir. Nevertheless, on reaching adulthood, Prince Hamu had succeeded to the estate of the late Prince Nzibe, and took charge of his father's homestead at kwaMfefe at Ngome in northern Zululand. Here, astutely exploiting the divisions within the ruling elite within the country, and his physical separation from Mpande's seat of power at kwaNodwengu, Prince Hamu became one of the most powerful and independent of the regional *izikhulu* - the 'great ones' of the nation. In time he accrued his own *isigodlo*, his household of female attendants given to him in tribute by important neighbours, a prerogative usually reserved for the king, and even held his own *umkhosi* harvest festival. He appointed his own *izinduna* within his chiefdom, and maintained an impressive array of personal attendants. Like King Cetshwayo, he enjoyed the support of a number of white traders – Herbert Nunn, James Michael Rorke, and William Calverley – who acted as his intermediaries in his commercial and political dealings with his Transvaal and Natal neighbours.

Hamu's prestige within the kingdom, his significant power base, and his geographical position astride the routes into the interior made Prince Cetshwayo wary of any threat he might pose to the legitimate succession. Prince Cetshwayo was anxious to maintain a good relationship with Prince Hamu, while at the same time suspicious of Hamu's independent inclinations. In 1856, Hamu had sided with Cetshwayo, and his support had been a significant element in Cetshwayo's battle to win support within the country. Shortly after 'Ndondakusuka, some of Hamu's followers, known as the Ngenetsheni, had clashed with members of Cetshwayo's faction in a clear warning that by his support Hamu considered that he had earned the right to expect no intervention from the heir apparent.

Throughout the last years of King Mpande's reign, Cetshwayo remained acutely sensitive to possible challenges to his succession. When the old king died in 1872, Cetshwayo prepared to assume the mantel of kingship but he was wary of any intervention by the powerful northern *izikhulu*, chiefly Prince Hamu and his equally independent-minded neighbour, Zibhebhu kaMaphitha. When the northern contingents arrived to join the coronation cere- monies in August 1873, John Dunn records a moment's apprehension as Cetshwayo found himself placed between the Ngenetsheni and Zibhebhu's approaching followers. Cetshwayo's determinedly calm manner – backed up by 200 of John Dunn's armed hunters – diffused the situation.

Prince Hamu's status ensured that he was a member of the inner circle of King Cetshwayo's council, which met at the new king's royal homestead at oNdini. In December 1877, however, a violent altercation between members of the uThulwana and iNgobamakhosi *amabutho* precipitated an open rift between Cetshwayo and Prince Hamu. The outbreak was itself symptomatic of wider generational and political tensions within the kingdom. At the annual *umkhosi* ceremony at the end of 1875, King Cetshwayo had given permission for the iNdlondlo *ibutho* to marry. He directed that they should take their brides from among members of a younger female guild, the iNgcugce. Many of the iNgcugce had already formed attachments to men closer to their own age, including members of the iNgobamakhosi. To the king's surprise, many girls simply refused to obey the edict, and, after stern warnings, Cetshwayo – worried about the erosion of royal authority implicit in the management of the *amabutho* – directed a number of girls to be killed. The rest promptly married, but resentments between the regiments surfaced at the following *umkhosi* ceremony, in December 1877. Members of the senior uThulwana and the young iNgobamakhosi were both quartered in the huts of the oNdini homestead itself. The uThulwana, insisting the younger men show them proper respect, aroused the indignation of the iNgobamakhosi, the more so since the iNdlondlo had been incorporated into the uThulwana, and the iNgobamakhosi had to watch as a number of their former girl-friends paid their new husbands conjugal visits. On the evening of 24 December an argument broke out between the commanders of the two regiments, and on the following morning a stick-fight broke out as the two regiments formed up to march out of the homestead to take part in a ceremony. Prince Hamu, who was a commander of the uThulwana, was apparently struck and, outraged by this assault on his dignity, ordered the uThulwana to take up spears against the iNgobamakhosi. A running fight broke out which lasted until nightfall, and cost the lives of as many as seventy men, the majority iNgobamakhosi. The king was furious, particularly as he had been enrolled in the uThulwana, yet had regarded the iNgobamakhosi with particular affection. When Prince Hamu demanded that the leader of the iNgobamakhosi, Sigcwelegcwele kaMhlekehleke – a personal friend of the king's –

be executed, King Cetshwayo refused. Prince Hamu then left oNdini to return to kwaMfefe, and did not return until the threat of war in late 1878 caused the king to insist that he should.

In the tense discussions that preceded the outbreak of war, Hamu was a vehement proponent of a peaceful solution to the crisis. He argued that a war would have disastrous consequences for the kingdom, and he damned *inkosi* Sihayo for provoking the British wrath. Hamu argued that King Cetshwayo should rather put Sihayo to death than risk the future of the kingdom on his account. In fact, his position was no doubt shaped by the tentative and very secret approaches he had already made to the British to secure his own neutrality. King Cetshwayo, well aware that when war broke out he could not be assured of Hamu's loyalty, insisted that the Prince remain at oNdini throughout January. Men from Hamu's area attended the muster of the great *impi* in the middle of the month, and subsequently took part in the Isandlwana campaign.

In February, with the country reeling from the shock of the first wave of fighting, Hamu found an excuse to slip away from oNdini and return to kwaMfefe. Here he opened negotiations with Colonel Evelyn Wood, whose No. 4 Column represented the most powerful concentration of British troops in the northern districts. Hamu assured Wood that he was sympathetic to the British cause, and hinted that he wanted to defect with his followers. Wood, who hoped that the Zulu kingdom might collapse if enough important *izikhulu* could be persuaded to abandon the king, responded favourably, and instructed Colonel Hugh Rowlands – whose No. 5 Column, on the Swazi border, was also close to Hamu's territory – not to attack Hamu's followers.

By this time the Prince's position was becoming dangerous. King Cetshwayo attempted to woo back his support with a gift of cattle, but at the same time ordered Zulu loyalists in the region to watch for any signs of dissent among the Ngenetsheni. Hamu's position was difficult, because he found himself hemmed in on one side by *inkosi* Zibhebhu's Mandlakazi – who were committed to the war – and on the other by the royalist abaQulusi and by Prince Mbilini waMswati, both of whom lay between

Ngenetsheni territory and Wood's column. On 17 February, two of Hamu's messengers arrived at Wood's camp at Khambula, and begged for British assistance. Prince Hamu, they said, was hoping to defect with thirty of his wives, 1,300 followers, and hundreds of head of cattle. No sooner had Hamu begun assembling his followers, than he was attacked by members of the Mandlakazi, and he abandoned his homestead and took refuge in a cave close to the Phongolo River. Here he sent a message via contacts in Swaziland to Rowlands to say that he intended to escape to the Transvaal through Swaziland. After several tense days, the British agent in Swaziland, Captain MacLeod, finally intercepted Hamu at Makhosini, the royal burial place of the Swazi kings, on 1 March. Hamu was then escorted first to Derby – where Rowlands was based – and then to Khambula, where he arrived on 10 March. He was accompanied by his wives and followers, and by his white advisers, Nunn, Rorke and Calverley. Hamu excited considerable curiosity in the British camp, and was found to be a large, fleshy man. He had 'escaped with difficulty', commented MacLeod succinctly, 'being enormously fat', with heavy facial features which took after his biological father, King Mpande. His fondness for gin was also noted. One of his white advisers caused something of a stir when it was noticed that he was riding a horse belonging to an officer killed at Isandlwana, looted, presumably, by one of Hamu's warriors.

Hamu himself was then relocated close to Utrecht, and some 300 of his followers were drafted into Wood's auxiliary unit, Wood's Irregulars. They played a prominent part in the Battle of Hlobane on 28 March, and indeed it is said that one of them – a member of the uThulwana *ibutho* – fell in with his old comrades, who did not know of his defection, that night, and slipped away to bring Wood news of the Zulu intention to attack Khambula on the 29th. Most of Wood's Irregulars dispersed on the night of the 28th, however, in reaction to their defeat at Hlobane.

Prince Hamu remained at Utrecht throughout the war, where he was visited by Lord Chelmsford, and photographed; the Prince was a valuable source of intelligence about the internal politics of the kingdom. Hopes that his defection would precipitate the break up of the kingdom proved unfounded, however, for he was the only member of the king's powerful inner circle to defect during the hostilities.

Hamu's defection earned him the lasting resentment of Zulu loyalists, but he was rewarded by the British at the end of the war, when he was one of the thirteen *amakhosi* appointed by Sir Garnet Wolseley to rule Zululand. Wolseley was not impressed by the Prince as an individual. He commented in typically caustic style in his journal:

> I never saw such an unwieldy and disgustingly obese individual before. He had to be helped to sit down, and when on the ground, his stomach and his fat thighs so inconvenienced him that he could not sit quiet for a moment. He gazed at one in an uninterested manner and with a semi-foolish stare. I hear he drinks two bottles of bad Holland's gin every day. I was glad to see the last of him.

Nevertheless, Hamu's standing within the kingdom, and his open alliance with the British, had made him a perfect counterbalance to royalist sympathizers in the north, and Wolseley expanded his existing territory, placing under Ngenetsheni control the strongly loyalist abaQulusi and Mdlalose sections.

One flaw in Wolseley's logic was that, in the eyes of many Zulu who had fought for King Cetshwayo, most of the British appointees were traitors to their countrymen. During the king's exile, many of his former supporters began to agitate for his return, and thereby provoked the wrath of the new administration. The abaQulusi were reluctant to acknowledge Hamu's authority, and he in turn reacted by confiscating cattle. When royalist supporters who found themselves in a similar situation across the country appealed to the British authorities in Natal for redress, the British upheld the authority of the appointed chiefs. In northern Zululand, Prince Hamu and his neighbour, Zibhebhu of the Mandlakazi, emerged as leading opponents of the royalist cause. Zibhebhu drove members of Cetshwayo's family out of his territory, while Hamu openly attacked royalist supporters in Ngenetsheni territory. By 1882, Zululand appeared to be on the brink of civil war, a fact which prompted the Colonial Office to sanction the restoration of King Cetshwayo to Zululand.

154

When the king returned in February 1883, it was to a much reduced kingdom. Acknowledging the divisions within the country, the British assumed direct control over the southern part of the country, north of the Natal border, while both Hamu and Zibhebhu were allowed to retain their independence. Cetshwayo rebuilt his oNdini homestead, and his supporters, encouraged by his return, began to plan their revenge on their recent oppressors. Friction between the abaQulusi and Ngenetsheni intensified. When a royalist army moved to attack Zibhebhu, however, it was heavily defeated in the Msebe valley in March 1883. King Cetshwayo then began to assemble his followers in force at oNdini; in July, Zibhebhu struck first, however. Supported by a contingent of Ngenetsheni, supplied by Hamu, Zibhebhu made a rapid night march down the Black Mfolozi River and caught Cetshwayo's followers by surprise at dawn on the 21st. The royalists were utterly defeated. Cetshwayo fled to seek British protection at Eshowe, where he died in February 1884.

The death of the king freed a younger generation of royalist supporters to seek redress by desperate measures. The king's successor, Prince Dinuzulu, appealed to Boers from the Transvaal Republic to intervene in Zululand on his behalf, and in June 1884 Zibhebhu was defeated by a combined royalist and Boer force at the Battle of Tshaneni. Prince Hamu had distanced himself sufficiently from his ally to avoid direct action, although Boer forces were moved into his district to guard against his intervention. In the aftermath of the battle, Dinuzulu was crowned king by the Boers in the shadow of Hlobane Mountain, but in return was forced to recognize their extortionate demands for land in payment. Only the timely intervention by the British – unsettled by the possibility of Boer influence extending to the sea – prevented the Boers from annexing much of Zululand. In the event, the Boers still retained a sizable tract of the old northern districts, which they designated a 'New Republic'.

The Ngenetsheni were incorporated within the boundaries of the New Republic. The Boers, however, allowed Prince Hamu to retain his authority over his followers, but he died soon after, in February 1887, of natural causes.

Manyanyoba Khubeka

Manyanyoba was *inkosi* of the section of the Khubeka people living in the Ntombe valley in 1879. Details of Manyanyoba's parentage are difficult to determine; some sources give his father as Magonondo Khubeka, while others suggest that Magonondo was a much earlier Khubeka leader, and that Manyanyoba's father was Magonondo's grandson, Tulasizwe.

The Khubeka lived in a particularly troubled frontier zone, which had been disturbed as early as 1819 by raids by the Zulu king, Shaka. Some sources suggest that the Khubeka had placed themselves voluntarily under Shaka's authority, an act which conferred a degree of prestige and which may account for their sympathetic treatment by the Zulu royal house a generation later. Indeed, the Khubeka appear to have been disrupted by the rise of the Swazi kingdom under King Mswati in the mid-1840s, but were untroubled by Zulu raids in the area in 1848. Nevertheless, it is likely that the Khubeka also gave tribute to the Swazi kings, as their geographical position close to the Phongolo River – generally recognized as the Zulu/Swazi border – left them vulnerable to both sides.

With the arrival of white settlers in the area the Khubeka's position became even more precarious, since the spread of Boer farmers along the Phongolo River brought with it the claims of the Transvaal republic. In addition, the German Hermannsberg mission, acting with the permission of King Mpande, established a settlement at nearby Lüneburg in the 1860s, and a mission church was built by the Revd. F.A. Meyer in the Ntombe valley itself.

Despite royal approval for the Hermannsberg settlement, the Khubeka seem to have resented the intrusion of whites into the Ntombe valley itself, and this may explain the close relationship forged between Manyanyoba and Prince Mbilini waMswati, who established a homestead on the Tafelberg, overlooking Meyer's Drift on the Ntombe, in 1867.

Mbilini was a prince of the Swazi Royal House, and had fled Swaziland after unsuccessfully disputing the Swazi succession. He was keen to build up his support by raiding cattle and followers among the Swazi living along the border, and he adroitly exploited the rival territorial claims in the area. In 1870 Manyanyoba joined Mbilini in a raid in southern Swaziland, but was so badly wounded that he was left on the field, and only recovered after a Boer farmer found him there.

With the annexation of the Transvaal by Britain in 1877, the Ntombe valley achieved a greater strategic significance. Not only was King Cetshwayo determined to discourage Boer encroachment in the area, but the Ntombe lay across a possible Zulu route into Swaziland – a line of retreat the king at least considered, should the pressure from the British become too great. In November 1877 King Cetshwayo sent an *induna*, Faku, into the region to build a royal homestead a few miles from Lüneburg, to serve as a focus for his authority. Both the Khubeka and abaQulusi – living further south, around Hlobane Mountain – were directed to assist. Although Faku subsequently withdrew, the move highlighted the importance of the Khubeka, and of Mbilini's followers nearby, as supporters of the Zulu cause.

By late 1878, with British troops beginning to muster on the Zulu borders, the Khubeka found themselves sandwiched between Colonel Wood's No. 4 column, to the south-west, and Colonel Rowlands' No. 5 column to the north-east. Wood, concerned that Manyanyoba's relationship with Mbilini would make the German settlements vulnerable, established a garrison at Lüneburg. In mid-October Wood interviewed Manyanyoba personally, but formed the opinion that he was 'nervous', and therefore no great threat.

Certainly, Manyanyoba was worried by his vulnerable position after the British ultimatum of 11 December, but reassured by Cetshwayo of royal support, he assembled his warriors and ritually prepared them for war on 24-25 December. On 10 January the Revd. Meyer's abandoned mission was looted and burnt. The war began, however, with aggressive action from the British, who dispersed the abaQulusi around Hlobane Mountain in running fights on 22 and 24 January. Manyanyoba moved to threaten Lüneburg with his followers – perhaps as many as 1,000 – but retired after a brief skirmish with troops from the Lüneburg garrison on the 26th. As they had learned to do many times over the past sixty years, the Khubeka abandoned their homesteads scattered along the foot of the rugged hills above the Ntombe, and retired into caves higher up.

Nevertheless, the Zulu supporters along the northern frontier soon rallied. On the night of 10-11 February Manyanyoba joined forces with Mbilini, and a detachment of Qulusi under Tola kaDilikana, to raid farms belonging to the Hermannsburg community at Ekhombela, a few miles west of Lüneburg. They attacked before dawn, using spears in preference to firearms, and went from farm to farm. Most of the white farmers had fled to the safety of the Lüneburg laager, but over fifty of their Christianized African workers – men, women and children – were killed. The raiders retired at dawn, under pressure from the Lüneburg garrison, who sallied out to intercept them.

This bold raid prompted Wood to try to dislodge the Khubeka from the Ntombe altogether. On 15 February a force of mounted men and black auxiliaries, led by Redvers Buller, swept into the valley, apparently taking the Khubeka by surprise. A shell was dropped into Manyanyoba's personal homestead, and as the Zulus emerged from their huts, Buller's men tried to catch them in a pincer movement. The Khubeka were too quick, however, and most reached their caves, where the British could not dislodge them. Buller retired having fired all the homesteads his men could reach; over thirty Zulus were killed, including two of Manyanyoba's sons. A large quantity of Khubeka livestock was also captured.

Despite such determined British attempts to reduce Manyanyoba's military effectiveness, he and Mbilini remained a formidable combination, dominating the countryside around Lüneburg. In the first week of March, a convoy of supply wagons, bringing food and ammunition to the companies of the 80th Regiment who then comprised the garrison at Lüneburg, was delayed by wet weather. A company-sized detachment under Captain David Moriarty was sent from Lüneburg to escort it in; by 9 March the convoy had reached the Ntombe at Meyer's Drift, but the flooded river had prevented Moriarty bringing the majority of the wagons across. The convoy's difficulties were only too obvious to Manyanyoba, who appealed to Mbilini to assist him in attacking it. Mbilini was in any case assembling followers from the nearby areas, and on 11 March he boldly entered Moriarty's camp under the pretext of being a 'friendly'. Having satisfied himself of its vulnerability, he and Manyanyoba joined forces that night. Before dawn the following morning they launched a surprise attack on the convoy, easily overrunning it. Moriarty and over seventy soldiers and civilian wagon drivers were killed, although Moriarty is said to have killed two more of Manyanyoba's sons in the mêlée before he died. Mbilini and Manyanyoba carried away what cattle and loot they could carry, and dispersed to their respective strongholds before the Lüneburg garrison could hurry out to intercept them.

This was the most spectacular Zulu victory in the Lüneburg sector since the war began, but it was soon negated by events in the wider war. On 29 March the main Zulu army, hurrying from oNdini to attack Wood's base at Khambula, was heavily defeated, and a few days later Mbilini himself was killed. With British fortunes spectacularly restored, the Khubeka remained in their caves, harried by patrols from Lüneburg. As the war passed inexorably in favour of the British, the Lüneburg garrison was reduced, but this move proved premature; in early June Manyanyoba felt secure enough again to launch a series of raids on the abandoned white farms outside Lüneburg. It is interesting to note that throughout this period Manyanyoba seems to have drawn a clear distinction between British subjects – including the Lüneburg community – and the Boers. Many of the Afrikaners living along the Phongolo frontier held stoutly republican views and were embittered by the British annexation of the Transvaal; some were said to have advised Manyanyoba on the choice of subjects for his raids, and in return Manyanyoba warned them of any impending military activity.

With the British victory at Ulundi on 4 July, King Cetshwayo's power to support his allies on the border was irretrievably broken. In the north, Manyanyoba and the abaQulusi remained under arms, and Sir Garnet Wolseley – who superseded Lord Chelmsford – sent two columns to pacify them. One column, commanded by Lieutenant Colonel J. Baker Russell, was directed to advance up the headwaters of the Black Mfolozi, from the south, while troops then based along the Transvaal border were

159

placed under the command of Lieutenant Colonel The Hon. George Villiers. As the two columns converged on the Lüneburg district, the abaQulusi *izinduna* surrendered on 1 September, leaving Manyanyoba effectively the only *inkosi* still armed and in the field. Manyanyoba tentatively offered to surrender, but Wolseley, growing impatient, ordered Baker Russell to 'clear Manyanyoba out'. On 4 September some of Russell's troops entered the Ntombe valley. The Khubeka were ordered to surrender, and several elderly men emerged from the rocks and were given into the care of an auxiliary unit. As troops advanced further towards the caves however, one of the Khubeka fired a shot – perhaps accidentally – and the auxiliaries promptly panicked and speared their captives to death. The sight of this discouraged any further surrender. Left with little choice Baker Russell decided to force them out. On 5 September he drove through the valley, and when the Khubeka still refused to surrender, he ordered brushwood to be piled up at the mouths of the caves and set alike, in an attempt to smoke the Zulus out. It was not successful, if only because Manyanyoba and most of his people had already escaped. On 8 September Russell directed his Engineers to use explosives to blow up the entrances to Manyanyoba's caves. That same day a party of the 4th Regiment also attempted to clear the last of Prince Mbilini's followers out of the Tafelburg caves. When two NCOs of the 4th were shot as they approached the caves, the British decided to blow them up without further ado, and they were sealed regardless of the fact that at least thirty Zulus – including women – were still inside.

The operations of 8 September were the last real shots of the war. Manyanyoba himself had gone into hiding, but he lacked any capacity to resist further, and he finally surrendered on 22 September.

By that stage, Wolseley was already proceeding with the participation of Zululand. He decided to neutralize Manyanyoba by relocating him in the territory of one of the British appointees, the BaSotho chief Hlubi. On 8 October Manyanyoba and ninety-four of his surviving adherents arrived at Rorke's Drift, and were allocated territory in the Batshe valley opposite, close to the ruins of *inkosi* Sihayo's old homestead, and squarely under the eye of

Hlubi himself.

Together with Prince Mbilini, Manyanyoba had emerged as one of the best guerrilla leaders to fight the war in the Zulu cause. Yet his protracted defiance had proved hugely costly to Manyanyoba. A number of his immediate family had been killed, together with a larger number of his followers, while many of the survivors had been dispersed. Their homes had been destroyed, they had been impoverished by the capture of their cattle, and ultimately they had been driven from the land by the British in a way which earlier Zulu and Swazi attacks had failed to do. Like the Ngobese and others among King Cetshwayo's erstwhile favourites, the Khubeka had born the true brunt of the British invasion.

Matshana kaMondise

In about 1820, King Shaka kaSenzangakhona extended his influence along the central and upper reaches of the Mzinyathi River. Among those groups who submitted to his authority were the Sithole people, whose territory straddled both sides of the river. The ruling *inkosi* of the Sithole was overturned, and a junior branch, led by Jobe kaMapitha, was raised up by Shaka to represent his interests. Under Jobe, the Sithole became a powerful tool of the Zulu Royal House, controlling much of the western approaches to the kingdom. Jobe himself crossed the Mzinyathi, and established his principle homestead in the region of Ilenge Mountain, in the modern Msinga district. Jobe survived the purges of Shaka's supporters which followed Shaka's assassination in 1828, and remained on good terms with his successor, King Dingane. In 1838, however, Jobe's position beyond the physical barrier of the Mzinyathi left him exposed to pressure from the Boer Voortrekkers, who had recently occupied central Natal. He attempted to remain aloof from the cataclysmic war between the trekkers and Dingane in 1838, and took the opportunity afforded by the Boer ascendancy, after the Battle of Ncome, to sever his links with Dingane. The Sithole enjoyed a brief period of autonomy, but when Prince Mpande defected to the Boers in 1840 he denounced Jobe as a supporter of Dingane's regime. Following the final victory over Dingane by Mpande's followers, with Boer support, Jobe was the subject of cattle raids intended to reduce his power and authority, and which resulted in his submission to the Trekker government in Natal.

Natal came under British control in 1843, and by the time Jobe died his heir Mondise had predeceased him. The chieftainship then passed to Matshana kaMondise, who was still young, and for whom one of Jobe's brothers, Vela, acted as regent. With the implementation of the location system in Natal, however, the Sithole found their territory in Msinga increasingly overcrowded, and Matshana's authority – like that of all the Natal *amakhosi* – limited by the colonial authorities. In 1858, Matshana allowed a number of men to be killed on suspicion of witchcraft. Since these included his uncle, the former regent Vela, this may have reflected Matshana's attempts to assert his independent authority. Matshana was ordered by the authorities to hand over to white justice the men accused of the killings. He refused, and the Secretary for Native Affairs, Theophilus Shepstone, sent his younger brother John, with a party of colonial troops, to arrest Matshana. John Shepstone lured Matshana to a meeting on the pretext of being unarmed, then produced guns and tried to arrest him. Matshana, described at that time as 'an agile chief', spotted the trap and managed to jump over several rows of sitting followers and make his escape; he was, however, wounded in the attempt. Shepstone ordered that the Sithole cattle be confiscated to pay for Matshana's 'defiance', and a number of Sithole were killed attempting to defend them. A local missionary later commented that Matshana had been well respected as an *inkosi* among the Sithole and his white neighbours alike, and that the Shepstones had bungled the affair.

Matshana kaMondise himself then fled to Zululand with some of his retinue, and offered his allegiance to Prince Cetshwayo. Cetshwayo, who had recently secured his succession by his defeat of his rival Prince Mbuyazi, was at that time building his support within the country, and was keen to welcome *amakhosi* from outside the Zulu borders, particularly those who had conspicuously rejected white authority. Through Cetshwayo's influence, King Mpande appointed Matshana *inkosi* of that section of the Sithole still living downstream of Rorke's Drift, in the rugged country at the confluence of the Mzinyathi and Mangeni rivers.

Matshana himself built a homestead at Nsingabantu, in the steep Mangeni river-valley. Cetshwayo further sealed his alliance with Matshana by giving Matshana two of his sisters in marriage.

By placing Matshana in such a strategic situation, Cetshwayo had increased his personal support along Zululand's vulnerable western border (Matshana's neighbour, towards the crossing at Rorke's Drift, was another of King Cetshwayo's favourites, *inkosi* Sihayo). Matshana's experiences in Natal had made him a valued observer of white affairs; he is said to have warned that 'in less than three years the English will have advanced over the western portion of Zululand'.

Nonetheless, Matshana's position within the kingdom as a whole remained an ambiguous one. When war broke out in 1879, Lord Chelmsford's political advisers were convinced Matshana could be persuaded to abandon King Cetshwayo, and be lured back within the colonial fold. In fact, this was based on a false assumption of the attractions of colonial rule; having endured it once, Matshana had no desire to do so again. Many of the king's inner council, however, regarded him as an upstart, a *khafula*, one 'spat out' by the Zulu kingdom, and tainted by his time under colonial authority. This ambivalence probably shaped the Zulu strategy in the early weeks of the war; with the destruction of Sihayo's homestead by Lord Chelmsford on 12 January, Matshana's followers found themselves directly in the path of the British advance. At the king's request, Matshana himself and 700 of his armed followers had remained in the border region, and had taken refuge in the Qudeni bush. By directing the main army to attack Lord Chelmsford's column, King Cetshwayo hoped to reassert his authority and prevent a collapse of support along the crucial central border.

In fact, by the time the main Zulu army reached Siphezi Mountain on 20 January, the British had already advanced towards Isandlwana. Lord Chelmsford himself declared his intention to move next against the territories of 'the two Matyanas' – Matshana kaMondise, and Matshana kaSitshakuza, whose amaChunu followers lived around Siphezi hill. Suspicion among the Zulu high command of Matshana kaMondise's intentions were apparently confirmed by British probes to Mangeni on the 20th. The Zulu commanders instructed Matshana to join them at Siphezi, but in the meantime, wary that he was already compromised, moved their army away from his territory, and into the Ngwebeni valley. Matshana responded to their command and his men began to move from Qudeni, across the hills above the Mangeni and towards Siphezi. It was this straggling movement which Dartnell first encountered on the evening of the 21st, and which Chelmsford himself further interrupted on the 22nd. So far from being a deliberate decoy, working in association with the commanders of the main *impi*, Matshana himself seems to have been entirely taken by surprise by the British movements. On the morning of the 22nd, accompanied only by his personal retinue, he went forward to greet what he assumed was the king's force, then moving through the hills above Mangeni. One Zulu account said:

> As they drew near [it became clear that the warriors were not King Cetshwayo's but men of the British NNC, and] they heard the sound of the enemies' firearms. His people tried to make him go back, and they too fired, so that Matshana might have an opportunity of escaping. So he mounted and rode off, but all his force died, only Noju and another were left. They chased him a long way, but he dismounted, and ran away on foot, and escaped them.

Matshana was chased by Captain Theophilus Shepstone Jnr., of the Natal Carbineers, and escaped by scrambling down a steep precipice, where Shepstone could not follow. Thus Matshana twice escaped the clutches of the Shepstone family.

The Zulu victory at Isandlwana on 22 January diverted British attention from Matshana. Although his followers abandoned their homes and took to the Qudeni bush several times through-out the hostilities – particularly during May, when the 2nd Division enthusiastically raided the northern Nquthu district – the incursion of 21 January was the only time the war really touched them. Matshana surrendered to the border agent Henry Fynn Jnr. with a number of other local chiefs on 20 August. For the most part, the Sithole had escaped the British retribution which was heaped on their neighbours, the Ngobese family of *inkosi* Sihayo. Matshana was allowed to retain his authority over them, and they were placed under the control of John Dunn. In 1882 this area was taken directly under the control of the British as the Reserve Territory. Their geographical separation from the principle areas of conflict meant that Matshana and the Sithole were not heavily involved in the Zulu civil war of the 1880s.

In 1906, the border districts were disturbed by the outbreak of the so-called Bambatha Rebellion, and Matshana's neighbour, Mehlokazulu kaSihayo, joined the rebels, passing through Matshana's territory with his warriors on his way to the rebel concentration in the Nkandla forest. Matshana, no doubt wary of a further clash with white authority, declared firmly for the government, although a number of young men from his people, including his own son Gudla, rebelled. The colonial militia promptly confiscated a large number of cattle from Matshana's followers, despite protestations of their loyalty. At the end of the rebellion Matshana was tried for sedition, but acquitted.

In 1904 the missionary, A.W. Lee, met Matshana and described him as 'an elderly man of immense dignity ... a tall, spare man, who regarded lesser folk with considerable hauteur and demanded from them full recognition of his importance ...' Lee noted that he was customarily addressed with a term of respect usually reserved for the Zulu kings – 'Ndabazitha' – reflecting his relationship by marriage with the royal house.

Mavumengwana kaNdlela

Mavumengwana was a son of Ndlela kaSompisi, a great warrior of King Shaka's day, and a councillor to King Dingane. Mavumengwana was born in the late 1820s to Ndlela's wife Nozidlodlo, and was the younger brother of Godide kaNdlela, who succeeded his father as *inkhosi* of the principle group of the Nthuli people, who lived on the Zulu bank of the middle Thukela River. In adulthood, Mavumengwana became the head of a branch of the Ntuli, living downstream from Godide, and extending inland towards the headwaters of the AmaTigulu River.

Mavumengwana was of the same age group as King Cetshwayo, and was a close personal friend of his. In view of the fact that King Mpande took a personal interest in the well being of Ndlela's sons, this friendship probably had its origins in time spent growing up together in one of the royal homesteads. Some sources suggest that Mavumengwana was subsequently enrolled in the uThulwana *ibutho* alongside Prince Cetshwayo; in fact, however, he seems to have been enrolled in the amaPhela regiment, which was formed in the late 1840s. By rights, the young Cetshwayo should also have joined this regiment, but King Mpande delayed his enrolment to counter growing rivalry among the royal princes, and Cetshwayo was enrolled instead in the younger uThulwana (formed in the early 1850s).

Nevertheless, Mavumengwana remained a firm friend and close ally of Cetshwayo's, and the two took part in Mpande's expedition against the Swazi in 1847 (when the uThulwana were still cadets). The Swazi army refused to meet the numerically stronger Zulu army in open battle and retired instead to natural strongholds. The Zulu tried – without much success – to drive them out, and both Cetshwayo and Mavumengwana are said to have shot a Swazi warrior each by shooting into caves. When Cetshwayo became king, he appointed Mavumengwana as commander of a wing of the prestigious uThulwana.

When the British invaded Zululand in January 1879, Mavumengwana's brother, Godide kaNdlela, was given command of the forces assembled in the coastal district to oppose Colonel Pearson's advance. The main army, assembled at oNdini and subsequently dispatched to the Rorke's Drift front, was given to Ntshingwayo kaMahole, and Mavumengwana was appointed his co-commander. Mavumengwana, who had not long turned fifty, was arguably too junior for such a position, despite the reputation he enjoyed as a warrior; King Cetshwayo retained a lingering wariness of the older councillors of his father's time, and Mavumengwana's appointment reflected a desire to have a royal favourite of his own generation at the heart of the command.

During the Isandlwana campaign, Mavumengwana seems to have worked well with Ntshingwayo – himself an ardent supporter of the king – although the older and more experienced Ntshingwayo dominated the command. After the battle, Mavumengwana retired to his personal homestead near the headwaters of the amaTigulu. Here he found that Pearson's force, despite its victory over Godide at Nyezane on 22 January, was invested in the old KwaMondi mission at Eshowe. Together with Prince Dabulamanzi kaMpande, who lived nearby, Mavumengwana took command of the Zulu forces which isolated Pearson. Large numbers of warriors were assembled at royal homesteads near Eshowe, and a cordon drawn from these kept Pearson under constant surveillance, harassing his patrols and preventing messengers reaching the British garrisons at the Thukela. When, at the end of March, Lord Chelmsford crossed the border to relieve Eshowe, the Zulu forces there were reinforced by fresh troops sent from oNdini. Under the overall command of Somopho kaZikhala, the Zulus attempted to halt Chelmsford's advance at kwaGingindlovu on 2 April; both Mavumengwana and Prince Dabulamanzi held commands during the subsequent battle. The British victory at kwaGingindlovu effectively destroyed the Zulu concentration in the coastal sector, however, and Eshowe was relieved. Mavumengwana apparently retired again to his homestead. Despite the growing numbers of British troops active in the area, some of Mavumengwana's Nthuli took part in the successful raid across the Thukela at the Middle Drift as late as 25 June, which destroyed African homesteads on the Natal bank and carried away cattle.

Mavumengwana did not formally surrender to the British until 5 August, over a month after Lord Chelmsford had defeated the main Zulu army at oNdini. Under the post-war settlement drafted by Sir Garnet Wolseley, Mavumengwana's territory, together with the Ntuli section headed by his brother Godide, was placed under that of the 'white *ikhosi*' John Dunn. Rather than risk antagonizing such an influential family, however, Dunn allowed them to retain their positions. When King Cetshwayo returned to Zululand in 1883, control of Dunn's territory passed to the British. Large numbers of Ntuli remained loyal to the king, however, and crossed into Cetshwayo's districts to pay their respects. *Inkosi* Godide was among them; he was killed when Zibhebhu kaMaphitha attacked oNdini on 21 July 1883.

Mavumengwana died about 1893.

Mbilini waMswati, Prince

Mbilini was one of the most dynamic and able guerrilla leaders to emerge from the war of 1879 and his prominence was all the more remarkable because he was outside the often close-knit circle of royal favourites who commanded the king's *amabutho*. He was not even, in fact, a Zulu but a member of the Swazi Royal House, the eldest son of King Mswati by his wife laMakhasiso. Mbilini was born about 1843 and was apparently raised to be a warrior. It was said that at the age of twelve he had been wrapped in the bloody pelt of a particularly savage dog in the hope that he would absorb some of its ferocious nature. In the 1850s, when still a boy, he accompanied a Swazi punitive expedition along the Lebombo Mountains and in 1865, when his father died, he felt confidant enough to challenge the succession. Although the eldest of Mswati's sons, and something of a favourite, he was nevertheless ineligible as an heir because his mother had been outranked by Mswati's later wives. Mbilini refused to back down but his ambitious nature had made him unpopular within the country and, with little support to back him up, he decided to flee.

He moved to Zululand and offered his allegiance to Prince Cetshwayo who was himself building his own support base within the Zulu kingdom. Cetshwayo offered Mbilini his protection since Mbilini afforded a long-term opportunity to influence events within Swaziland. Cetshwayo allowed Mbilini to settle in the sparsely populated northern border region, close to Swaziland, in the Ntombe valley. At that time Mbilini had only a handful of supporters and built himself a homestead close under the protective cliffs of a hill known as the Tafelberg. This area was remote from the centres of African and colonial metropolitan power, and Mbilini used the proximity of the nearby Swazi and Transvaal borders to facilitate a programme of raiding designed to build up his cattle and followers. The main targets were Swazi, some of them living on the Transvaal side of the border. As a result, in 1877, the Transvaal Republic complained about Mbilini's activities to King Cetshwayo who gave them permission to punish him but – significantly – did nothing himself. Mbilini adroitly avoided Boer punitive efforts by hiding in the caves of his 'stronghold'.

He had also cultivated close links with a strongly royalist group, the abaQulusi, whose settlements lay further south around the Zungwini and Hlobane mountains. After the Boers withdrew, Mbilini built himself a new homestead on the southern flank of Hlobane and named it wryly *iNdlabeyetibula*, 'they gave my huts a shove'. Over the next two years he would move freely between the two to avoid the repercussions of his actions. With the annexation of the Transvaal by Britain in April 1877, Mbilini's propensities were seen to have implications for the British, the more so because his Ntombe stronghold was just a few miles from the border settlement of Lüneburg. With tension mounting, British troops were moved to garrison Lüneburg, a move that was widely interpreted inside Zululand as proof of their aggressive intentions.

When the Anglo-Zulu War broke out in January 1879, Prince Mbilini was still a young man. He was in his thirties, unmarried but wore the polished gum ring of a married man because, he said, he was head of his own estate. He had a slight build and a pleasant manner but a shrewd, ambitious and ruthless mind which had caused one of his Zulu relatives to dub him 'a hyena'. He could ride and shoot, had a wealth of recent guerrilla experience and from the first allied himself entirely with the Zulu cause.

At first, he moved his followers south to join forces with the stronger abaQulusi near Hlobane. The local British commander, Colonel Wood, recognized the threat they posed and on 20 January marched out from his camp at Fort Thinta to disperse them. A running fight broke out over several days as the abaQulusi were driven from Zungwini and skirmished along the foot of Hlobane. On the 24th, Wood received news of the disaster which had befallen the Centre Column at Isandlwana, and he retired to Fort Thinta. Nevertheless, the Zulus had been impressed by his resolution and the eclipse which took place on 22nd was seen as a sign that Mbilini's power – associated with the sun – was waning. Mbilini himself moved back to the Ntombe valley where he found a more vulnerable target. Although the white settlers at Lüneburg had gone into a protective laager, they had left their African retainers to protect their farms. On the night of 10-11 February Mbilini led a combined force of his own men, abaQulusi and retainers of the local *inkosi* Manyanyoba Khubeka who fell on the unsuspecting farm workers, going from property to property to kill forty-one men, women and children. Before daylight the Zulu force scattered, Mbilini himself hurrying back to Hlobane. He was back a month later, however, to scout a convoy of wagons, escorted by a company-strength detachment of the 80th Regiment, which had been stranded by the wet weather on the banks of the Ntombe, within sight of his Tafelberg stronghold. For several days the convoy was stuck in the mud, drenched by daily downpours. On 11 March a civilian wagon-driver with the convoy claimed to recognize Mbilini among a party of unarmed Africans who entered the camp to chat and to sell mealies. That night, having thoroughly scouted the position, Mbilini led a force of some 800 men – abaQulusi, Manyanyoba's followers and men from the Zulu king's army who lived locally, whose regiments were then dispersed – down from the Tafelberg. Under cover of a dense mist they advanced to within fifty yards of the camp on the north bank of the Ntombe before being dis-covered. They fired a volley then rushed in, spearing the confused garrison as they emerged from their tents. Having carried the camp on the north side they crossed to the south side. Here they were met by a handful of determined soldiers but still successful-ly captured the wagons. They were able to thoroughly loot the camp of supplies, arms, ammunition and cattle and withdraw before troops from the Lüneburg garrison could hurry out to intercept them.

In the aftermath of the attack Mbilini returned to Hlobane to avoid British retribution. His presence there intensified Colonel Wood's desire to deprive the Zulu of that particular stronghold. When, shortly afterwards, Lord Chelmsford asked Wood to make a diversionary attack to draw attention away from his own planned march to relieve Eshowe, Wood decided to attack Hlobane. His plan was to assault it at either end of the mountain with mounted parties at dawn on 28 March. Although the British achieved their start positions without opposition, the plan proved to be based on poor intelligence and badly coordinated. One party, attacking the western end of the mountain, failed to reach the summit. The other, attacking from the eastern end, successfully forced its way up through the cliffs onto the plateau but was then cut off by abaQulusi filtering round the shoulders of the mountains in its wake. Wood himself, following his assault parties, came under fire and two of his staff, Captain Campbell and a civilian interpreter named Llewellwyn Lloyd, were killed in a fierce scramble among the boulders at the foot of the cliffs. The exact role played by Prince Mbilini in the battle is difficult to determine. The abaQulusi credit the victory to their senior military commander, Sikhobhobo, although the British at the time were convinced Mbilini was the architect. Certainly, the skirmishing on the southern flanks took place above Mbilini's homestead, and contemporary reports that he shot Captain Campbell among the rocks may well have been true. In all likelihood Mbilini and Sikhobhobo had worked together to develop a contingency plan for the defence of the mountain since it was an obvious enough target. Certainly, they had between them already disrupted the British attack before the coincidental arrival of the king's main army which appeared at the height of the battle, en route to attack Wood's base at Khambula. In the event, the British troops were driven across the summit, their lines of retreat closed off, until they were forced down a rocky staircase at the far end in conditions very closely resembling a rout. Mbilini himself received two light wounds, to his head and upper body, during the battle – perhaps the result of the firefight with Wood's staff.

The following day the main army, supported by the abaQulusi, attacked Khambula and was defeated after several hours of hard fighting. Mbilini did not take part in the second battle and instead moved north again to the Ntombe to recover from his injuries. Within days he was back in action, launching an attack on the descendants of Africans known to have joined the British auxiliaries and raiding the farm workers outside Lüneburg again. Yet, with the victory at Khambula the British were now in the ascendancy and many Zulu supporters across the northern region had gone into hiding. On 5 April Mbilini's luck ran out. Together with just a handful of men on horseback he was looting cattle from deserted farms close to Lüneburg when a British patrol, led by Captain Prior of the 80th Regiment, intercepted him. Two Zulus were shot down as they fled and a third was wounded and fell from his horse; he was stabbed by auxiliaries chasing him and proved to be Tshewane kaSihayo, a brother of the famous Mehlokazulu, and a known associate of Prince Mbilini. A fourth man attempted to escape by riding his horse down into a steep donga. One of the auxiliaries, running up behind him, fired down and saw him stagger in the saddle. He managed to keep his seat and ride away, but the injury was a fearful one – the bullet had hit him above his right shoulder and passed out at his left hip. The man was Prince Mbilini. Although his followers hurried him away towards Hlobane, it is doubtful if he ever reached it and within a few days the British were confidently able to report that the most feared guerrilla leader of the war, 'the hyena of the Phongolo river', was dead.

Mehlokazulu kaSihayo

Mehlokazulu was born about 1853, the senior son of *inkosi* Sihayo kaXongo Ngobese of the amaQungebeni people. Sihayo was a personal favourite of (then) Prince Cetshwayo, and at his instigation had succeeded his brother, Mfokozana kaXongo, as *induna* on the western approaches to Zululand, opposite Rorke's Drift.

Mehlokazulu spent much of his youth at his father's kwaSoxhege homestead, nestling in the foothills of Ngedla Mountain. As a boy he would have herded his father's cattle, and hunted birds and rock rabbits with sticks before attending his first muster as a cadet in the *amabutho* system. Mehlokazulu was enrolled in the iNgobamakhosi *ibutho*, which was formed in 1873. The iNgobamakhosi was a particularly large regiment, reflecting King Cetshwayo's attempts to revitalize the *amabutho* system, and one for which he held a great affection, having supervised its cadetship in the last years of his father's reign.

Mehlokazulu benefited from the prestige enjoyed by the Ngobese family from an early age. He was selected with a number of other youths – all of them from the families of important *amakhosi*, including that of Mnyamana Buthelezi – to become a personal attendant of the king, and his duties included fetching water from a particularly pure spring on a mountainside several miles from the king's homestead at oNdini. He also served as one of the king's 'eyes', a network of official observers who reported news in the outlying districts and along the borders to Cetshwayo personally.

He held a junior command within his regiment. Although senior commanders were appointed from among older men by the king himself, a number of youths who had displayed leadership during their cadetship were appointed as officers when the regiment was formally enrolled. Mehlokazulu's exact status is uncertain, but typically such men commanded either a company, or a group of companies which had served at the same royal homestead during their cadetship. Although Mehlokazulu's standing as the son of an *inkosi* would undoubtedly have influenced his selection, he was already possessed of a strong and self-confidant personality. In later life he would show himself to be a nationalist, a committed supporter of the Royal House, and a believer in traditional Zulu values. At the same time, he belonged to a generation who had grown up against the reality of the economic penetration of Zululand by the European world, and he lacked the awe of the whites which characterized many of his father's generation. He appreciated the benefits whites had to offer, but recognized their shortcomings and was more than prepared to stand his ground against them. Even as a young man, he had earned an uneasy reputation among white traders and missionaries who had found him unwilling to tolerate a poor bargain, and more than ready to act decisively if he felt cheated.

In December 1877 the iNgobamakhosi famously clashed with the older uThulwana *ibutho* at the annual first fruits ceremony. Mehlokazulu's part in the incident is not recorded, but it is unlikely that he would have escaped involvement in an incident which left as many as seventy iNgobamakhosi dead. The king held the iNgobamakhosi to blame for the incident, and many of them were individually fined.

In July 1878 Mehlokazulu was the instigator of the famous 'border incident', which was cited in the British ultimatum. Two of his father's unfaithful wives had crossed into Natal with their lovers, seeking protection at the homesteads of two border policemen, Mswagele and Maziyana. To abandon an *inkosi* for a commoner was a serious slight according to Zulu custom, but what made this case so galling to the Ngobese family was the open defiance expressed by the women. Neither had troubled to move more than a mile or two from the border, and one is said to have taunted Mehlokazulu in response to his complaints, saying 'tell Mehlokazulu to come and kill [me]'. As guardians of the western borders on the king's behalf, Sihayo's family could ill afford to allow Natal's authority to be so easily invoked to undermine their prestige.

On 28 July, before dawn, some thirty Zulus mounted and carrying firearms, and 200 more on foot with traditional weapons, surrounded Mswagele's homestead. They were led by Mehlokazulu, but accompanied by his brothers Mkhumbikazulu and Bhekuzulu, and Sihayo's own brother, Zuluhlenga. Taking care to offer no harm to Natal citizens, they nevertheless dragged out one of the errant women, and took her back across the border. Once on Zulu soil, they killed her. Accounts differ, but since it was against custom to shed the blood of a high-ranking woman, she was probably strangled with hide reims, and shots fired into the air in celebration. The following morning the woman hiding at Maziyana's homestead was also taken and killed.

So public an execution was clearly intended to send a warning to the African population along the border that Sihayo's family could not be insulted with impunity, and indeed it was not unknown for fleeing criminals to be chased across the border by both sides. Coming at a time of tension between Natal and the Zulu kingdom, the repercussions of the incident went far beyond anything Mehlokazulu had anticipated. The British authorities complained strongly to King Cetshwayo, demanding cattle in compensation and that he surrender the guilty parties. The king was prepared to offer cattle – and directed Sihayo to provide them from his own herds – but he could not surrender Mehlokazulu without damaging his own prestige. For several months, Mehlokazulu and Tshekwane left their home in the Batshe valley, and went to live with Prince Mbilini in northern Zululand, another royal favourite whose territory was conveniently inaccessible to both white authority and King Cetshwayo's administration.

With the coming of war, Mehlokazulu rejoined his regiment, the iNgobamakhosi. He was at oNdini when Lord Chelmsford crossed the Mzinyathi on 12 January 1879, and attacked Sihayo's homestead at kwaSoxhege. Mehlokazulu's brother Mkumbikazulu had been left in charge of a force of amaQungebeni guarding their homesteads and cattle; the force was scattered by the British and Mkhumbikazulu was killed.

The main Zulu army set out from oNdini on 17 January. Once it reached Sihayo's territory, both Sihayo and Mehlokazulu acted as mounted scouts, advising the commanders of British movements in the country they knew so well. According to Mehlokazulu, there was 'no intention of making an attack that day (at Isandlwana) because it was the day of the New Moon … what led to the attack was the fact of their being themselves fired upon'. Mehlokazulu later gave a remarkable and detailed account of the battle, recalling how the iNgobamakhosi attack stalled in front of Durnford's stand in the Nyogane donga, but then broke into the camp as the British line collapsed. He was modest about his own role, commenting that 'he supposed he must have killed someone, but there was a great deal of confusion'. In later years, he enjoyed teasing *inkosi* Hlubi, who led a detachment of mounted auxiliaries under Durnford's command, that he spotted Hlubi in retreat, and chased him some way down the fugitives' trail – and nearly caught him. By that time, of course, the story had an extra poignancy, for Sihayo had been deposed, and the British had set up Hlubi in his stead.

The Zulu army dispersed after Isandlwana. It is unlikely that Mehlokazulu returned to the Batshe valley, for most of the amaQungebeni had abandoned their homes for inaccessible bush or mountain strongholds further from the British advance. By March, however, it was clear that a new phase of fighting was imminent, and the king reassembled the *amabutho*. Mehlokazulu was present at the attack on Wood's camp at Khambula on 29 March, recalling dolefully the part played by his regiment in the subsequent Zulu defeat. The iNgobamakhosi had been in the right horn, and had been stung into launching a premature attack by the British horsemen:

The English fired their cannon and rockets, and we were

fighting them and attacking them for about an hour. I mean the Ngobamakhosi regiment. Before the main body of the Zulu army came up, we, when the Zulu army did come up, were lying prostrate – we were beaten. So many were killed that the few who were not killed were lying between their bodies ...

The British pursuit after Khambula was severe, and Mehlokazulu noted that he only just managed to escape, a bullet having creased his skull and cut away a line of his hair. He was present, too, at Ulundi, but admitted that 'we did not fight with the same spirit, because we were then frightened. We had had a severe lesson.'

After Ulundi, Mehlokazulu joined the general surrenders, but was recognized and arrested, and sent to Pietermaritzburg at the beginning of September. Here he gave a long account of his participation in the war to the magistrate, and it was thought that he would be tried for his part in the border incident of 1878. In the event, he was released, 'as anyone who gave the moment a matter's thought', commented the traveller Bertram Mitford, 'might have foreseen would be the case'.

By October Mehlokazulu was back on the border, but to a very changed world. His father was no longer an *inkosi*, having been deposed by the British, and the outsider Hlubi Molife given his territories instead. Mehlokazulu hoped to rebuild kwaSoxhege, but with Hlubi in residence nearby it was an uncomfortable situation. There had been a further dramatic decline, too, in the family fortunes. In August, King Cetshwayo's senior *induna*, Mnyamana Buthelezi, who blamed Sihayo's family for provoking the catastrophe of the British invasion, had sent men to carry off Sihayo's cattle as punishment. Their impoverishment left the Ngobese family suddenly without authority or influence, and emboldened Hlubi to act against them. He ordered them to move to the far western fringes of his territory.

Here the traveller Mitford found them in 1882, and left a revealing portrait of Mehlokazulu:

'...a fine, well-made man, of about five or six and twenty, with an intelligent face and brisk, lively manner. A sub-chief of the Ngobamakhosi regiment and a good shot, he is much looked up to by his younger compatriots as a spirited and daring warrior ... '.

To my inquiries as to how he was getting on since the war, Mehlo-ka-zulu replied that it hadn't made much difference to him individually; his father had been a powerful chief but now was nobody, and had been driven out of his former country. Still they managed to live.

'Did he regret having fought?'

'No, he couldn't exactly say that; he was a young man and he wanted to prove himself as a warrior. He had been in all the principle engagements: Isandlwana, Kambula and Ulundi, and now he wanted to "sit still".'

'Always?'

'Well, that he couldn't say either; he liked a fight now and then; there was no mistake about it.'

For those Zulus who adhered to the king, the 1880s offered little chance, in any case, to 'sit still'. In 1883 King Cetshwayo was restored by the British to part of his old territories, but almost immediately was disastrously defeated by Zibhebhu kaMaphitha, who had risen to prominence during his absence. Mehlokazulu's part in these events is not known, but his father Sihayo was present at the rebuilt oNdini homestead when Zibhebhu attacked it on 21 July 1883. So, too, were many of the iNgobamakhosi, and it is likely Mehlokazulu was among them; when the royalist stand collapsed however, and many of the young warriors were agile enough to flee, many of the old royal councillors could not, and Sihayo was among the dead. Significantly, Mehlokazulu's name emerges as one who acted as an intermediary in the negotiations for the Boers to intervene in the aftermath of the disaster.

When the tangled chain of post-war events led inexorably to Dinuzulu's revolt against British authority in 1888, Mehlokazulu took to the field briefly once more in the royalist cause. Hlubi, that usurper of Ngobese fortunes, had raised a unit of auxiliaries to support British troops, leaving his territory largely undefended. For Mehlokazulu, it was an opportunity to settle old scores, and he assembled an *impi* to attack Hlubi's homesteads. The move came to nothing, however, for Dinuzulu's rebellion soon collapsed, and Mehlokazulu was forced to recognize it as a lost cause.

The rebellion of 1888 did at least cause the British authority to reconsider their policies, and to a shift away from a decade of 'divide and rule' which had proved so destructive. Rather than suppress royalist aspirations, they began instead to accommodate them – and to some extent subvert them. Since 1883 they had refused to recognize Mehlokazulu's claim as *inkosi* of the Qungebeni, but in 1893 they finally did so, and he returned to the Mzinyathi region.

Yet the final years of the nineteenth century would prove no kinder to the African peoples of Natal and Zululand. Unsettled by the conflict of the Anglo-Boer war, increasingly impoverished and forced to work as migrant labourers for the growing white industrial economy, they suffered, too, from a succession of natural disasters which withered crops and killed their cattle. Traditional forms of leadership, the *amakhosi*, could only survive with the approval of the colonial administration, and the *amakhosi* found themselves trapped between the demands of the white government and the expectations of their people. For many the situation had already become intolerable, even before Natal added an additional financial burden in 1905 – a Poll Tax. In April 1906 a Natal *inkosi*, Bambatha kaMancinza, broke under the strain, attacked a police patrol, and fled across the border to Zululand, hoping to invoke the legendary spirit of the old Zulu order.

Few Zulu *amakhosi* joined him; one who did was Mehlokazulu kaSihayo. It seems that over the years his resentment against white authority had grown, particularly since large tracts of traditional Zulu territory had been given over to European settlement in the aftermath of the Anglo-Boer War. When called upon to pay the Poll Tax, he failed to comply, pleading ill health. By this stage Natal troops were hurrying to the border in pursuit of Bambatha, and Mehlokazulu began to fear he would be attacked. About this time a local missionary, A.W. Lee, encountered Mehlokazulu while paying a visit to a neighbouring chief, Makafula kaMahawuta:

> I entered [Makafula's] own hut to find myself confronted by
> the big chief of the Nquthu area, Mehlokazulu ka Sihayo of
> the Maqungebeni people. We were both taken aback, I

because I had not expected to thrust myself into such distinguished company, and he, because the last thing he wished to see there was a person with a white face. Mehlokazulu was a Zulu of the old school, a fighting man with a distinguished record ... He glared at me out of his prominent, rather blood-injected eyes, and, turning to Makafula, he asked 'Who is this white boy? Why does he come here? What does he want?' ... It was an uncomfortable moment. I felt I had blundered into a secret meeting between the two chiefs at which they had been discussing the situation.

In fact, Mehlokazulu had probably hoped to avoid any involvement, but with troops passing perilously close he was acutely aware that his reputation counted against him. As a precaution he assembled his fighting men at Mangeni – the same area Lord Chelmsford had searched on the day of Isandlwana, years before – in early May. Mehlokazulu made no move to join the fighting, but some of his men began to slip away, moving along the Qudeni foothills to join the rebel concentrations in the Nkandla forest. This provoked a column of colonial troops to move down from Helpmekaar and cross into Zululand at Rorke's Drift, camping near the old Isandlwana battlefield. With the heavy-handedness that characterized colonial operations in 1906, they began burning homesteads – including Mehlokazulu's own – and carrying away cattle. When they spotted groups of men lingering on the hillsides of Malakatha Mountain, they shelled them with artillery. Unknown to them, Mehlokazulu was among them; he was apparently unhurt, but the concussion of a shell bursting nearby knocked him off his horse.

The incident confirmed his opinion that the authorities were deliberately targeting him, and with no other options available to him, Mehlokazulu joined the rebellion. With those armed men still under his command, he moved towards Nkandla, and in early June affected a junction with Bambatha's forces in the rugged country not far from King Cetshwayo's grave. By this time, there were considerable concentrations of colonial troops sweeping the Nkandla, and Mehlokazulu and Bambatha decided between them to make for the narrow gorge of the Mome stream, a spot so inaccessible that it had long been regarded as an impenetrable stronghold. Indeed, King Cetshwayo had briefly sheltered there after his defeat by Zibhebhu at oNdini.

After a difficult march, the rebel force reached the mouth of the gorge on the evening of 9 June. They were reluctant to enter it at night, because of the difficult terrain, and Mehlokazulu, who was by now stout and feeling the effect of his exertions, insisted they camp on flat ground by the entrance. As one embittered survivor later commented, Mehlokazulu had refused to enter the gorge 'because he was very stout, and wore boots, and was tired'. That night, in the inky darkness, a herd boy claimed to hear the sound of wagon wheels in the distance, but Mehlokazulu dismissed the report, commenting tartly that the whites were incapable of making such an approach at night.

He was wrong. News of the rebel movements had reached the colonial troops who, with remarkable coordination, converged on the gorge overnight. They had expected the rebels to have already slipped into its recesses, and were surprised at first light to see them still sleeping in the open. They immediately began to rain shell, machine-gun and rifle fire on the rebel encampment. Caught entirely by surprise, the rebels streamed into the gorge, only to find themselves trapped by troops on the heights all round.

Both Bambatha and Mehlokazulu were reported killed, along with hundreds of other rebels. While there were persistent rumours that Bambatha had actually escaped, there is no doubt of Mehlokazulu's fate. He was seen trying to get away; he was dressed in European clothing, and followed by an attendant carrying a new pair of riding boots. Mehlokazulu was shot dead.

The slaughter at Mome effectively crushed the rebellion in Zululand, and the loss of Mehlokazulu was in particular a serious blow. His death was sadly appropriate to his life, which was characterized by a determined but unequal resistance to encroaching European authority. Where he had once embodied the spirit of defiance which had carried the Zulu army to victory at Isandlwana in 1879, he had endured afterwards years of dispossession and hardship. Whereas many Zulu *amakhosi* had recognized the essential futility of Bambatha's rebellion, and had refused to join it, Mehlokazulu had responded to the impossible situation in which he found himself in characteristic style.

Mkhosana kaMvundlana Biyela

Mkhosana kaMvundlana was *inkosi* of the Biyela people, and played a decisive role in the Battle of Isandlwana, where he was killed.

The Biyela, whose ancestral lands lay south-east of the middle reaches of the White Mfolozi River, enjoyed a particularly close relationship with the Zulu Royal House, with whom they claimed common ancestors. This privileged position within the kingdom was enhanced by their decision to ally themselves to King Shaka early in his career, rather than resist the Zulu ascendancy. Indeed, Mkhosana's father, *inkosi* Mvundlana kaMenziwa, was among a handful of distinguished warriors who were on close personal terms with Shaka. Mvundlana is remembered in particular for his participation in the campaign against the Ndwandwe in 1818, when he is said to have entered the enemy camp by stealth and attacked the Ndwandwe commander. Despite his conspicuous loyalty to Shaka, Mvundlana survived the purges which followed Shaka's assassination in 1828, and remained a member of the innermost royal council through the reigns of successive Zulu kings, a position he still enjoyed on Cetshwayo's accession in 1873. He died at some point in the mid-1870s, and was succeeded as *inkosi* of the Biyela by his son Mkhosana.

Mkhosana was born about 1835, and enrolled in the iNdlondlo *ibutho*. The iNdlondlo were allowed to marry and don the *isicoco* about 1875. Mkhosana seems to have retained King Cetshwayo's friendship, although his youth debarred him from sitting on the king's inner council. Following the usual Zulu practice of appointing older men as senior officers among newly-formed regiments, Mkhosana had, by 1879, been given a high-ranking command among the uKhandempemvu (uMcijo) *ibutho*. He is listed among the three most senior officers of the regiment, although overall command rested upon Vumandaba kaNthathi, who was both older and one of King Cetshwayo's most trusted councillors. Nevertheless, Mkhosana was the senior *induna* of kwaKhandempemvu, the royal homestead in the amaBedlana hills, near oNdini, where the uKhandempemvu were based.

With the outbreak of war in January 1879, Mkhosana accompanied his regiment on the advance towards Isandlwana. It was the uKhandempemvu who, having been discovered at about noon on 22 January by mounted parties sent out from the British camp, launched the spontaneous attack which precipitated the battle. Mkhosana, along with many senior regimental officers, was apparently attending a command conference with the generals Ntshingwayo kaMahole and Mavumengwana kaNdlela when *impi* was discovered; he did not apparently rejoin his men but remained with the generals as they followed behind the advancing regiments. By the time the generals took up a commanding position above the iNyoni rocks on the escarpment overlooking Isandlwana, the Zulu centre – including the uKhandempemvu – had already descended to the dongas below, and had come under heavy fire from the main British firing line. The men of the uKhandempemvu took cover among the dongas and, with the open ground in front of them swept by fire, their advance stalled. Realizing that if the centre failed the whole assault would collapse, Ntshingwayo sent Mkhosana hurrying down the steep escarpment to urge his men on.

When he reached the dongas, Mkhosana strode up and down fearlessly in front of his men, oblivious to the British bullets striking rocks all around him, berating the sheltering warriors and urging them to renew the attack. Family sources have rationalized his apparent invulnerability by suggesting that he presented such a magnificent spectacle, dressed in his finery, alone and in the open, that the British were reluctant to shoot him down; sadly, no evidence has survived from British sources on the point, although the tradition does at least suggest that Mkhosana was wearing the full finery of an *inkosi*, resplendent in leopard-skin shoulder-cape and with Scarlet Louie and Blue Crane feathers in his headdress. Famously, Mkhosana rallied his men by calling out lines from King Cetshwayo's praises – *'uhlamvana ubul'mlilo ubaswe uMantshonga no uNgqelebana kashongo njalo'* ['the little branch of leaves that extinguished the great fire kindled by Mantshonga and Nqgelebana' – a reference to Prince Cetshwayo's victory at the Battle of 'Ndondakusuka in 1856, and to the perceived role two white men, 'Mantshonga' Walmsley and

'Ngqelebana' Rathbone, played in inciting the conflict – 'gave no such order as this!']. Stung by this allusion to their royal duty, the uKhandempemvu rose up from the donga and rushed forward. Their attack coincided with the British withdrawal towards the camp, and the uKhandempemvu were able to drive between the 24th companies facing them, and prevent the British reforming. The moment was a decisive one and precipitated the British collapse.

At the moment of his triumph, however, Mkhosana was killed, shot through the head. Family sources suggest that he was in fact killed by one of his own men in the confusion of the rush, since his body was later found to have a conspicuous wound in the back of the head. Given his role in encouraging the attack, which had made him an obvious target, this is more likely to be a folk-memory of the terrible exit wound inflicted by the British Martini-Henry rifle. After the battle, Mkhosana's body was identified by his kinsmen and, like most of the Zulu dead, covered over and left on the field.

So far from being 'an old Zulu commander' popular in tourist mythology, Mkhosana was about forty-three years old at the time of his death, and in the prime of life.

Mkhosana kaSangqana Zungu

Mkhosana was born about 1830, the head of a junior lineage of the Zungu people. He was enrolled in the amaShishi section of the iSanqu regiment, which was formed in 1852. Mkhosana became a personal attendant of King Mpande, and later a leading friend, confidant and adviser of King Cetshwayo. In the closing stages of the Anglo-Zulu War, Mkhosana and his son Maphelu accompanied the king in his flight from oNdini. When Major Marter's Dragoons tracked Cetshwayo to a homestead in the remote Ngome forest on 28 August and surrounded it, it was Mkhosana who attempted to delay them at the gate. He was, however, captured with the rest and accompanied the king into exile at the Cape. Mkhosana Zungu features in a number of photographs of the king's attendants, photographed at that time. In 1881, Bishop Colenso secured permission for Mkhosana to return briefly to Zululand, where he attempted to quell the rising tension between royalist and anti-royalist factions. He returned to join King Cetshwayo for his visit to London in August 1882. When Cetshwayo was restored to part of his former territory in early 1883, Mkhosana again attended him. During the disastrous attack by *inkosi* Zibhebhu on the rebuilt oNdini complex in July 1883, Mkhosana helped the king to escape. In later life he was regarded as a great authority on Zulu tradition, and in 1914, when King Solomon Nkayishana kaDinuzulu organized a ceremonial cleansing hunt, *ihlambo*, as part of the mourning ceremonies for the late King Dinuzulu, he asked Mkhosana to preside. Mkhosana was by that time so old and frail that he had to be fetched from his home near Mahlabatini by wagon. He died shortly afterwards.

Mkhosana's son Maphelu was born about 1854 and was a member of the uVe regiment. He fought at Isandlwana and followed his father as an ardent royalist; he also had a fierce reputation as a warrior. Maphelu Zungu became a senior adviser to King Dinuzulu; he was also a leading source on Zulu history in the researches carried out by Colonel H.C. Lugg.

Mnyamana kaNgqengele Buthelezi

About 1817, the newly emergent Zulu king, Shaka kaSenzangakhona, attacked the Buthelezi people of *inkosi* Phungashe kaMvulane. This was one of Shaka's early military victories, and it was apparently decisive; the Buthelezi were defeated and Pungashe fled among the Ndwandwe people, where he subsequently died.

The early incorporation of the Buthelezi into the enlarged Zulu kingdom ensured them of a special place close to the Royal House. Shaka overturned *inkosi* Pungashe's line, raising up a junior lineage of the Buthelezi royal family to rule on his behalf. The head of this lineage was a friend of Shaka's, Ngqengele kaMvulana, who became both Shaka's trusted body-servant and a senior adviser. After the death of Ngqengele, his son Klwana retained an important role under Shaka's successor Dingane, and commanded a number of military expeditions on his behalf. During the war with the Voortrekkers in 1838, *inkosi* Klwana remained loyal to King Dingane, but when Prince Mpande defected to the Boers, Klwana tentatively changed his allegiance. Nevertheless, after Dingane's defeat by Mpande, Mpande remained wary of Klwana's true sympathies, and eventually Klwana was killed.

King Mpande then raised up another of Ngqengele's sons, Mnyamana, to be *inkosi* of the Buthelezi, and to fulfil the role increasingly played by the influential Buthelezi representatives on the royal council. *Inkosi* Mnyamana was born about 1813, his mother was Phangela of the Sibisi people, and he had been enrolled in the Mkhulutshane regiment in Dingane's time. He was to live until 1892, and during his career he was destined to become the senior state official – *induna'nkhulu* – under three successive Zulu kings, and to remain one of the most powerful men in the kingdom. His personal homestead, ekuShumayeleni, was on the Black Mfolozi River in Buthelezi territory, but he spent much of his life at court.

In 1854 Mpande formed a new *ibutho*, the uThulwana. It consisted of men born in the early 1830s, including a number of Mpande's own sons, Prince Cetshwayo among them. Mpande was particularly fond of this regiment which, basking in royal approval and containing so many young men of high rank, was soon known throughout the country for the airs it assumed. King Mpande appointed Mnyamana Buthelezi as the senior commander of the uThulwana, remarking that he was the only man in the country with the strength of character and the standing to overawe them.

It was an astute judgment. Sadly, no authenticated photograph of Mnyamana has yet emerged, possibly because he was no admirer of the European lifestyle, seeing it for the threat it was to the traditional Zulu way of life. In his prime, *inkosi* Mnyamana was a tall, slim man with a dark complexion who sported a neat pointed beard and moustache. He was a traditionalist by nature, conservative, wary of threats from outsiders, but a subtle thinker whose advice was always considered, and inclined against rash action, particularly when conflict was involved. He carried his authority in his manner, and the respect he engendered – even among the boisterous young men of the *amabutho* – was immense.

In his day-to-day management of the uThulwana, when they were assembled for duty at one or another of the royal homesteads, Mnyamana was frequently in the company of the royal princes, and often ate in the same hut as Cetshwayo. Cetshwayo came to share his hopes and ambitions with Mnyamana, and this created a friendship between them that lasted throughout their lives. In the succession dispute of 1856, Mnyamana naturally supported Cetshwayo's party, and from that time he was in effect the *induna'nkhulu* in waiting, a leading representative of the new order which would follow King Mpande's death.

Mpande died in September or October 1872, and his funeral arrangements were organized by his chief adviser, Masiphula kaMamba. As an act of public recognition – to stave off the threat of internal challenges – Prince Cetshwayo issued an invitation to the Natal authorities to attend the coronation ceremonies, which would take place after nearly a year of mourning. Masiphula endorsed the invitation, but many conservative councillors, including Mnyamana, were wary of the price of such intervention, and in the event Cetshwayo was installed as king in the middle of August 1873, a fortnight before Theophilus Shepstone arrived to preside over a rather farcical ceremony of his own. Old Masiphula was dead by then; no sooner had he played his part in the traditional ceremony than Cetshwayo discarded him. He was excluded from the new king's councils, but was too prestigious a representative of the old regime to be allowed long to live; after sipping water one night from a gourd reserved for his personal use, he was suddenly taken ill, collapsed, and died.

The death of Masiphula marked Mnyamana's emergence as the new *induna'nkhulu*. As King Cetshwayo set about establishing his new court, he relied heavily upon the trusted Mnyamana. When construction of his new royal residence at oNdini began, only the girls of Mnyamana's Buthelezi clan were allowed to cut grass for the thatch, while two of Mnyamana's sons served as royal attendants.

Inkosi Mnyamana used his influence to curb the young king's frustrations in his dealing with whites. When Cetshwayo wanted to raid Swaziland, to earn prestige for his reign and enrich the national cattle herd, Mnyamana was among those who dissuaded him, pointing out that the move would undoubtedly alienate Zululand's white neighbours. When, throughout 1877 and 1878, relations deteriorated with British Natal, Mnyamana came increasingly to argue that the British should be placated where possible; not because of any sympathy for the whites, but for fear of the consequences for the Zulu people.

The crisis came to a head with the British ultimatum in December 1878 and it was clear to the council as a whole that the British could not be bought off. While Mnyamana was prepared to countenance the surrender of *inkosi* Sihayo's sons, named in the British ultimatum, neither he nor the rest of the king's advisers could accede to the British demands to dismantle the *amabutho* system. The king was left with little alternative but to assemble his army, and await British movements.

Among Mnyamana's responsibilities as *induna'nkhulu* was the overall control of the army. When news came that Lord Chelmsford had crossed the border at Rorke's Drift and, on 12 January 1879, attacked *inkosi* Sihayo's followers, Mnyamana played a leading and crucial role in determining the Zulu response. With a leading royalist supporter on the fragile western border attacked, and others in danger of being compromised, Mnyamana was among those who urged that the Zulu army be dispatched to the Rorke's Drift front in response. When, on 17 January, the army, having been ritually prepared, set out from the kwaNodwengu homestead, near oNdini, for the border, a number of Mnyamana's sons went with it.

The army, of course, encountered the British column at Isandlwana, and overran that part of it guarding the camp. It was, however, a desperately costly victory, with at least 1,000 warriors killed outright, and hundreds more mortally wounded. Among those killed was Mnyamana's son Mtumengana. Indeed, so great were the Zulu losses – and so ominous the lessons for future fighting – that Mnyamana urged the king to make peace while he was in a favourable position to do so.

In fact, of course, the British had no intention of opening negotiations until they had overthrown the Zulu kingdom, and over the following months all King Cetshwayo's peace overtures were rebuffed. By the middle of March, with British reinforcements gathering once more on the borders, it was clear that a new phase of fighting was imminent, and the king once more assembled the *amabutho* who had triumphed at Isandlwana. This time it was the northern border that seemed most vulnerable, especially following the pressure by Colonel Wood on local royalists like the abaQulusi, and the defection of Prince Hamu. When the army set out again, it did so for the north.

This time, *inkosi* Mnyamana accompanied the army in person. It was a measure of the importance Cetshwayo placed in the campaign that he sent with it his most senior and respected councillor to represent his 'eyes and ears', and to personally direct the strategy. On 28 March part of the army encountered and drove off the British foray against Hlobane Mountain; on 29 March the whole army attacked Wood's camp at Khambula. On route from their bivouac along the streams which feed the headwaters of the White Mfolozi River, near modern Vryheid, the army was halted for the customary application of last-minute protective medicines. It was usual on these occasions for the senior commander to address the assembled regiments, and *inkosi* Mnyamana stepped forward, drawing all his considerable power of oratory to stress the importance of the coming fight, emphasizing that the fate of the kingdom might lie in the balance. He left the young warriors who heard him 'burning like fire'.

When the army advanced to the attack, tactical direction passed to Mnyamana's great friend, Ntshingwayo kaMahole. The difficult ground over which the army was forced to approach, and the eagerness of the younger *amabutho* on either wing, meant, that the attack got off to an uncoordinated start, and despite hours of gallant attacks, which came at times within an ace of penetrating the British defences, it was defeated. Exhausted and dispirited, the retiring warriors were cut down by a particularly ruthless British pursuit. Mnyamana apparently attempted to rally them, hoping to catch the British now that they had emerged from their entrenchments, but his commanders, including Zibhebhu kaMaphitha, pointed out that it was too late. The rout continued, and that night, many men simply wandered home; it was left to Mnyamana Buthelezi to assemble those who would listen, and led them back to carry the mournful news to the king at oNdini.

The defeat at Khambula was the turning point in the war, for it was clear that the Zulus had little hope of winning it by military means alone. The country was once again filled with mourning; among the dead were two more of Mnyamana's sons. King Cetshwayo tried with increased urgency to open negotiations, but the British were now even less prepared to listen.

By the end of June 1879 Lord Chelmsford had reached the White Mfolozi River, in the very heart of Zululand. The king assembled his army, and held one last meeting of his council; no doubt the strategy for the coming contest, which both sides realized was likely to be the final one, was discussed. *inkosi* Mnyamana's advice is not recorded, but he no doubt played his part in deciding a strategy which, it was hoped, would see the British forces trapped in the open country near oNdini.

On 4 July Chelmsford crossed the river, and drew up in formation on ironically the very ground where the Zulus had hoped to trap him. *Inkosi* Mnyamana was apparently watching the battle with Cetshwayo's representative, Prince Ziwedu, from a hillside nearby. Sadly, however, the encircling movements which had proved so destructive at Isandlwana, and which had nearly triumphed at Khambula, were checked by a careful British deployment in square, and again the Zulu were defeated. A spirited charge by the 17th Lancers chased them from the field, and the British then rode in triumph from one royal homestead to the next, setting each on fire.

King Cetshwayo had not waited to witness the disaster, but had abandoned oNdini before the battle began. Significantly, he made for Mnyamana's ekuShumayeleni homestead on the Black Mfolozi. He was to remain there for a month, fruitlessly attempting to negotiate terms for his surrender. The British would have none of it, however, even when, on 14 August, Mnyamana, Ntshingwayo and two of Cetshwayo's brothers entered the camp of Sir Garnet Wolseley – Chelmsford's successor – at oNdini and offered up a large herd of cattle in the hope a securing a promise that the king's life would be secured. Wolseley refused to bargain, and detained the delegation, including Mnyamana, whom, over the following days, he tried to prize from his support of the king with bribery and threats.

In the event, with Mnyamana effectively in captivity, Cetshwayo left ekuShumayeleni for the Ngome forest, where British patrols tracked him down and captured him on 28 August. With the king in captivity, Wolseley set about disposing of his country, setting up thirteen appointees to rule on Britain's behalf. He offered *inkosi* Mnyamana a chieftainship, but Mnyamana refused, partly out of loyalty to Cetshwayo, and partly out of uncertainty over the fate of his followers, most of whom were placed under the defector, Prince Hamu kaNzibe.

In one of his last acts as King, Cetshwayo had given the care of his son and heir, Prince Dinuzulu, into the care of *inkosi* Zibhebhu. Once it became clear, however, that Zibhebhu was committed to the new post-war order, and had no interest in Cetshwayo's return, it was Mnyamana who sneaked Dinuzulu away from Zibhebhu's Bangonomo homestead, concealing him instead at one of his own homesteads, Opisweni, before passing him into the care of his uncle, Prince Ndabuko. Mnyamana continued to agitate for the king's return, supporting the efforts of Ndabuko, Shingana and others, and complaining of the mistreatment of his followers by Hamu.

When Cetshwayo returned to Zululand in 1883, Mnyamana hurried to greet him, and assumed his old role of *induna'nkhulu*. Such was the anger at *inkosi* Zibhebhu, for the indignities heaped upon royalists during the king's absence, that Prince Ndabuko assembled a force to attack him. The force mustered at Mnyamana's ekuShumayeleni homestead, and included a contingent commanded by Mnyamana's principle son, Tshanibezwe. When the force advanced against Zibhebhu, it was ambushed at Msebe on 30 March 1883 and routed. One of Mnyamana's sons, Ndulunga, was captured by Zibhebhu's forces.

In the aftermath of Msebe, there was a general mustering of the remaining royalist forces. Mnyamana assembled his followers in the Buthelezi territory, while the king himself gathered an army at oNdini, intent on attacking Zibhebhu from different directions. In the event they were forestalled by Zibhebhu's sudden and spectacularly successful attack on oNdini itself on 21 July.

With the destruction of oNdini, and subsequent death of King Cetshwayo himself, the royalist cause was in tatters. A new generation of younger, reckless royalist leaders, crystallizing around Prince Dinuzulu himself, were prepared to offer land to the Boers in return for their military support.

Inkosi Mnyamana was now in his seventies. He retained an enormous influence over Prince Dinuzulu, but had lived to see the fall of the old Zulu order, and the inexorable advance of European encroachment. He recognized the futility of taking up arms against the British, and he dreaded – quite rightly – the Boer lust for land. Typically, the advice he gave Dinuzulu was cautious; he argued against the involvement of the Boers, and against further attacks of Zibhebhu, whom he characterized as 'a dog on a lead held by the British'. When Dinuzulu decided anyway to invite Boer participation, unleashing a chain of events which would lead inevitably to another clash with British arms, *inkosi* Mnyamana acquiesced, but he was to remain distanced from Dinuzulu's subsequent struggles. Zibhebhu was duly defeated at the Battle of Tshaneni, but the subsequent Boer land-grab provoked a British reaction, and in 1888 Dinuzulu found himself in open rebellion against them. The support of the Buthelezi people was split, a number of Mnyamana's sons joining the rebels, while Mnyamana himself tried either to hold aloof, or reluctantly supplied auxiliaries for the British.

The 1888 rebellion ended in defeat, as Mnyamana had expected, and Dinuzulu and his uncles Ndabuko and Shingana were sent into exile. It was the final ruin of the military traditions of the Royal House, for whom Mnyamana had been a leading councillor for three generations, and the throwing over of a way of life for which he had fought fiercely all his life. Perhaps fortunately, he did not live long enough to see much of the steady erosion of Zulu economic and political independence which followed; he died on 29 July 1892.

The House of Ngqengele continued to play a significant part in Zulu affairs. Mnyamana's son, Tshanibezwe, succeeded as *inkosi* of the Buthelezi, and was an adviser to Dinuzulu until his death in June 1906. Dinuzulu's successor, Solomon Nkayishana – whose life was dominated by a drive to restore the status and prestige of the Zulu monarchy – appointed Tshanibezwe's son, Mathole Buthelezi, as one of his principle councillors. A sister of

King Solomon, Princess Constance Magogo, married *inkosi* Buthelezi. In an attempt to heal the rift with *inkosi* Zibhebhu's followers, Solomon appointed Bokwe kaZibhebhu to serve him alongside *inkosi* Mathole. Mathole Buthelezi died in 1942; his son, Mangosuthu Buthelezi, born to Princess Magogo in August 1928, was not formally installed as *inkosi* of the Buthelezi until 1957. Mangosuthu Buthelezi has also served as a leading adviser to the present king, HM Goodwill Zwelithini. Dr Buthelezi is also, of course, a prominent politician, leader of the Inkatha Freedom Party, and a former Minister of the Interior of the South African government.

Ndabuko kaMpande Zulu, Prince

Prince Ndabuko was born to King Mpande and his wife Ngqumbazi Zungu about 1842. Prince Ndabuko was a full brother to King Cetshwayo, and was a close personal friend and political ally throughout his life, and a leader of the royalist cause after the king's death. During the succession crisis of 1856, the teenage Ndabuko was a prominent member of King Cetshwayo's party, and he would remain his confidant and adviser. He was a member of the uMbonambi *ibutho*, which was enrolled in 1863.

During the British invasion of 1879, Prince Ndabuko took part with his regiment, and was present during the Isandlwana campaign. The uMbonambi were credited by the Zulus as having been the first regiment to enter the British camp, and Prince Ndabuko, who was a decisive and energetic man, was among those who pursued the British survivors to Sothondose's Drift. Here, according to his own account, he saw a number of warriors attempting to cross the river, and, '...called to members of his own regiment, the Umbonambi, to join them; but they declined on the grounds that it was necessary to return to the field of battle to attend to their wounded'.

Many of the warriors were, in any case, exhausted, and at the river those who attempted to cross were reminded of the king's prohibition on doing so by the *induna* Vumandaba kaNthati.

With the capture of King Cetshwayo at Ngome on 28 August 1879, Ndabuko regarded himself as temporary head of the royal lineage. Before his capture, King Cetshwayo had passed his son and heir, Prince Dinuzulu, and a number of women from his *isigodlo*, into the care of *inkosi* Zibhebhu kaMaphitha of the Mandlakazi area. After the king's capture, the British confirmed Zibhebhu as one of their appointed rulers in Zululand, and the boundaries of his territory were extended to include the homestead of Prince Ndabuko. Shortly after the king's exile, as it became clear that Zibhebhu had little interest in furthering the cause of the Royal House, Mnyamana Buthelezi smuggled Prince Dinuzulu out of Zibhebhu's Bangonomo homestead, and sheltered him at his Opisweni homestead, before passing Dinuzulu into the care of Ndabuko; Zibhebhu, however, refused to give up a number of the royal women and the cattle which King Cetshwayo had allocated for their care, arguing that Cetshwayo was no longer king, and that he, Zibhebhu, was now a ruler in his own right. Prince Ndabuko was indignant that a member of a junior lineage should assume such airs; this incident was widely held to be the origin of the split between the Royal House and Zibhebhu's Mandlakazi section, and it marked the emergence of Prince Ndabuko as both Prince Dinuzulu's guardian and a leading spokesman in the royalist cause.

During the king's absence, Prince Ndabuko and a number of his brothers, including the Princes Shingana, Sitheku and Mpande, agitated for King Cetshwayo's return. In May 1880 Ndabuko headed a large contingent of prominent royalists who walked all the way to the colonial capital of Pietermaritzburg, and presented themselves to Bishop Colenso, complaining of the injustices perpetrated by the British appointees in Zululand, and begging for the king's return. Colenso was sympathetic, but the authorities merely told them that they should make their complaints to the British Resident in Zululand. Ndabuko returned to Zululand and promptly did so; this time he was told bluntly that he was now only a commoner and should not consider himself entitled to be involved in the politics of Zululand. In the meantime the situation in Zululand had deteriorated, with frequent violence between royalist supporters and the most strident of the British appointees. At the end of August 1881, the acting High Commissioner for south-east Africa, Sir Evelyn Wood, held a meeting of prominent Zulus at the seat of the British Residency at

Nhlazatshe. Forthright denouncements by leading members of the Royal House, including Ndabuko, only resulted in a reaffirmation of British policy, and furthermore a directive that Ndabuko and Dinuzulu should be removed from Zibhebhu's district and made to live under John Dunn. Since Dunn was an active ally of Zibhebhu, and regarded by the Royal House as a traitor for changing sides in 1879, this only increased Prince Ndabuko's resentment. For many Zulus the meeting at Nhlazatshe marked the beginning of the Zulu civil war.

In an attempt to stem the rising tide of violence, the British again partitioned Zululand, and restored King Cetshwayo to a portion of his former territory. Prince Ndabuko immediately rallied to his cause and attended the king's installation on 29 January 1883. The king's return merely increased the desire among his long-suffering followers to avenge themselves on those who had persecuted them during his absence. At the end of March 1883 Prince Ndabuko assembled a large force of royalist supporters which advanced to attack *inkosi* Zibhebhu in northern Zululand. Zibhebhu lured them into a trap, however, and ambushed them in the Msebe valley on 30 March. Thousands of royalists were killed during the subsequent rout, and their leaders, including Prince Ndabuko, only just managed to escape.

The disaster at Msebe led to widespread violence across Zululand. King Cetshwayo began to assemble his supporters at his rebuilt oNdini homestead, including many of the most influential councillors and *amakhosi* of his old regime. Prince Ndabuko gathered the surviving royalist forces in northern Zululand and hurried to the muster, but events forestalled him; on 21 July Zibhebhu launched a surprise attack on oNdini and utterly routed the forces assembled there. The king only just managed to escape; most of his councillors were killed. Prince Ndabuko's followers were within a few miles of the battlefield when they heard of the catastrophe, and turned back. King Cetshwayo himself fled to Eshowe, the seat of the British Reserve Territory, where he died in February 1884.

A number of the king's brothers visited him during his last days, among them Princes Ndabuko, Shingana, Ziwedu and Dabulamanzi. Cetshwayo is said to have given the care of his heir,

Prince Dinuzulu, into the hands of Dabulamanzi, but as the senior surviving member of his House, Prince Ndabuko was, after the king's death, both Dinuzulu's guardian and head of the royalist cause. In May 1884 Dinuzulu appealed to the Transvaal Boers to help him against Zibhebhu; on 20 May Ndabuko, Ziwedu and Shingana installed him as king in a traditional Zulu ceremony, and on the following day the Boers formally recognized him. The practical result of this alliance was a combined royalist/Boer expedition which defeated Zibhebhu at the Battle of Tshaneni on 5 June.

The price to be paid by the royalists for Boer involvement in their struggle was a high one. Dinuzulu was forced to accede to Boer demands for land which effectively alienated all of western Zululand. The spectre of unlimited Boer access to the sea – with the involvement by rival European powers in the region – provoked a reaction from the British authorities, who worked fast to limit Boer claims, and on 19 May 1887 formerly annexed what was left of Zululand, thereby assuming a responsibility they had steadfastly denied since 1879. The annexation was greeted with much bitterness by Prince Dinuzulu, who had striven to restore a part of his birthright; encouraged by his uncle Ndabuko, Dinuzulu assembled an armed following at Ceza mountain in northern Zululand. When a British patrol attempted to arrest him on 2 June 1888, they were chased from the field by Dinuzulu's men. The British then hurried troops into Zululand, and called upon long-standing supporters, like *inkosi* Zibhebhu, to support them. On 23 June a royalist force led by Dinuzulu and Ndabuko launched a daring attack on Zibhebhu's camp at Ivuna, and scattered him.

Yet the royalist ascendancy was short-lived. The Zulu people were divided against themselves by a decade of destructive civil war, and stood little chance of repeating even the limited successes of 1879. On 2 July 1888 the British broke up a royalist concentration at Hlopekhulu, near Ulundi, under the command of Prince Shingana kaMpande; after sporadic fighting, Dinuzulu and Ndabuko crossed into the Transvaal republic in the hope of finding sanctuary. The Transvaal was unwilling to protect them, and Ndabuko surrendered to the British on 17 September, and

Dinuzulu on 15 November.

Ndabuko, Dinuzulu and Shingana were all tried for high treason at the gaol at Eshowe between February and April 1889. All three were found guilty, and sentenced to be exiled. Prince Ndabuko received the severest sentence of fifteen years; Dinuzulu received ten years and Shingana twelve.

At the end of 1889 they were sent to the island of St Helena. They were allowed to take with them one male attendant each, Ndabuko and Shingana, being married men, were allowed two wives, while Dinuzulu was allowed two female attendants from his *isigodlo*.

In December 1897 all three were allowed to return to Zululand. Dinuzulu's position was severely limited by the British authorities, who refused to acknowledge him as king, but merely head of the royalist section. The experience of exile had severely dampened the will of all three senior representatives of the Royal House to resist the tide of Imperial control; in 1906 Dinuzulu refused to openly commit himself to the Poll Tax rebellion.

Nomguqo Dlamini, 'Paulina'

Nomguqo Dlamini was born about 1858 in the territory of the Buthelezi people, in north-central Zululand. Her father, Sikhunyane Dlamini, was a member of the Royal House of Swaziland, and had been captured as a herd boy during a military expedition in King Dingane's reign. He had been given into the care of a headman of the Buthelezi, and grew up to become a man of some importance. He was enrolled in the iHlaba *ibutho* (raised about 1837), was present at the death of the Boer leader Piet Retief, and was a royal messenger who maintained a household of five wives. Nomguqo was his daughter by his fifth and 'great wife', and was regarded as the senior of his children.

In 1872, Nomguqo was given on behalf of the Buthelezi into the *isigodlo* of Prince Cetshwayo kaMpande. The term *isigodlo* refers to both a senior man's private and secluded household, and the girls who attended him there. It was the custom of *amakhosi* to present likely candidates as tribute to join the royal *isigodlo*. The king had call upon their services, and could dispose of them in marriage, usually in order to build political alliances. The girls of

196

the *isigodlo* were forbidden contact with the outside world; they performed the menial tasks of the royal court, and a select number were used by the king as concubines. During the nineteenth century, the great Zulu kings maintained *isigodlo* containing several hundred such women.

Nomguqo first attended Prince Cetshwayo shortly before King Mpande's death. She then lived for a while at Cetshwayo's homestead near the coast, kwaNdlangubo. When Cetshwayo became king and established a new homestead at oNdini, Nomguqo was transferred there.

Nomguqo lived through the last crucial years of King Cetshwayo's reign. She witnessed the building of oNdini, Theophilus Shepstone's expedition to crown Cetshwayo king, saw the great ceremonies which took place in the royal homestead, and witnessed from the inside the growing tension which resulted from the growing crisis with Natal. She remained at one royal homestead or another throughout the British invasion, and was among those ordered to prepare for the king's flight on the eve of the Battle of Ulundi. Cetshwayo sent his heir Dinuzulu into *inkosi* Zibhebhu kaMaphitha's territory, and Nomguqo was one of the *isigodlo* girls appointed to accompany him. Once it became clear that Zibhebhu intended to appropriate the king's property – including the royal women – they fled, and in the political chaos that followed the post-war settlement, Nomguqo described how she and other Zulu non-combatants were forced to hide in caves to avoid the ravages of civil war.

It is her account of daily life in the inner recesses of oNdini which makes Nomguqo's story invaluable, however. Still a young girl, she describes the daily routine of fetching water and preparing food for the king, and records the rituals which circumscribed almost every aspect of the king's life:

When the king was about to partake of a meal, two of his grooms would move around the *umuzi*, calling out 'Ungathinti!' meaning literally, 'don't disturb!' but also that no one was permitted to cough. One of the menservants would walk round one side of the *umuzi*, the second one on the other side, all the time calling out 'Ungathinti!' Everyone then knew that the king was eating and that coughing was prohibited. When I suffered an attack of asthma during such times I had to leave the *umuzi*, together with others who felt the need to cough...

Nomguqo thought Cetshwayo 'very good looking and of a royal demeanour'. He was taciturn and thoughtful, but a stickler for the etiquette of Zulu custom, and frequently punished those who lapsed in this regard. Most punishments consisted of a fine of one head of cattle, but in extreme circumstances Cetshwayo consigned the miscreant to the long walk across country to the kwaNkatha hill, on the banks of the Mfolozi River, in the company of the state executioner. Nomguqo noted that Cetshwayo did have people killed, but that 'he was more considerate [than others] and did not have people killed without some reason, or merely for the sake of killing'.

In 1887 Nomguqo experienced a number of dreams which a trader named Gert van Rooyen interpreted as a sign that she was called to become a Christian. She was baptized at the Hermannsburg mission at Ehlanzeni in northern Zululand on 21 December 1887 and took the name Paulina. Thereafter, she became heavily involved in mission work in Zululand, and worked as a servant for van Rooyen. During the Anglo-Boer War, van Rooyen moved to Ladysmith and was caught up in the siege; he then fled to join a brother who farmed near Holkrans, outside Vryheid. In 1902 Paulina heard rumours of the impending abaQulusi action against the Boer commandos operating around Holkrans, and was able to warn van Rooyen, who left before the abaQulusi launched their attack.

In the 1920s, Paulina met the Hermansburg missionary Heinrich Filter who, from 1925, took an interest in her history. In 1939 Filter invited Paulina to stay at his mission at Elandskraal, near Rorke's Drift, with a view to transcribing her story. Written down in Filter's native German, it was finally translated by the noted linguist and expert on Zulu affairs, 'SB' Bourquin, and published in 1986 under the title *Paulina Dlamini; Servant of Two Kings*. It remains the only detailed account of life in the pre-conquest Zulu court from a female perspective.

Nomguqo Paulina Dlamini died on 12 December 1942.

Ntshingwayo kaMahole

Ntshingwayo was born about 1810 into the chiefly line of the Khoza people, who lived on the upper reaches of the White Mfolozi, north of Nhlazatshe Mountain. The link between the Khoza and the Zulu had been established early; Ntshingwayo's father had apparently been a friend and companion of the young Zulu *inkosi* Sezangakhona kaJama, and the two hunted and herded cattle together. In some versions of the story, Mahole was among those who was present when Sezangakhona first encountered Nandi, the girl from the Langeni people, as she gathered water at the riverside one day in the 1770s. Senzangakhona's relationship with Nandi, of course, led to the birth of the famous Shaka and to the dramatic changes in the course of Zulu history. Mathole had become one of King Shaka's advisers; his son, Ntshingwayo, went on to be a trusted confidant of no less than two of Shaka's successors.

Little is known about Ntshingwayo's early career. He was enrolled in the uDlambedlu *ibutho* and probably served with them during King Dingane's disastrous war against the Voortrekkers in 1838. Since by 1879 he was regarded as a distinguished and experienced warrior, he may well have held a junior or regimental command during some of Mpande's expeditions into Swaziland. He certainly enjoyed King Mpande's trust to a remarkable degree, and he was considered to be one of a small handful of councillors who were *pakathi* – on the inside – who enjoyed privileged access to the affairs of state at the highest level, and who were part of the national decision-making process. Ntshingwayo became a close personal friend of Masiphula kaMamba, King Mpande's senior *induna*, and Mpande appointed Ntshingwayo to the command of the eMlambongwenya royal homestead. Prince Cetshwayo spent a good deal of time during his youth at eMlambongwenya, sowing the seeds of a future relationship with Ntshingwayo which would last beyond Mpande's reign.

In 1856 the Royal House was split by a succession crisis between the rival sons of Mpande, Princes Mbuyazi and Cetshwayo. When Mbuyazi failed to secure sufficient support within Zululand, Mpande apparently entrusted Ntshingwayo with a secret message urging Mbuyazi to flee across the border and seek support from the colonial authorities in Natal. The message was never delivered because Ntshingwayo's mission was intercepted, and Cetshwayo's army in any case caught Mbuyazi's followers at Ndondakusuka, on the banks of the flooded Thukela, and all but destroyed them. Nevertheless, such was the regard in which Cetshwayo held Ntshingwayo's integrity as a royal servant that he never held Ntshingwayo to account for his actions on Mbuyazi's behalf, and indeed throughout the latter years of Mpande's reign Ntshingwayo enjoyed the respect of both the old king and the heir apparent. When, in the late 1860s, Mpande was increasingly troubled by intrusive Boer settlements along the border with the Transvaal republic, it was Ntshingwayo whom he instructed to establish a royal homestead in the area as an assertion of Zulu authority.

When Mpande died in 1872, Ntshingwayo survived Cetshwayo's succession well enough. Not all of the old order did so; Cetshwayo considered that Ntshingwayo's colleague Masiphula had been far too vocal in his earlier support of Prince Mbuyazi. Masiphula presided over the installation ceremonies in 1873, and promptly announced his intention to retire from public life. This did not save him, however, for he was far too influential within the kingdom for Cetshwayo to tolerate his presence. Invited to the royal homestead one day, Masiphula took a drink from a gourd reserved for his personal use – and within a few hours suddenly collapsed and died.

As king, one of Cetshwayo's first acts was to appoint Mnyamana kaNgqengelele, *inkosi* of the Buthelezi, as his new senior *induna*. Mnyamana and Ntshingwayo were of a similar age, and were also personal friends; Ntshingwayo soon found himself enjoying a similar relationship as a supporter and political ally of Mnyamana as he had previously enjoyed with Masiphula. King Cetshwayo appointed Ntshingwayo as commander of the kwaGqikazi royal homestead, and seems to have regarded him as commander-in-chief of the Zulu army.

When, from 1877, the increasingly strained relationship with British Natal seemed likely to spill into open conflict, both Mnyamana and Ntshingwayo advocated a cautious policy. They were fearful of the consequences of going to war with the British, and advocated appeasing them where possible. Nonetheless, both men recognized that the central demands of the ultimatum of 1878 – the disbandment of the Zulu army and the acceptance of a British envoy at the Zulu court – were incompatible with the country's independent status, and they regretfully accepted the inevitability of armed resistance. Both were intimately involved with planning the national defence, and when the Zulu army left oNdini on 17 January for the border, Ntshingwayo marched with it as senior commander.

On the eve of war Ntshingwayo is described as being about seventy years old, a stocky, powerful man whose grey hairs and paunch belied a physical toughness and commanding presence. He was both an astute strategist and a charismatic leader, renowned as an orator and for his knowledge of Zulu history and the praise-poems of the Zulu kings. He had a natural air of authority, the result of years of experience in marshalling the often-unruly *amabutho*. It says much of his character that when the army marched to the front, Ntshingwayo and his colleague Mavumengwana kaNdlela walked at the head of their men rather than riding horses as many *izinduna* did, setting a comfortable and practical pace which would not exhaust the army.

By 20 January – the same day that Lord Chelmsford's column advanced to Isandlwana – the Zulu army reached Siphezi Mountain, about fifteen miles away. Ntshingwayo sent messengers to open communications with *inkosi* Matshana kaMondise of the Sithole people, whose territory lay along the Mangeni River, but, discovering that British patrols were active in the area and wary of Matshana's intentions, Ntshingwayo directed the army to move away from Sithole territory, towards the sheltered Ngwebeni valley. That the move was accomplished on the 21st, without discovery by the British, was arguably one of the great Zulu masterstrokes of the war.

Although King Cetshwayo had given responsibility for the field command to Ntshingwayo and Mavumengwana, he had instructed them not to provoke the British, in the hope that a negotiated settlement to the crisis might prove possible. This effectively allowed the British the military initiative, but Ntshingwayo was discussing his options for an attack on the camp with his officers late on the morning of the 22nd when British patrols, following up foragers from the uKhandempemvu regiment, stumbled upon the hidden Zulu army. The uKhandempemvu promptly launched an attack, sucking in the other regiments behind them. Ntshingwayo managed to hold back only those *amabutho* furthest from the British incursion, administering to them only the last-minute pre-battle rituals and command directives, before hurrying after his attacking army. Many of the regimental commanders who had been in discussion with him were, in the meantime, able to rejoin their regiments and impose some direction on the attack. By the time Ntshingwayo reached the edge of the iNyoni escarpment, overlooking the camp at Isandlwana, the battle was already underway. His choice of personal viewpoint again testifies to his skill and experience; it allowed him a panoramic view of almost the entire battlefield, in contrast to the limited perspective of the British officers at the foot of Isandlwana below. From his position – which was within easy range of the British artillery – Ntshingwayo was able to direct the attack with runners. In particular, when the uKhandempemvu regiment in the Zulu centre, directly below his viewpoint, stalled under the heavy fire of the British 24th, Ntshingwayo recognized the danger this posed to the Zulu assault, and he reacted quickly, sending Mkhosana kaMvundlana to rally the uKhandempemvu and urge them on.

Despite the impromptu nature of the Zulu attack, Isandlwana was very much Ntshingwayo's victory. He had outmanoeuvred Lord Chelmsford, moving his army to within five miles of the British camp without being detected, and his thorough scouting and command briefings had laid the basis for the Zulu success. He had, moreover, managed to regain command after the initial confusion, and had intervened at key points to direct the victory. Only his failure to properly prepare the entire army with the necessary rituals – the result of the spontaneous nature of the attack – which resulted, in the eyes of many Zulu, in the terrible casualty rate, detracted from his achievement. Two of Ntshingwayo's own sons were badly wounded in the battle, perhaps mortally.

It was customary for a Zulu army to return to report to the king after a great victory, but such was the exhaustion following Isandlwana that many warriors simply went home to recover. Ntshingwayo accompanied the rest to oNdini, although they straggled into the royal homestead looking more like a defeated army than a victorious one.

For two months Cetshwayo allowed the men to rest at their personal homesteads, but by late March it was clear that the British were on the verge of a new offensive and the *amabutho* were re-assembled. This time they were sent north to attack Colonel Wood's column at Khambula hill. Ntshingwayo was again in military command, but such was the importance the Zulu placed upon this campaign that Cetshwayo's senior *induna*, *inkosi* Mnyamana Buthelezi, accompanied the expedition as the king's personal representative. On 28 March part of the army encountered the British foray against Hlobane Mountain, but there is no evidence that Ntshingwayo himself directed the attack. The following day, after Mnyamana had addressed the assembled regiments, the army attacked Khambula.

Once again, Ntshingwayo took up a commanding position, observing the British positions from a low knoll within artillery range. This time, however, his skills were frustrated by the British preparedness, and by the indiscipline of the younger *amabutho*, who allowed themselves to be provoked into launching uncoor-dinated attacks. Ntshingwayo was never able to regain the initiative; the British concentrated to meet each Zulu attack, breaking them piecemeal, and the Zulus were at last driven off with heavy losses.

After Khambula, it was increasingly obvious to both King Cetshwayo and his advisers that the Zulu stood little chance of winning the war on purely military grounds. Nevertheless, after the king's attempts to open negotiations with the British had failed, and Lord Chelmsford had advanced to the White Mfolozi River, the *amabutho* were summoned in a last-ditch attempt to defend the Zulu heartland. On 2 July the king convened a command council which was attended by Mnyamana, Ntshingwayo and others. It was decided that, if possible, the British should be lured onto the oNdini plain, towards an exposed spot close to the kwaNodwengu homestead, and attacked from all sides.

Ironically, Chelmsford had selected the same spot himself as his preferred battleground. Early on the morning of 4 July he crossed the White Mfolozi and formed his troops into a square. The Zulu *amabutho* promptly surrounded them and attacked, but the devastating curtain of British fire prevented their charges from striking home. They were eventually driven from the field by a ruthless cavalry charge.

The senior Zulu commanders survived the battle. Over the following weeks, the British paraded through the countryside, overawing those who were still inclined to resist while at the same time attempting to persuade the influential *amakhosi* to surrender. On 14 August a deputation of senior men entered Lord Wolseley's camp near the ruins of oNdini to ask that Cetshwayo – who was still then at large – should be spared. Mnyamana and Ntshingwayo were among them, and they were adamant that they had not 'run away to the Whites', but had merely asked for the king's life. The capture of the king a fortnight later nevertheless brought home the realities of defeat.

It was Wolseley's decision to divide the country into thirteen independent chiefdoms and to overthrow the authority of the Zulu Royal House. King Cetshwayo's influential brothers were all excluded from the settlement, and two of the appointees were men who had fought for the British during the war. Because of Mnyamana's influence throughout the kingdom, Wolseley was particularly keen that he should accept a chieftainship, but Mnyamana refused and the post was offered to Ntshingwayo instead. Seeing that Mnyamana had effectively isolated himself from political power in the new order, Ntshingwayo accepted. Ntshingwayo's territory included that of his own people, the Khoza, and lay between Hlobane Mountain in the north and Nhlazatshe in the south. Nevertheless, Ntshingwayo remained loyal to the royalist cause, and in 1880 was among those who went to Bishop Colenso in Natal to petition for King Cetshwayo's return. Like most of those dependent upon the British for his authority, however, he was still resented by die-hard royalists who felt that he should not have accepted the chieftainship; his frustration with this view probably explains a comment, on the eve of Cetshwayo's restoration, that he no longer supported the House of Shaka, and would rather move into the newly-designated British Reserve.

In fact, when Cetshwayo was restored in February 1883 Ntshingwayo did not move into the British Reserve. He travelled to the new oNdini homestead to *konza* - pay his respects – to King Cetshwayo, but while there was apparently insulted by royalists. Perhaps because of this he was not involved in the disastrous Msebe expedition in March, when his military expertise was sorely missed. Nevertheless, he was at oNdini again in July when Cetshwayo summoned all prominent royalists to address the violent rift with *inkosi* Zibhebhu's Mandlakazi. Ntshingwayo was present at the royal homestead when Zibhebhu launched his surprise attack at dawn on the morning of 21 July.

Little information has survived on Ntshingwayo's role in his last battle. King Cetshwayo had appointed him to command the uDloko *ibutho* – veterans of Rorke's Drift – which formed part of the royalist centre, but in fact the royalist forces had hurried out to meet the enemy in a state of great confusion, many of them without their officers who were still conferring with the king, and it is quite possible that they had already collapsed by the time Ntshingwayo reached the front. In the subsequent rout most of the young warriors managed to escape, but the elderly senior officers of the old order were caught and killed. Ntshingwayo was among them. It is said that *inkosi* Zibhebhu regretted the deaths of very few among the royalist notables, most of whom he recognized as bitter enemies; one exception he made was that of Ntshingwayo, whose bravery, loyalty and military skills he much admired.

It is, of course, a bitter irony that Ntshingwayo, the great Zulu victor of Isandlwana, should be killed along with more than fifty distinguished men, many of whom had served not only Cetshwayo but King Mpande before him, not by foreign enemies but by his fellow countrymen, and in a civil war which was the logical conclusion of the policy of 'divide and rule' pursued by the British since the invasion. Nor was there redemption, even in death; the British Resident, Henry Fynn Jnr., noted that ten days after the battle some of Ntshingwayo's sons visited the battlefield in the hope of burying their father's remains. They were unsuccessful, however, 'owing to the decomposed state of the dead about Ulundi ... they were unable to identify Ntyingwayo's remains'.

It is uncertain whether Ntshingwayo kaMahole was ever photographed. A photograph, depicting a man fitting his description sitting holding a firearm and surrounded by members of his family, has been identified as him and has been widely reproduced as such. An element of doubt remains, however, because of the notoriously casual way many such portraits were captioned at the time, and indeed other copies of this portrait exist which have been variously identified, quite inaccurately, as Cetshwayo himself or Prince Hamu. Photographs of Ntshingwayo kaMahole's younger kinsman, Ntshingwayo kaSikhonyana (head of a section of the Khoza living in the Eshowe district) have often been mistaken for him. Ntshingwayo kaSikhonyana was a heavy man with famously pendulous breasts and posed for a number of photographs at his homestead, surrounded by his wives and *izinduna*, his body usually hidden beneath a white shirt.

There is one contemporary image which undoubtedly represents Ntshingwayo kaMahole. His body was sketched by W.A. Walton, the 'special artist' for the *Pictorial World*, as it lay stretched out and disfigured by stab wounds on his great war shield on the battlefield of oNdini. It remains one of the most poignant images of the post-war catastrophe inflicted upon the Zulu people.

Phalane kaMdinwa

Phalane was born about 1813, and enrolled in the uMkhulutshane regiment in King Dingane's time. He became a royal *induna* during King Mpande's time, and served as regent for the Dube people on the coast during the minority of their *inkosi* Lokothwayo kaMadlebe. When Lokothwayo achieved his majority late in Mpande's reign, Phalane was made senior *induna* of the Dlangezwa section – descended from a royal homestead established by King Shaka – on the lower Mhlatuze River. Phalane was regarded as a senior royal representative in the affairs of the coastal people, and he sat on the royal council. He was described as a tall, dignified man who habitually wore brass bangles around his neck and ankles, and cultivated the long fingernails of the Zulu aristocrat. In December 1878, he was one of the Zulu representatives who crossed the Lower Thukela to hear Frere's ultimatum. When war broke out, he was a commander of the force dispatched under Godide kaNdlela to halt Colonel Pearson's advance, and he fought at the Battle of Nyezane on 22 January. When Lord Chelmsford advanced to relieve Eshowe at the end of March, Phalane again held a command among the Zulus assembled to oppose him, and he fought at the Battle of kwaGingindlovu on 2 April. He surrendered to Major General H.H. Crealock's forces, together with a number of other notables from the coastal districts, on 4 July.

Sigcwelegcwele kaMhlekehleke

Sigcwelegcwele was *inkosi* of the Ngadini people who lived in the foothills of the Ngoya Mountains, not far from KwaMagwaza. Born in the late 1820s, Sigcwelegcwele was one of a group of younger *amakhosi* and distinguished warriors who were associated with King Cetshwayo in his youth, before his accession, and who were broadly his contemporaries in age. Such men formed a clique of favourites whom King Cetshwayo used to offset the influence of the King Mpande's elderly councillors and to assert his position against the independent aspirations of the powerful regional nobles. Such considerations influenced Sigcwelegcwele's appointment as commander of the iNgobamakhosi *ibutho*. Formed during the last years of Mpande's reign, at a time when Prince Cetshwayo was increasingly asserting his influence over state affairs, the iNgobamakhosi were heavily patronized by Cetshwayo, and the choice of Sigcwelegcwele as their senior *induna* placed this large, young and notoriously boisterous regiment directly under Cetshwayo's control. Nevertheless, following Mpande's death in 1872 Cetshwayo remained wary of challenges to his accession, and Sigcwelegcwele was prominent among his supporters during the installation ceremonies of 1873. On this occasion Sigcwelegcwele was slightly injured during an exuberant volley by the regiments. Although not loaded with shot, a gun discharged by a man standing behind him burnt a hole in Sigcwelegcwele's ceremonial dress of cow-tails and scorched his shoulder.

In 1882 Bertram Mitford described Sigcwelegcwele as 'a fine-looking man, in the prime of life, tall and broad-shouldered, [who] carried his shaven head as erect as if it ought to wear a crown instead of a shiny ring of mimosa'. He was self-assured and a confident and aggressive fighter, qualities which were essential given his position at the centre of the kingdom's generational and regional conflicts. At the great *umkhosi* ceremony – the annual gathering of the nation designed to bless the new harvest – which took place in December 1877, these tensions irrupted into open violence, with Sigcwelegcwele himself at the centre of events. The entire army was mustered in its finery and quartered at the cluster of royal homesteads on the Mahlabatini plain, which constituted King Cetshwayo's capital. The great oNdini homestead had traditionally been the quarters for the uThulwana *ibutho* on such occasions. The uThulwana enjoyed a high status within the kingdom, as Cetshwayo himself had been enrolled in them as a youth, together with a number of other royal princes. They were, moreover, commanded by Prince Hamu kaMpande, arguably the most powerful regional magnate in the country, and *inkosi* Mnyamana Buthelezi, the king's most trusted councillor. The uThulwana were married men in their mid-forties who had recently been bolstered by having the younger iNdlondlo incorporated into their ranks. When the king had given permission for the iNdlondlo to marry in 1875, to take on an equal social status with the uThulwana, there had been disturbances across the country because the iNdlondlo had been directed to take their brides from among a group of younger girls, many of whom had already given their affections to men from younger regiments, including the iNgobamakhosi.

These resentments still festered in 1877 when King Cetshwayo decided to quarter the iNgobamakhosi at oNdini for the *umkhosi*, alongside the uThulwana and the iNdlondlo. Tensions between the two immediately ran high – the uThulwana resenting the insolence of the younger men, and the iNgobamakhosi the airs of the older – and these were reflected one night during an exchange over the beer pot between the two commanders. *Inkosi*

Mnyamana made disparaging remarks about the untested fighting abilities of the iNgobomakhosi, and Sigcwelegcwele snapped back 'you shall see tomorrow when they go out'. The following morning, the uThulwana and iNdlondlo formed up to march out of the homestead to take part in the ceremonies, but the iNgobamakhosi sullenly hung back. At last the iNgobamakhosi were brought out of their huts and formed up, but as they marched towards the homestead's narrow gate they became mixed up with rear guard of the uThulwana, who were just ahead. In the congestion a scuffle broke out and soon exploded into a general stick-fight which raged through the huts and out onto the plain beyond. When Prince Hamu was told of the clash he lost his temper at the insult afforded to his dignity by a regiment of youths – and ordered the uThulwana to arm with spears. The men hurried to their huts and returned to attack the iNgobamakhosi with a vengeance, driving them out of oNdini and into the open veld. King Cetshwayo tried several times to halt the fighting but his messengers could not get close to the scene for fear of being attacked themselves. Sporadic clashes continued throughout the day, and only died down when the uThulwana returned victoriously to their huts that night, leaving the iNgobamakhosi to sleep in the hills. The following day the two *amabutho* were reformed and kept apart. Prince Hamu was furious at Sigcwelegcwele, blaming him for allowing the incident to happen; he demanded that Cetshwayo put Sigcwelegcwele to death, but the king stood by his favourite, opening a rift with Hamu which had not healed by the time of the British invasion a year later. Sigcwelegcwele was sent home under a cloud of royal disapproval, but according to John Dunn, the elderly councillors attempted to secure their objective by other means, and complained to King Cetshwayo that Sigcwelegcwele was using magic to secure the king's good offices, sending a familiar spirit in the form of a hyena to visit the king's quarters at night. They planned to summon Sigcwelegcwele to the king under a false pretext, then have him executed for witchcraft. Dunn, knowing that Sigcwelegcwele was one of the king's most loyal supporters, sent to him to warn him to make excuses and keep out of the king's way until at last Dunn persuaded Cetshwayo that the accusations were false.

In 1879, Sigcwelegcwele commanded the iNgobamakhosi during the Isandlwana campaign. After the battle he returned to his homestead on the Mhlatuze, and helped to direct the investment of Colonel Pearson's force at Eshowe. Some 3,000 Zulus were quartered in temporary barracks within a few miles of the British position, and were rotated to provide a cordon sealing off the escape route towards the Natal border; Sigcwelegcwele shared the command with Prince Dabulamanzi and Phalane kaMdinwa. When Lord Chelmsford crossed the Thukela to march to Pearson's relief, the Zulus moved forward to block him, and Sigcwelegcwele was present at the Battle of Gingindlovu on 2 April 1879.

The British victory at Gingindlovu and the relief of Eshowe was a severe blow to Zulu hopes in the coastal sector, and these were reduced still further by the reorganization of British troops and by the advance across the region of the 1st Division under Major General H.H. Crealock. Crealock worked hard to persuade Zulu notables living locally that King Cetshwayo's cause was finished and that they should surrender. Among these was Sigcwelegcwele, who was approached by messengers employed by John Dunn, including one of Sigcwelegcwele's brothers, Fanane. Sigcwelegcwele reportedly admitted that the war seemed hopeless, and he refused to attend a call from the king to join the final mustering of the *amabutho* at oNdini; nevertheless, he was unwilling to surrender while the country was not yet conquered. Sigcwelegcwele did not in fact surrender until after the final defeat of the Zulu army at oNdini (Ulundi) on 4 July.

After the war, Sigcwelegcwele's territories were placed under the control of John Dunn. Sigcwelegcwele himself, perhaps as a result of his realization that traditional Zulu fighting methods were no match for a powerful European army, took little part in the royalist movement to have Cetshwayo restored. Unlike most of the other 'great ones' of the old order, he did not answer Cetshwayo's summons to the rebuilt oNdini in July 1883, and so escaped the slaughter which followed the attack by Zibhebhu kaMaphitha. Sigcwelegcwele seems to have died in due course of natural causes.

Sihayo kaXongo Ngobese

The emaQungebeni people, who originally inhabited the country close to the original Zulu heartland west of the White Mfolozi River, apparently allied themselves to King Shaka early in his career, about 1817. Their *inkosi* at that time was one Ntusi, whose line was interrupted, either by Shaka himself, or by his successor, King Dingane. A junior branch, under Xongo kaMtintisi, was raised up and became functionaries of the Zulu Royal House.

About 1850, Xongo was appointed by King Mpande as *induna* on the western borders of the kingdom, along the Mzinyathi River, opposite the crossing at Rorke's Drift. The gradual reconstruction of Zulu state authority, in the aftermath of the disastrous war against the Voortrekkers (1838-40) was a characteristic of Mpande's reign, and Xongo's appointment reflected the need to establish a reliable royal favourite in a vulnerable area exposed to white penetration. A number of emaQungebeni moved from the White Mfolozi to settle under Xongo.

On his death, Xongo's following passed to his son Mfokazana. During the succession dispute of 1856, however, Mfokazana's younger brother, Sihayo kaXongo, established himself as a favourite of Prince Cetshwayo by his firm support for Cetshwayo's cause. When Mfokazana died without issue, Cetshwayo confirmed Sihayo as his successor.

Inkosi Sihayo was a member of the iNdabakawombe *ibutho*, and aged about sixty in 1879. He had built his principle homestead, kwaSoxhege, 'the maze', at the foot of a horseshoe indentation at the northern end of the Ngedla mountain, facing out across the open Batshe valley. This position commanded the traders' road into Zululand from Rorke's Drift and, as well as providing valuable intelligence of affairs along the border for King Cetshwayo, Sihayo also engaged in trading activity with passing whites on his own account. He was regarded as a wealthy and powerful man in his own right, and sat in the king's inner council. He owned suits of European clothes, several wagons, horses and saddles, his followers were well armed with European trade guns, and he entertained local missionaries in some style. kwaSoxhege consisted of a dozen neatly built huts surrounding a

211

large, well-built cattle pen which reflected his wealth in cattle. The valley of the Batshe was largely fertile, and British observers noted that it was covered with a patchwork of fields, efficiently tilled by means of draft oxen and European ploughs. Sihayo had the command of at least 300 men from the emaQungebeni, who were formed for service by him into *amabutho*.

It was probably *inkosi* Sihayo's involvement in the white world across the border which led to the famous incident of July 1878 which was subsequently cited in the British ultimatum. Two of his wives had abandoned him, crossed the river, and placed themselves beyond his authority, moving in with lovers on the Natal bank. One had taken refuge at the homestead of a Natal border policeman named Mswagele, who lived below Rorke's Drift. Indeed, neither woman had troubled to move far from their border, and their open defiance of Sihayo's authority struck a blow not only at the prestige of his family, but seemed to undermine his wider position, both as a representative of the king, and as a man highly regarded by colonial society along the border. The reaction of Sihayo's sons can therefore be seen as an attempt to reassert their father's authority. Taking advantage of Sihayo's absence, attending the king at oNdini, Sihayo's chief son, Mehlokazulu, his brother Tshekwane and their uncle Zuluhlenga, crossed the border on two separate occasions, arrested the errant wives, and dragged them back into Zululand, where they were executed according to Zulu law.

In fact, both sides had generally tolerated 'hot pursuit' actions, chasing runaways across the border, but coming at a time of heightened tension between British Natal and the Zulu kingdom, Mehlokazulu's actions were seen as inflammatory. Bartle Frere cited them in the ultimatum of 11 December 1878, demanding that the perpetrators be surrendered to British justice.

The demand placed the king in a dilemma. As well as a personal friend, Sihayo was also widely known as a royal appointee, and by acceding to British demands Cetshwayo would have been seen to abandon something of his own authority. He refused to surrender Sihayo's sons, but offered to pay cattle in compensation instead, missing the essential truth that Frere was not interested in justice, but in bringing down the kingdom as a whole. Sihayo's predicament split public opinion within Zululand; Mehlokazulu was a well-known and popular man, and many ordinary Zulus were indignant at the British presumption. A strong party within the royal council, led by Prince Hamu and *inkosi* Mnyamana Buthelezi, urged the king to comply with the British demands rather than risk the destruction of the kingdom as a whole. This led to heated exchanges within the council, and Sihayo was on one occasion spat upon by an angry member of the appeasement party.

In the event, the British ultimatum could not be acceded to on a number of levels, and on 11 January 1879 war broke out. The first act of the British general, Lord Chelmsford, was to attack Sihayo's homestead, in keeping with the view that British policy was essentially punitive by nature. Both Sihayo and his son Mehlokazulu had left kwaSoxhege to attend the general muster of Zulu forces, although Sihayo had left a number of his followers, under his younger son Mkhumbikazulu, to watch British movements and protect his property. On 12 January Chelmsford attacked Mkumbikazulu's positions in the rocks at the foot of the cliffs lining the Ngedla Mountain. The Zulus were dispersed, Mkhumbikazulu and about sixty of his men were killed, and the British looted and burnt kwaSoxhege, carrying away several hundred of Sihayo's cattle.

Both Sihayo and Mehlokazulu were present with the main Zulu army during its advance to the Rorke's Drift front. On 21 January, the decision to move away from *inkosi* Matshana kaMondise's territory, compromised by British incursions, and into the Ngwebeni valley was largely conditioned by Sihayo's presence as a scout and adviser on local conditions. On the 22nd, both Sihayo and Mehlokazulu scouted the British positions at Isandlwana before the battle began, and Mehlokazulu was involved in the thick of the fighting.

After the battle, many of the emaQungebeni abandoned their homes along the border and retired to natural strongholds further away from the British border garrisons. Both Sihayo and his sons remained committed to the war; Mehlokazulu subsequently fought at Khambula and Ulundi. Tshekwane kaSihayo was an associate of Prince Mbilini kaMswati, and fought in a number of

Mbilini's raids; he was killed in the same skirmish which claimed Mbilini's life. Sihayo seems to have spent much of the war at oNdini, although he may have returned on occasion to the border to report on affairs there, and may have been involved in the skirmishes with British patrols which took place in the northern Nquthu districts in May and June 1879. He was probably present at both Khambula and oNdini.

At the end of the war, during the widespread surrenders of August and September 1879, Sihayo was recognized at Fort Cambridge and detained, while his son Mehlokazulu was captured after Ulundi and sent to Pietermaritzburg for trial. Both men were subsequently released, and returned to their old territory. Mehlokazulu attempted to rebuild kwaSoxhege, while Sihayo took up temporary residence in another of his homesteads, kwaNusa.

Yet in the aftermath of the war the political situation along the border had changed radically, and the profile of the Ngobese family was too high to allow them to return to their former lifestyle. The Zulu bank of the Mzinyathi River had been given over by the British to their appointee, the Sotho *inkosi* Hlubi, who had built his own homestead in the Batshe valley. The presence of Sihayo was a considerable embarrassment to Hlubi, who clearly needed to assert his authority over the representatives of the former regime, but was reluctant to adopt a forthright solution for fear of provoking Zulu loyalists under his control. Hlubi appealed to the British for a solution, but Wolseley brusquely told him that, as a ruler on his own account, he must trust his own judgement. In the event, Hlubi's dilemma was resolved by none other than *inkosi* Mnyamana Buthelezi, King Cetshwayo's former chief councillor. Mnyamana still blamed Sihayo for the British invasion, and in September 1880 Mnyamana's followers confiscated over 1,000 head of cattle from the emaQungebeni as punishment. This move, by a leader of impeccable royalist credentials and enormous prestige within the kingdom, not only impoverished Sihayo's family but effectively undermined their standing. Capitalizing on this, Hlubi took the opportunity to move Sihayo and Mehlokazulu away from the Batshe valley, and resettle them on the fringes of his territory, in the Qudeni district.

Thus, by 1881, Sihayo had suffered the full weight of British retribution, his home destroyed, several of his sons killed, his followers dispersed, and his cattle plundered. The traveller Bertram Mitford could not conceal a twinge of sympathy at his predicament when he met Sihayo about that time:

> From what I heard of the old chief – his deep-rooted hostility to us before the war, and his anti-English proclivities generally, I expected to see a grim, scowling savage; instead, whereof, I beheld an urbane, jovial-looking old Zulu advancing to meet me with outstretched hand, and grinning from ear to ear … [He] rejoiced in a head-ring and a pair of boots (of course not omitting the inevitable 'mutya') [and] the pedal extremities of this worthy were cased in a huge pair of bluchers, which, he being a great sufferer of gout, seemed about the worst line of adornment he could have struck out in. The old fellow lumbering along (he is enormously fat), with a barbed assegai in his hand, and trying to look as if he were not on hot bricks, cut a slightly ridiculous figure … An outcast, where formerly he had been powerful and respected; his cattle gone; one of his sons killed in battle; an alien reigning in his stead; his friend and benefactor a captive and in exile, and himself old, sick, and broken down. Yes, I think one could afford to pity him.

Not surprisingly, the restoration of King Cetshwayo in January 1883 was greeted with delight by those of his former supporters, like Sihayo, who had suffered most by the British victory in 1879. Although legally required to remain under his appointed chief, Sihayo hurried to offer his allegiance to the king. He was among a large number of powerful figures from the old regime who had rallied to the newly rebuilt oNdini homestead in the middle of 1883 in response to the outbreak of civil war with *inkosi* Zibhebhu kaMaphitha. On 21 July Zibhebhu launched a surprise attack on oNdini. Royalist forces hurrying out to meet him were easily dispersed, and many of the king's councillors, being elderly and overweight, were overtaken during the pursuit. Over fifty of the most important men of the old kingdom – *izikhulu*, council-

215

lors, *amakhosi* and *izinduna* – were killed by Zibhebhu's men, and their bodies left on the Ulundi plain.

Among them was Sihayo kaXongo Ngobese.

Sikhobobo kaMabhabhakazana Sibiya

In the early 1820s, King Shaka extended Zulu influence along the upper Mzinyathi and Ncome Rivers, and towards the broken country along the banks of the Phongolo. To exert his authority in the region, he established a royal homestead, known as ebaQulusini, to the east of the Hlobane Mountain, and gave it into the care of his formidable aunt (sister of *inkosi* Senzangakhona), Queen Mnkabayi. The descendants of men attached to that homestead settled the area and, together with the remnants of the groups conquered there by Shaka, became known as abaQulusi. Because of their close relationship with the Royal House, they were regarded not as a hereditary chiefdom, but as a section of the Zulu state, directly under the control of the king. They were not governed by *amakhosi*, but by *izinduna* – state officials – appointed by the king. Because the abaQulusi owed their origins to Shaka himself, they were particularly loyal to the Royal House, of which they considered themselves an extension, and as such they were a dependable element on the northern borders, an area otherwise dominated by strong regional *amakhosi* whose interests did not always coincide with those of central government.

By the 1870s, the abaQulusi could muster several thousand armed men, who assembled at ebaQulusini – which still existed, although it had perhaps moved location and been rebuilt in the years since it was established – and fought as their own *ibutho*, rather than with the king's age-based regiments.

In 1879 the senior *izinduna* of the abaQulusi were Mcwayo kaMangeda, Tola kaDilikana, Msebe kaMadaka, Mahubulwana kaDumisela and Sikhobobo kaMabhabhakazana. Of these, Sikhobobo was regarded as the senior military commander, and was to emerge as the abaQulusi's most dynamic strategist.

Sikhobobo was of the Sibiya people, and had apparently enrolled as a youth in the uMdlenevu *ibutho*, which was formed in the early 1840s from men born in the early 1820s. It is not

216

clear when he was attached to the ebaQulusini homestead, although a contingent of abaQulusi played a prominent part at the Battle of 'Ndondakusuka in December 1856, fighting on behalf of Prince Cetshwayo. This cemented their relationship with the heir apparent, and it is possible that Sikhobobo was present on that occasion. Certainly, by the 1870s, he was heavily involved in events on the northern border. In the tense months leading up to the British invasion, King Cetshwayo was keen to assert his authority along the exposed northern border and to drive back the claims of the expanding Transvaal farmers; Sikhobobo was involved in the task of establishing new homesteads on the king's behalf. At the end of 1877, while building cattle posts along the Phongolo River, a party of abaQulusi under Sikhobobo's command was involved in a tense stand-off with Boers from the Wakerstroom district, who demanded they withdraw; the incident was only resolved when a Swazi *impi*, sent by the Swazi king to investigate, arrived and reinforced King Cetshwayo's claim to the area, forcing the Boers to back down. On 11 November, Sikhobobo personally entered the settlement of Lüneburg to warn the British garrison, on King Cetshwayo's behalf, to leave the area; he was not allowed into the settler laager because local blacks denounced him as a spy.

At the end of 1878, with war apparently inevitable, the abaQulusi mustered their warriors and ritually prepared for war. Throughout the coming campaign, they would provide an effective focus of resistance to the British invasion, and worked in close alliance with Prince Mbilini – who had a homestead on the slopes of the abaQulusi stronghold at Hlobane mountain – and with *inkosi* Manyanyoba in the Ntombe valley. Together they harassed British movements across the region, and worked as an effective check against British ambitions to persuade other local *amakhosi* to submit.

The threat posed by the abaQulusi was recognized by Colonel Wood who, from the beginning commanded the largest British concentration in the north. On 20 January he dispatched a mounted reconnaissance to feel out abaQulusi positions along the Zungwini, Hlobane and Ityenka mountains, but the British were forced to retire after provoking a stiff response. On the 20th,

Wood set out with a larger force and succeeded in capturing Zungwini Mountain by surprise; looking across the valley at Hlobane opposite, however, Wood was disconcerted to see about 4,000 Zulus drilling with skill and precision on the lower slopes of the mountain. On the 24th he attempted to disperse this concentration, and a running fight broke out over the Nek between Zungwini and Hlobane, and along the northern foot of Hlobane itself. At one point, Wood's infantry advanced too far from their wagons, and were nearly cut off by a party of abaQulusi who rushed down to intercept them. Only a quick move by Wood's cavalry commander, Redvers Buller, prevented the wagons being taken. The Zulus were eventually dispersed and retired up the mountain under shellfire, but Wood was forced to break off the action when a messenger arrived bringing news of the Zulu victory at Isandlwana.

The abaQulusi were apparently commanded on this occasion by Msebe kaMadaka; Sikhobobo's involvement is not entirely clear. It may be that Msebe's poor showing allowed Sikhobobo to emerge as the natural commander in future engagements.

On 1 February, Buller followed up this advantage by a long-range raid, which destroyed the ebaQulusini homestead and carried away hundreds of head of cattle. Despite this setback, the abaQulusi were fully involved in skirmishing throughout February and March, lending detachments to reinforce Prince Mbilini's raids in the Lüneburg area. After Mbilini's success at the Battle of Ntombe (12 March), he retired to his homestead on the slopes of Hlobane. Colonel Wood, well aware of the danger posed to British movements by the concentrations around Hlobane, resolved to clear the mountain by a dawn attack on 28 March. Two British parties ascended the range at either end, intending to drive off the Zulu cattle which had been herded onto the summit for safety. The plan was based on poor intelligence, however, and soon began to go awry. Although Prince Mbilini is often credited as the architect of the Zulu victory at Hlobane, the descendants of the abaQulusi are adamant that Sikhobobo was in fact behind the contingency plans which led to the British retreat. Given that a British attack on the mountain was an obvious possibility, this is quite possibly the case. Large numbers of abaQulusi had been assembled in temporary huts beneath the north-eastern slopes of the mountain and once the British attack developed, they were hurried up under Sikhobobo's command. Some elements swept round the foot of the cliffs surrounding the summit – cutting off the British line of retreat – while others drove the British across the flat-topped mountain, trapping them at the famous 'Devil's Pass' at the far (western) end. The coincidental arrival of King Cetshwayo's main army – en route to attack Khambula camp – completed the British rout.

That night Sikhobobo addressed the assembled abaQulusi warriors; they had, he said, fulfilled their obligation by driving off the invaders that day, but any among them who wished to join the main army's attack on Khambula might do so. Accordingly, a large force of abaQulusi moved in support of the main army during its advance on Khambula the following day, although after its exertions at Hlobane it was slow to march. During the attack on Khambula (29 March) the Zulu army was defeated, and in the retreat the abaQulusi, falling back towards their stronghold on Hlobane, suffered heavily from the British pursuit.

The losses at Hlobane greatly reduced the abaQulusi's ability to resist, and many of their warriors dispersed to their homes across the region. Nonetheless, a few remained in the vicinity of Hlobane, to shout defiance at passing British patrols, or continued to join the skirmishing around Lüneburg. The abaQulusi remained technically under arms until news reached them of King Cetshwayo's capture in the Ngome forest on 28 August. On 1 September Mahubulwana kaDumisela formally surrendered on behalf of his people.

In the post-war settlement, the abaQulusi were deliberately placed under the control of Prince Hamu kaNzibe, in the hope that this would check their royalist sympathies. In fact it merely created tension between them and Hamu's supporters, and Hamu's attempts to exert his control by confiscating abaQulusi cattle were met with armed resistance. With the return of the king in January 1883, the abaQulusi felt sufficiently encouraged to attack their oppressors, but the resurgent royalist cause was dealt at devastating blow by their utter defeat by *inkosi* Zibhebhu at oNdini on 21 July 1883. A detachment of abaQulusi was present on that occasion, but arrived too late to play a part in the battle.

The defeat and subsequent death of King Cetshwayo at least allowed a young element, headed by Cetshwayo's heir, Prince Dinuzulu, to emerge within the royalist cause. Dinuzulu took the drastic step of appealing to the Transvaal Boers to fight against Zibhebhu on his behalf, promising farms in return. Dinuzulu met a commando of Boer volunteers in the heart of the abaQulusi territory, near Hlobane Mountain, and on 21 May 1884 they crowned him king before embarking on an expedition to defeat Zibhebhu. Dinuzulu's own warriors included a large number of abaQulusi, apparently commanded by Sikhobobo in person. On 5 June this combined Boer/royalist force encountered Zibhebhu's forces lying in ambush beneath the Tshaneni Mountain on the banks of the Mkhuze River. Initially, a determined attack by Zibhebhu's men drove back the royalist centre and right, but these rallied on the Boers following behind, who fired over their heads and broke up Zibhebhu's attack. Sikhobobo's abaQulusi then made a decisive movement on the royalist left, throwing out a 'horn' which advanced along the river bank, crossed over, and fell upon Zibhebhu's non-combatants sheltering in the hills on the far bank. Zibhebhu's force then collapsed and fled, with the abaQulusi in particular, causing heavy casualties in the pursuit.

The price of this victory was high. Dinuzulu was obliged to grant the Boers a huge tract of land along the northern borders, which included the entire abaQulusi district. The Boers declared this to be a New Republic, and built a capital at Vryheid ('Freedom'), near Hlobane. The country was marked out for farms, and most of the abaQulusi found themselves suddenly dispossessed, living on land now claimed by the Boers. A festering sense of resentment fuelled support for Dinuzulu's attempts to resist white encroachment further into Zululand, and in 1888, when Dinuzulu went into open rebellion against the British authorities, large numbers of abaQulusi crossed over from the New Republic to join him.

The antipathy felt by the abaQulusi towards the Boer government came to a head during the Anglo-Boer War of 1899-1902. Generally, both sides were wary of provoking the Zulus by campaigning too obviously in Zululand, although the Boers made a number of strikes through the country in an attempt to divert pressure from the gradual British successes in the Free State and Transvaal. Vryheid had remained a centre of Boer republican sympathies, and had been occupied by British troops. Towards the very end of the war, one of the last active Boer commandos was operating in the Vryheid area, drawing support from sympathizers among the farming community. The British were reluctant to act directly against it because peace negotiations were already under way. Such was the effectiveness of the British 'scorched earth' policy, that by this stage the 'bitter ender' commandos were desperately short of supplies, and those near Vryheid had been reduced to plundering the cattle and food of local abaQulusi, who the Boers accused of sympathizing with the British. According to the abaQulusi, homes were destroyed and herdsmen shot out of hand. In April 1902, acting under Louis Botha's personal orders, Sikhobobo's own homestead had been destroyed, and he and a large number of abaQulusi took refuge on the outskirts of Vryheid. Sikhobobo appealed to the British to curb the Boer excesses, but was told that it was politically impractical due to the delicate stage of the negotiations. When the leader of the commando, Field Cornet Jan Potgeiter, heard of Sikhobobo's appeal, he sent an indignant message saying that if Sikhobobo wanted the abaQulusi cattle back, he should come and get them himself; Potgeiter declared that he did not think the Zulus would do anything, however, as they were no longer the men their fathers were, and were no better than 'chicken lice'.

On 5 May Sikhobobo informed the British garrison at Vryheid that he was taking some of his men out to recover their cattle. That night his men marched to a hill known as Holkrans (Ntatshana), not far from Khambula, where Potgeiter's commando of seventy men was camped. The abaQulusi surrounded the camp before dawn, intending to attack at first light – 'in the horns of the morning' – but a premature shot gave the Boers some warning. The Zulus rushed forward but were shot down in some numbers. According to oral tradition, they retired and lay down among the corpses lying in the long grass. As the sun rose, the Boers tentatively emerged from their positions, when Sikhobobo stood up and shouted 'No! It is not yet over!' The abaQulusi sprang up and rushed in among the Boers before they could return to their cover, driving them back up the slopes of Holkrans hill. Of Potgeiter's men, fifty-six were killed and three taken prisoner; over fifty Zulus were killed and a large number wounded. The British garrison reported the *impi* returning in triumph that evening, singing war songs and carrying their wounded.

The Holkrans incident represented the most severe reaction by the African population to British and Boer troop movements during the Anglo-Boer War, and it contributed to the peace process. It raised the latent fear of attack by Africans on Boer commandos and farms, and persuaded a number of hitherto recalcitrant 'bitter-ender' of the necessity to end the hostilities. At the same time it created further bitterness, for the Boers regarded it as a shameful attack, and accused the British of complicity. In fact the abaQulusi response was the product of years of ill feeling over the occupation of Vryheid, and of specific provocation which Sikhobobo in particular considered intolerable.

The abaQulusi played no significant part in the 1906 distur- bances, and the Battle of Holkrans was to prove their last significant military operation. Sikhobobo was by then in any case an old man – he died peacefully of old age and was buried in the modern Paulpietersburg district. The abaQulusi today regard Holkrans as one of his greatest victories as a commander, on a par with his defeat of the British force at Hlobane in 1879.

Sitshitshili kaMnqandi

Sitshitshili was the senior son of *inkosi* Mnqandi kaMatshana of the esiBizini (Sibisi) people who lived near Nhlazatshe Mountain, north of the White Mfolozi. Sitshitshili's grandfather Matshana had been an *induna* under King Shaka, and Mnqandi was a coun- cillor to both King Mpande and King Cetshwayo.

Sitshitshili was born about 1850 and was enrolled in the uKhandempemvu *ibutho*. He was present during the Isandlwana campaign, although no details of his participation have survived. He was already recognized by that stage as an *induna* – presum- ably commanding a company or group of companies within his own regiment – and since he was a noted horseman he may well have commanded the uKhandempemvu's scouts. After the battle, it was Sitshitshili who complained to the king that the army had suffered heavy losses because it had embarked on the battle before the necessary preparatory rituals had been completed. When the army reassembled for the Khambula expedition in late March, Sitshitshili again served with the uKhandempemvu. Arriving in the vicinity of the abaQulusi stronghold of Hlobane Mountain at dawn on 28 March, and finding Hlobane under attack by British detachments from Khambula, the senior commanders dispatched the army's right wing to aid the defenders. As they approached the mountain the regiments divided, the uVe and iNgobamakhosi *amabutho* moving to cut off the British retreat at the western end of Hlobane while the uKhandempemvu advanced to the eastern end. Here they intercepted elements of the Border Horse and Frontier Light Horse descending the mountain and drove them over Ityenka Nek. Small parties of British troops fled across the open country north of Hlobane, with elements of the uKhandempemvu in pursuit. Among those killed in the rout were Captain R.J. Barton of the Frontier Light Horse and Captain J. Poole of the Border Horse. Passing through the area in May 1880 while in command of the Empress Eugenie's escort, Colonel Evelyn Wood made enquiries among the Zulus as to the fate of Barton and Poole. He was told by Mehlokazulu kaSihayo that Sitshitshili had been in command of the group who had pursued and killed the two officers. Wood promptly sent a message to the esiBezini at Nhlazatshe to summon Sitshitshili:

Chicheeli came, and talked quite frankly, giving me a still higher opinion of the powers of observation of the savage than I already had. After describing the coat and other clothes that Barton wore, he said 'the White Man was slightly pitted by smallpox'. Now I had lived at Aldershot for two years in daily intercourse with Robert Barton, and at once said, 'Then it is not the man I mean'. Chicheeli, however, declined to be shaken from his statement, and repeated that the marks on his face were slight, but that there was no doubt that he had had smallpox. Opening my portmanteaux, I took out a cabinet sized photograph and a magnifier, and, examining the face closely, I then perceived that what I had for two years taken to be roughness of skin was really the marks of smallpox, which Chicheeli had noticed as he stood over the dead body.

Chicheeli told me that on the Ityenka Nek he followed several white men and killed them, one man, as he approached, turning his carbine and shooting himself. When he, with several others, got down onto the plain, 7 miles from the mountain, he overtook Captain Barton, who had taken Lieutenant Poole up on his horse. He fired at them, and when the horse, being exhausted, could no longer struggle under the double weight, the riders dismounted and separated. Chicheeli first shot Lieutenant Poole, and was going up towards Barton, when the latter pulled the trigger of his revolver, which did not go off. Chicheeli then put down his gun and assegai, and made signs to Barton to surrender. I asked, 'Did you really want to spare him?' 'Yes', he replied, 'Cetywayo [sic] had ordered us to bring one or two *indunas* to Ulundi, and I had already killed seven men.' Barton lifted his hat, and the men were close together when a Zulu fired at him, and he fell mortally wounded; and then, said Chicheeli, 'I could not let anyone else kill him, so I ran up and assegaid him'. I said, 'Do you think you can find the body?' 'Yes, certainly', he said, 'but you must lend me a horse for it is a day and a half.' I sent Trooper Brown, V.C., with him next day, and with the marvellous instinct of a savage, he rode to within 300 yards of the spot where, fourteen months previously, he had killed my friend, and then said 'Now we can off-saddle, we are close to the spot,' and, casting round like a harrier, came in less than five minutes upon Barton's body, which had apparently never been disturbed by any beast or bird of prey. The clothes and boots were rotten and ant-eaten, and tumbled to pieces on being touched. Brown cut off some buttons from the breeches, and took a Squadron Pay book from the pocket filled with Barton's writing, and then buried the remains, placing over them a small wooden cross painted black, on which is cut 'Robert Barton, killed in action, 28th March 1879', and then he and Chicheeli buried the body of Lieutenant Poole.

Sitshitshili survived the war. By temperament he was a man who believed it his duty to acknowledge the established authority.

Thus, while he remained loyal to the exiled King Cetshwayo, he was also prepared to serve the interests of the British who supplanted him. In 1882 Sitshitshili was working as an occasional messenger for the newly appointed British Resident, Melmoth Osborne, at Nhlazatshe. When King Cetshwayo was restored in February 1883, both Sitshitshili and his father Mnqandi renewed their allegiance to the Royal House. Following the outbreak of internecine violence which followed, both men attended the general muster of royalist supporters at the newly rebuilt oNdini homestead in July; they were both present when, on the morning of 21 July, oNdini suffered a surprise attack by the forces of *inkosi* Zibhebhu kaMaphitha. By now an elderly man, Mnqandi was among those senior royalist councillors who were too portly and slow to make good their escape and, along with fifty-two other *amakhosi* and *izinduna*, he was killed in the royalist rout. Sitshitshili himself survived, and helped escort Prince Dinuzulu, the king's teenage heir, to safety as the fighting engulfed the royal homestead.

The years which followed were chaotic for royalist supporters. King Cetshwayo died at Eshowe in February 1884, and Dinuzulu appealed to the Transvaal Boers to intervene on his behalf. Although this was successful, large tracts of central Zululand were lost to European settlement as a consequence. Sitshitshili, now installed as *inkosi* of the emiBazini, moved his homestead south to the eThaleni hill, in the northern Nkandla district. During the Anglo-Boer War, Sitshitshili was one of a number of Zulu *amakhosi*, including Zibhebhu kaMaphitha and Mehlokazulu kaSihayo, who were authorized by the British to loot Boer cattle along the Transvaal border to prevent hostile commandos crossing into Zululand.

By 1905 Sitshitshili was regarded as a committed ally of the colonial administration in Natal. That year the Natal government introduced a Poll Tax in an attempt to repair the damage wrought to the colonial exchequer by the Anglo-Boer War. This tax was widely resented by the African population, many of whom had recently been impoverished by cattle diseases and drought. The crisis highlighted the ambiguous position of the *amakhosi*, who were dependent on the government for their authority, but who were facing determined resistance to the tax among their followers. Sitshitshili publicly declared his willingness to comply in an attempt to quell widespread disturbances across the Nkandla district. When, however, protest spilled over into open violence in April 1906, Nkandla became a focus for rebellion. While several prominent Nkandla *amakhosi* sided with the rebels, Sitshitshili became a rigorous ally of the government troops. He attacked the homesteads of his own followers who had joined the rebellion, destroying their huts and confiscating their cattle, he provided warriors to join the government's auxiliary units, and rode out to serve himself in the capacity of a scout.

The rebellion in Nkandla was effectively crushed by the spectacular colonial victory at Mome Gorge on 10 June. In the aftermath, however, there was considerable bitterness among surviving rebels directed against the *amakhosi* who had supported the government, and who were therefore considered to have betrayed their own people. A handful of young men led by Sukabekhuluma kaGezindaka, who had played a key role in the rebellion, orchestrated attacks on prominent *amakhosi*. Throughout the first half of 1907 several *amakhosi* were killed or wounded. Sitshitshili himself expressed disquiet about this development in a comment which hints at a growing disillusion with his decision to so closely ally himself with the authorities. 'We cannot understand how matters stand at present', he said, 'Although we are British subjects we still seem to be subject to danger, we do not seem to be protected in the way we ought to be.' On 8 August, 1907, Sitshitshili was murdered on the instructions of Sukabekhuluma. His murderer, a youth named Njombolwana, had previously entered the *inkosi*'s homestead pretending to be a messenger from the Royal House. Njombolwana had a revolver hidden in his old greatcoat; waiting until Sitshitshili was dozing on his bed that evening he had entered his hut and shot Sitshitshili twice in the chest before running off.

An attempt was later made by the government authorities to implicate King Dinuzulu in Sitshitshili's murder. Although Dinuzulu had publicly distanced himself from the Rebellion, many whites suspected that he had secretly supported it, and, when the gun used in the murder was later found in Dinuzulu's district, cited Sitshitshili's murder as proof. In fact, Dinuzulu deplored Sitshitshili's murder, and paid tribute to Sitshitshili's distinguished record as a warrior both in 1879, and in the royalist cause in the 1880s.

Somopho ka Zikhala

Somopho was the head of a lineage of the Mthembu people who lived along the middle reaches of the Nseleni River in the coastal district. An *induna* in King Mpande's time, Somopho was attached to the emaNgweni royal homestead which acted as the principle centre of royal authority on the coast. Prince Cetshwayo spent much of his youth at emaNgweni, and formed a close personal friendship with the older Somopho. After his accession in 1873, Cetshwayo made Somopho head *induna* of emaNgweni. He was also trusted with the charge of the king's powder stores, which were housed several miles to the north-east of oNdini. The powder was made by Sotho gunsmiths employed by Cetshwayo, under Somopho's supervision, and was stored in a cave nearby.

Somopho's role in the early stages of the 1879 war is unclear, but when Lord Chelmsford massed on the Thukela border in late March in preparation for the relief of Eshowe, Somopho was given command of Zulu troops which, reinforcing the cordon already around Eshowe, were concentrated in the Nyezane valley, across the road from Natal. When Chelmsford began his advance, Somopho was the senior commander of the force which attempted to halt him at the Battle of kwaGingindlovu on 2 April. After the Zulu defeat and subsequent relief of Eshowe, Somopho seems to have returned to the emaNgweni homestead. The battle signalled the end of the ability of the Zulu in the coastal districts to resist, and this became increasingly apparent as the 1st Division occupied the area in overwhelming numbers in May and June. Somopho was among a number of important local *amakhosi* and *izinduna* who surrendered to Major General H.H. Crealock on 4 July.

After the war, Somopho continued to live in the coastal districts, which, during the 1888 uprising, largely supported Dinuzulu. Somopho is mentioned among those *amakhosi* who called out men to fight on Dinuzulu's behalf, and on 30 June they were present during an unsuccessful attack on a British outpost, Fort Andries. When British troops concentrated in the area, however, the rising on the coast collapsed. Somopho himself evaded a column sent to capture him.

Vumandaba kaNthathi

Vumandaba was born about 1818, apparently among the Khumalo people. Enrolled as a youth in the uMkhulutshane *ibutho* he may have taken part in the Battle of Ncome (Blood River) in December 1838, and during the reign of King Mpande he became an *inceku* – a personal servant of the king – and later a state official, an *induna*. As such he became intimately acquainted with the affairs of the court, and his position depended upon his trustworthiness and tact. He kept aloof from the succession intrigues of the 1850s, a crisis from which he emerged both trusted by King Mpande and respected by the heir apparent, Prince Cetshwayo. When Cetshwayo became king in 1873 he confirmed Vumandaba in his position. By that time Vumandaba was both an *inceku* – his duties apparently included tasting the royal food and drink to ensure it was not poisoned – a royal messenger and an officer in the king's army. He was the senior commander of the uKhandempemvu regiment. On 11 December 1879, Vumandaba headed the Zulu delegation which assembled on the Natal bank of the Lower Thukela to hear the long-awaited report of the Boundary Commission, and with it the British ultimatum. He appears in the centre of the famous group portrait taken of the Zulu envoys taken by the photographer James Lloyd of Durban.

In 1879 he commanded the uKhandempemvu in the Isandlwana campaign and in 1882 the traveller, Bertram Mitford, found him living in a long-established homestead near KwaMagwaza, and left not only a telling impression of Vumandaba the man, but something of Vumandaba's recollection of the battle:

> Vumandaba is a tall, thin old man, with grizzled hair and beard, a rugged countenance ... a good specimen of the high class Zulu, dignified in manner and speech ... I found him a very genial and pleasant old fellow. Not the least pleasing

228

feature about him was his feelings of attachment and loyalty towards his late [i.e. deposed] master. He was full of Cetywayo, [sic] nearly his first question being about the King and his welfare. 'Why hadn't we brought him back? All the people wanted him' ... The uKhandempemvu regiment was in the thick of the battle at Isandlwana, and foremost in carrying the camp, though it suffered severely in the earlier stages of the conflict from the fire of the outlying companies; and now its chief told me how stubbornly some of our soldiers had fought to the last, many of them using their pocket-knives when their bayonets were wrenched from them. Some even astonished their savage enemies by a well-directed 'one-two', straight from the shoulder, flooring the too exultant warriors like ninepins. The Zulus could not understand how men could use their hands as knobkerries, for the native is quite a stranger to the art of fisticuffs. 'A few of the soldiers', said the chief, 'shot a great deal with "little guns" (revolvers), but they didn't shoot well. For every man they killed, they fired a great many shots without hitting anybody' ... as I was getting up to go, the old chief laid his hand upon my arm in his eagerness. 'Bring us back Cetywayo', he said; 'we want to see our king again. Bring him back!' I declare I felt quite small for the moment, call it foolish sentimentality who will. Many a time since I seemed to see the old man's rugged, earnest face, and to hear his emphatic tones – the loyal old warrior – pleading for his fallen and exiled king.

During the closing stages of the battle. Vumandaba, mounted on horseback, led some of his regiment in pursuit of the British survivors. When he reached Sothondose's (Fugitives') Drift, he found some men of the young iNgobamakhosi regiment had just crossed the Mzinyathi River. Vumandaba 'shouted with a loud voice' across to them, saying 'Has he said you were to cross? He is not invading! He is only defending the land of the Zulus! Come back'. Some of the NNC who survived later commented that 'we were saved by that alone; for, if they had come across, we should just have been killed, being utterly exhausted'.

Not surprisingly, when King Cetshwayo was restored to Zululand in January 1883, Vumandaba was among thousands of

Zulus who gathered to greet him at Mthonjaneni. He resumed his post as one of the king's senior *izinduna,* and remained with the king as Cetshwayo directed the building of a new oNdini homestead. He was still there when, on the morning of 21 July, oNdini was attacked by Zibhebhu kaMaphitha. The royalist supporters, marshalled into their old regiments, attempted to make a stand but collapsed in the face of a determined attack. Most of the young warriors were able to run away, but many of the elderly notables of the old kingdom were caught and killed. Zibhebhu's followers overran the royal homestead, setting fire to the huts, snatching what loot they could, and killing any royalists who lingered there. These included a detachment of the uThulwana regiment, who, cut off and unable to escape, turned to fight; Vumandaba was seen among them, stabbing about him and killing several of the enemy until at last 'they finally overcame him by showering him with a flight of spears'.

Zibhebhu kaMaphitha

Zibhebhu kaMaphitha was one of the most able military commanders to emerge from the 1879 conflict although, ironically, the full extent of his abilities only became apparent afterwards, to the desperate cost of his countrymen. Zibhebhu was *inkosi* of the Mandlakazi, a section of the Zulu Royal House who traced their descent from King Shaka's grandfather, Jama. The exact relationship remains obscure for it concerns the 'raising up' of a child named Sojiyisa into Jama's household; when Sojiyisa grew to manhood he founded a homestead known as *kwaMandlakazi,* the place of the mighty seed or great power. He was regarded as being genealogically a brother of *inkosi* Senzangakhona. When Senzagakhona's son, Shaka, expanded the Zulu kingdom in from about 1816, Sojiyisa's heir, Maphitha, became a firm ally. He was given command of the northern reaches of the kingdom to rule of Shaka's behalf and the Mandlakazi became one of the most powerful sections within the kingdom, their prestige a reflection of their close association with the Royal House. Maphitha survived Shaka's assassination and the turmoil of King Dingane's reign and during Mpande's time was regarded as the most influential of the regional barons, given a decisive voice in the royal council and allowed to appoint his own *izinduna*, state officials. Zibhebhu was the eldest son in Maphitha's 'great house', and was born in 1841 and enrolled in Mpande's uMxapho *ibutho*, formed in 1861. From an early age Zibhebhu showed himself to be shrewd, ambitious and aggressive. Maphitha controlled an extensive trade network extending from northern Zululand through to Delagoa Bay in Mozambique and through it Zibhebhu developed an unusual degree of interest, for his time, in the workings of the white world. In due course he would prove to be completely at ease in white company and he understood fully the principles of trade and profit which motivated white society. In later years, despite a quiet and controlled manner, he proved to be utterly ruthless and unusually acquisitive.

In 1856 the Mandlakazi played a decisive role in Prince Cetshwayo's defeat of his rival, Prince Mbuyazi. Although Zibhebhu was too young to have played a prominent part he was probably present at the Battle of 'Ndondakusuka as a mat-carrier and certainly his conspicuous support for Prince Cetshwayo's party attracted the prince's gratitude. In later years Maphitha became convinced Zibhebhu was plotting against him and appealed to Mpande for permission to kill him; Cetshwayo intervened and refused to allow it. Both Maphitha and Mpande died in 1872 and Cetshwayo and Zibhebhu succeeded to the leadership of their various houses. For Prince Cetshwayo this meant the crown and, despite a last-minute fear that the Mandlakazi might dispute his succession, Zibhebhu in fact rallied to join him in the installation ceremonies in 1873. Indeed, Cetshwayo seems to have felt confident enough of Zibhebhu's support to allow the Mandlakazi to manage their own affairs with the minimum of royal interference. Zibhebhu himself developed further his father's European trading connections and by 1878 had become unusually wealthy. This position placed him squarely in the peace camp on the king's council, determined if he could to head off a confrontation with the British; when he failed to do so, however, and war broke out in January 1879, Zibhebhu committed himself wholeheartedly to the fighting.

Zibhebhu had seen little military action prior to 1879 but his flair soon became apparent. He was commanding the Zulu scouts who, on 21 January, brushed aside a British patrol which very nearly intercepted the movement of the main Zulu army from Siphezi to the Ngwebeni valley, near Isandlwana. The following day, during the Battle of Isandlwana, he commanded the reserve which cut the British line of retreat to Rorke's Drift. He harried the British survivors until they reached the Mzinyathi River where he abandoned his command and crossed into Natal to plunder cattle on his own account. During the second phase of the war, in March 1879, he took part in the Battle of Khambula. Such was the nature of the action that Zibhebhu was granted no opportunity to distinguish himself although his pragmatism is evident in an anecdote that during the retreat he cautioned *inkosi* Mnyamana Buthelezi against attempting to rally the fleeing *amabutho* because to do so would only expose them to further losses.

During the last phase of the war, when the British had advanced close to oNdini, it was Zibhebhu who was entrusted with guarding the drifts on the White Mfolozi River. Zibhebhu organized a screen of riflemen who harassed British watering parties and when, on 3 July, parties of British mounted troops crossed the river, it was Zibhebhu who very nearly lured them into an ambush. He allowed himself to be seen, on horseback and with a group of scouts, and as the British pursued him he led them towards a carefully prepared trap. Long grass had been plaited to trip the horses and Zibhebhu's own uMxapho regiment lay concealed in a great arc around it; only the instincts of the British commander, Lieutenant Colonel Redvers Buller, prevented him from falling into the trap. In the event the British halted before they were in position, and the uMxapho narrowly failed to trap them. Nevertheless, they chased the British back to the river and inflicted several casualties upon them. The following day, when Lord Chelmsford crossed the river at the head of his army and formed up in a large square near the oNdini royal homestead, it was Zibhebhu who led the Zulu left in a determined charge on a British corner. The charge failed but afterwards the nearest Zulu dead were found just nine paces from the British lines.

In the aftermath of the defeat Zibhebhu returned to his Bangonomo homestead in northern Zululand. The British had not penetrated this area, and he offered the defeated king a place of refuge. King Cetshwayo refused for himself but sent his young son, Dinuzulu, and a number of attendants and cattle into Zibhebhu's keeping. Ironically, it was this incident which would dramatically poison the relationship between the Royal House and the Mandlakazi. After the king was captured by the British in August, Prince Ndabuko -the king's full brother – objected to the arrangement, commenting tartly that it was not fit for the heirs of the House of Senzangakhona to eat off the meat-tray of the House of Sojiyisa. Zibhebhu took offence, and while he gave up Dinuzulu into Ndabuko's care he flatly refused to give up the royal cattle. His reaction became a point of contention with the Royal House which would ultimately lead to catastrophic consequences for the kingdom as a whole.

When the British divided up the kingdom after the war, Zibhebhu was one of the thirteen appointees they set up to rule on their behalf. Despite his impressive war record in the national cause, he was regarded as a natural ally because of his 'progressive' attitude towards the developing European economy. This set him apart, in white eyes, from the majority of his countrymen and made him appear a natural counter to the resurgence of the Royal House. That he accepted the position was entirely in keeping with his ambitious nature; and in doing so Zibhebhu broke irrevocably with his allegiances of old. From that point he regarded himself as a ruler of equal status who acknowledged no loyalty to a Royal House which, in his view, was a thing of the past. To make his point he demanded the submission of prominent royalists who found themselves living under him, including the Prince Ndabuko and Shingana. Where they objected to the new order, Zibhebhu confiscated their cattle.

The British system soon proved unworkable, however, and the divisions it unleashed within the country led to escalating violence. By the end of 1882 the British were contemplating a reversal of policy and considering restoring Cetshwayo to at least part of his old territory in the hope that he might be able to stabilize the country. Clearly he could not be given control over those *amakhosi* who had harried his supporters in his absence; the British solution was partition. A large swathe of the southern reaches of the country were placed directly under British control; in the north, those who most bitterly opposed Cetshwayo's return – Prince Hamu and Zibhebhu – were allowed to retain their independence.

Cetshwayo was returned to Zululand in February 1883 and trouble flared immediately. Prince Ndabuko, determined to redress the wrongs he had suffered at Zibhebhu's hands, mustered an army of 5,000 men on the southern Mandlakazi borders. At the end of March it crossed into Zibhebhu's territory. Zibhebhu lured it into the Msebe valley where, on 30 March, he ambushed it. The royalists were formed in a long straggling column and, suddenly attacked on three sides, they collapsed and fled. Hundreds were slain in the rout. The battle was undoubtedly a defining moment in Zibhebhu's career; he had finally taken up arms against the Royal House in spectacular fashion, and his skills as a military commander were all too apparent.

In the months that followed King Cetshwayo assembled his followers at the newly rebuilt oNdini homestead. Zibhebhu waited for the right moment then, on 20 July 1883 he assembled 3,000 of his followers at his ekuVukeni homestead on his southern borders. That night he made a daring forced march across the wild Black Mfolozi valley, only to appear at first light on the hills overlooking oNdini. The royalists were taken by surprise and although the king's *amabutho* hurried out to oppose them, they soon collapsed in the face of a determined Mandlakazi attack. They broke and fled and Zibhebhu's warriors overran oNdini, looting it and setting it on fire; King Cetshwayo himself narrowly escaped. The battle marked the true end of the 'old Zulu order', for among the dead were scores of elderly *amakhosi* and royal councillors who had enjoyed the highest prominence since the days of King Mpande.

King Cetshwayo fled to British protection at Eshowe, and in February 1884 he died. His death ushered in a new phase of the bitter struggle between the Royal House and the Mandlakazi. His heir, Prince Dinuzulu, appealed for white volunteers from the Transvaal to intervene on his behalf promising land in reward. A Boer commando duly declared Dinuzulu king of the Zulus in the shadow of Hlobane Mountain on 21 May 1884, and a combined royalist and Boer force advanced to attack Zibhebhu. The Mandlakazi fell back, luring the royalists down the valley of the Mkhuze River towards the Tshaneni Mountain, where Zibhebhu had laid a typical trap. He had hidden an advanced guard in a donga flanking the riverbank; it was ordered, on being discovered, to fall back towards the foot of Tshaneni, drawing the royalists after it. Zibhebhu's main body was concealed so as to be able to sweep down on the royalist flanks and pin them against the river. The plan might well have succeeded had not one of his men accidentally discharged his rifle when the royalists approached on 5 June. Realizing that he had been discovered, Zibhebhu ordered the Mandlakazi forward and they swept down on the royalists, only to be driven back by their Boer supporters. A strong royalist counter-attack by the abaQulusi split Zibhebhu's line and carried among the Mandlakazi non-combatants sheltering behind. Zibhebhu's forces were scattered, and the triumphant royalists carried away as many as 60,000 of his cattle and hundreds of women and children. 'I wonder I have lived so long' Zibhebhu was heard to say, 'but oh! My poor children!'

Nevertheless, Zibhebhu was by no means spent. He rallied a few hundred supporters around him and slipped through the royalist lines, marching the length of the country to appeal to the British in the Reserve Territory for help. The British were not prepared to intervene militarily but they did offer sanctuary to a man who, after all, had been a cornerstone of their policy in Zululand since 1879. Zibhebhu and his followers were settled close to Eshowe. In the meantime, events moved on. The Boers duly presented their bill for their help and claimed such a huge area of Zululand that British officials – prompted not by humanitarian concerns but by a fear of Boer influence extending to the coast – were driven at last to object. The Boer claims were limited to the area along the old Transvaal border – which was now declared to be a 'New Republic' – and in May 1887 the British formerly extended their authority over what was left of Zululand.

One of their first official acts was to return Zibhebhu to his old territories around Banganomo. It was, of course, a fitting reward for a trusted ally but it was anathema to the Royal House. In particular, Prince Dinuzulu, who lived nearby, could not tolerate it.

Frustrated at successive royalist failures to drive back the tide of European encroachment, he was prepared to risk everything rather than accept Zibhebhu's return. The British established a magistrate's post at Ivuna, on top of the Nongoma ridge, squarely placed between the two opposing sides to keep them apart. Both Dinuzulu and Zibhebhu assembled their followers for war, however, and when the magistrate tried to arrest Dinuzulu at Ceza Mountain on 2 June 1888 he found an *impi* waiting for him. He bid a hasty retreat to Ivuna, where Zibhebhu moved to support him. Nothing daunted, Dinuzulu made a surprise move on the magistracy on 23 June. He caught both the British and Mandlakazi by surprise, feinted towards the British post then fell upon the Mandlakazi with a vengeance, scattering them across the hilltops. It was the first act in a rebellion which would see British redcoats fighting once more in Zululand and which led, in the end, to the capture and exile of King Dinuzulu as it had once to his father.

The Mandlakazi sided with the British throughout the rebellion, but to Zibhebhu's surprise he was not allowed to return immediately to Banganomo. The British at last had begun to question the cost of their old 'divide and rule' policies, and Zibhebhu was called to Eshowe to account for his actions. He was released, but it was not until 1898 that he was actually allowed to return to the Mandlakazi heartlands. Dinuzulu, recently pardoned, returned about the same time. The rifts between them went largely unhealed and in the aftermath of the Anglo-Boer War the old quarrel about King Cetshwayo's cattle broke into fresh life. Zibhebhu appeared as ready as ever to resort to an armed solution but he was now an old man. He was nearly seventy and his health was failing; on 27 August 1904 he died at his Banganomo homestead.

His death prevented another crisis, and the Mandlakazi were for a while preoccupied with a succession dispute between his sons. Nevertheless, a partial reconciliation between the Mandlakazi and the Royal House was only engineered by Dinuzulu's successor, King Solomon Nkayishana, as late as 1927.

No individual's legacy summed up the bitterness of the British conquest more than that of Zibhebhu kaMaphitha. Hailed in his time as the greatest Zulu general since King Shaka, he had exercised his abilities courageously in defence of the kingdom in 1879, but ultimately it was his own people who had felt them most keenly. For all his personal skills, his courage, his dynamism and his extraordinary military flair, he was, in the end, an agent of the destruction of the Zulu Royal House no less than Lord Chelmsford or Evelyn Wood, and in his victory at oNdini in 1883 he shattered the human fabric of the old kingdom far more efficiently than had the British.

In the career of Zibhebhu kaMaphitha the terrible chain of events unleashed by Sir Bartle Frere reached their logical conclusion.

Select Bibliography

Ballard, Charles, *John Dunn; The White Chief of Zululand*, A. D. Donker, Johannesburg, 1985

Bancroft, James W., *The Zulu War VCs*, J. W. Bancroft, Manchester, 1992

Bayham-Jones, Alan, and Stevenson, Lee, *Rorke's Drift; By Those Who Were There* , Lee Stevenson Publishing, Brighton, 2003

Bendall, Simon, 'A Minor Military Dynasty of the 18th and 19th Centuries', *Journal of the Society for Army Historical Research Vol. 83*, no. 334, Summer 2005

Bennett, Ian, *Eyewitness in Zululand*, Greenhill, London, 1989

Best, Brian, and Stossel, Katie, *Sister Janet*, Pen & Sword Books Ltd., Barnsley, 2006

Binns, C.T., *The Last Zulu King; The Life and Death of Cetshwayo*, Longmans, London, 1963

—*Dinuzulu; The Death of the House of Shaka*, Longmans, London, 1968

Bryant, A.T., *Olden Times in Zululand and Natal*, Shuter & Shooter, London, 1929

Butterfield, Paul H., (ed), *War and Peace in South Africa; The Writings of Philip Anstruther and Edward Essex*, Scripta Africana, Melville, 1987

Castle, Ian and Knight, Ian, *Fearful Hard Times; The Siege and Relief of Eshowe*, Greenhill, London, 1994

Clarke, Sonia (ed), *Invasion of Zululand*, Brenthurst Press, Johannesburg, 1979

—*Zululand at War*, Brenthurst Press, Johannesburg, 1984

Child, Daphne (ed), *The Zulu War Journal of Colonel Henry Harford, C.B.*, Shuter & Shooter, Pietermaritzburg, 1878.

Coghill, Patrick, *Whom The Gods Love; A Memoir of Lieutenant Nevill Josiah Aylmer Coghill VC*, private publication, Gloucestershire, 1966

Cooper, Barbara, 'George Hamilton Browne; An Investigation into his Career in New Zealand', *Bay of Plenty Journal of History*, Vol. 33, n. 2, November, 1985

Cope, Nicholas, *To Bind the Nation; Solomon kaDinuzulu 1913-1933*, University of Natal Press, Pietermaritzburg, 1993

Drooglever, R. W .F., *The Road To Isandhlwana; Colonel Anthony Durnford in Natal and Zululand*, Greenhill, London, 1992

Emery, Frank, *The Red Soldier; Letters from the Zulu War*, Hodder &

Stoughton, London, 1977

—*Marching Over Africa; Letters from Victorian Soldiers*, Hodder & Stoughton, London, 1986

Faye, Carl, *Zulu References*, City Printers and Publishers, Pietermaritzburg, 1993

Filter, H. (compiler), and Bourquin, S. (translator), *Paulina Dlamini; Servant of Two Kings*, Killie Campbell Library, Pietermaritzburg, 1986

Greaves, Adrian, and Best, Brian (eds), *The Curling Letters of the Zulu War*, Pen & Sword Books Ltd., Barnsley, 2001

Greaves, Adrian, *Isandlwana*, Cassell, London, 2002

—*Rorke's Drift*, Cassell, London, 2002

—(ed), *Redcoats and Zulus*, Pen & Sword Books Ltd., Barnsley, 2004

—*Crossing the Buffalo*, Cassell, London, 2005

Guy, Jeff, *The Destruction of the Zulu Kingdom*, London, 1979

—*The Heretic; A Study of the Life of John William Colenso 1814-1883*, University of Natal Press, Johannesburg, 1983

Hale, Frederick, *The Missionary Career and Spiritual Odyssey of Otto Witt*, unpublished PhD thesis, University of Cape Town, 1991

Holme, Norman, *The Noble 24th*, Savannah, London, 1999

Hope, Robert, *The Zulu War and the 80th Regiment of Foot*, Churnet Valley Books, Leek, 1997

Hummel, Chris (ed), *The Frontier War Journal of Major John Crealock 1878* Van Riebeeck Society, Cape Town, 1988

Johnson, Barry C., *Hook of Rorke's Drift*, Johnson-Taunton Military Press, Birmingham, 2004

Jones, Huw M, 'Hlobane; A New Perspective', *Natalia*, Natal Witness, no. 27. December 1997

—*Biographical Register of Swaziland to 1902*, University of Natal Press, Pietermaritzburg, 1993

Knight, Ian and Castle, Ian, *The Zulu War; Then and Now*, Plaistow Press, London, 1992

Knight, Ian, *Brave Men's Blood; The Epic of the Zulu War*, Greenhill, London, 1990

—*Zulu; The Battles of Isandlwana and Rorke's Drift*, Windrow and Greene, London, 1992

—*The Anatomy of the Zulu Army*, Greenhill, London, 1994

—*Great Zulu Commanders*, Arms & Armour Press, London, 1999

—*With His Face to the Foe; The Life and Death of Prince Louis Napoleon*, Spellmount, Staplehurst, 2001

—*The National Army Museum Book of the Zulu War*, Sidgwick & Jackson, London, 2003

Laband, John P.C., *Lord Chelmsford's Zululand Campaign*, Alan Sutton, Stroud, 1994

—*Kingdom in Crisis; The Zulu Response to the British Invasion of 1879*, Manchester University Press, Manchester, 1992

—*Rope of Sand; The Rise and Fall of the Zulu Kingdom in the Nineteenth*

Century, Jonathan Ball, Johannesburg, 1995

— 'Longcast in Zululand; The Paradoxical Life of a Transfrontiersman, 1850-1909', *Journal of Natal and Zulu History*, Vol. XV, 1994/1995

Lloyd, W.G., *John Williams VC; A Biography*, Three Arch Press, Cwmbran, 1993

Lottering, Agnes, *Winnefred and Agnes; The True Story of Two Women*, Kwela Books, Cape Town, 2002

Lugg, H.C., *Historic Natal and Zululand*, Shuter & Shooter, Pietermaritzburg, 1949

Lummis, Cannon William M., M.C., *Padre George Smith of Rorke's Drift*, Wensome Books, Norwich, 1978

MacKinnon, J.P. and Shadbolt, Sydney, *The South Africa Campaign 1879*, Sampson Low & Co., London, 1880

Mitford, Bertram, *Through the Zulu Country; Its Battlefields and its People*, Kegan Paul Trench & Co., London, 1883

Mossop, George, *Running the Gauntlet*, Thomas Nelson & Sons, London, 1937

Nzimande, Themba, *King Mpande's Children; The Blood-Royal Zulu Princes and Princesses*, KwaZuluMonuments Council, Durban, 1997

Preston, Adrian (ed), *Sir Garnet Wolseley's South African Journal 1879-80*, A. A. Balkema, Cape Town, 1973

Stevenson, Lee, *The Rorke's Drift Doctor; James Henry Reynolds and the Defence of Rorke's Drift*, Lee Stevenson Publishing, Brighton, 2001

Uys, Ian, Rearguard; *The Life and Times of Piet Uys*, Knysna, 1998

Vijn, Cornelius (translated by Bishop Colenso), *Cetshwayo's Dutchman*, Longmans, London, 1880

Webb, C. de B., and Wright, John, (eds), *The James Stuart Archive of Recorded Oral Evidence relating to the history of the Zulus and Neighbouring Peoples*, Vols 1 (1976), 2 (1979), 3 (1982), 4 (1986), 5 (2001). University of Natal Press, Pietermaritzburg

Whitehouse, Howard (ed), *A Widow-Making War; The Life and Death of a British Officer in Zululand*, 1879, Paddy Griffith Associates, Nuneaton, 1995

Williams, W. Alister, *Commandant of the Transvaal; The Life and Career of General Sir Hugh Rowlands VC*, KCB, Bridge Books, Wrexham, 2001

Wood, Field Marshal Sir Evelyn VC, *From Field Midshipman to Field Marshal*, Methuen, London, 1906